IN SEARCH OF
A DREAM

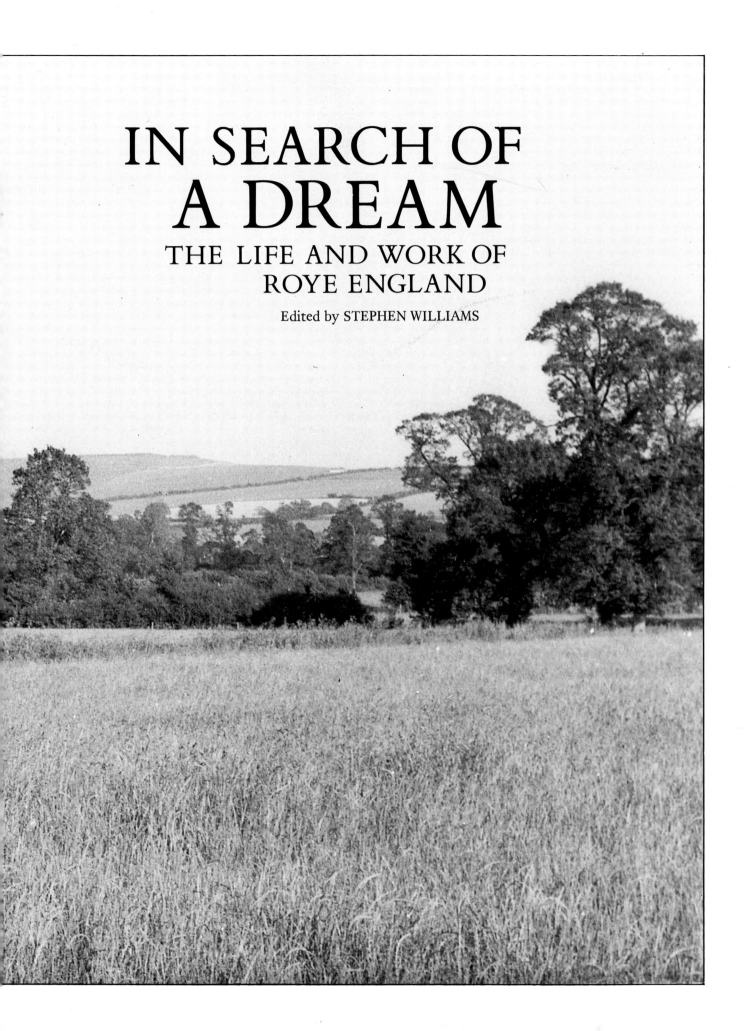

IN SEARCH OF
A DREAM

THE LIFE AND WORK OF
ROYE ENGLAND

Edited by STEPHEN WILLIAMS

ISBN 1 874103 62 3

Harvest time near Hinton Parva, August 1933.   ROYE ENGLAND

Title page: A distant prospect of the White Horse Hill, seen from the meadows below Bishopstone.   ROYE ENGLAND

Designed by Paul Karau
Printed by Amadeus Press, Cleckheaton

Published by
WILD SWAN PUBLICATIONS LTD.
1-3 Hagbourne Road, Didcot, Oxon, OX11 8DP

Cottages at Compton Beauchamp, July 1941.   ROYE ENGLAND

CONTENTS

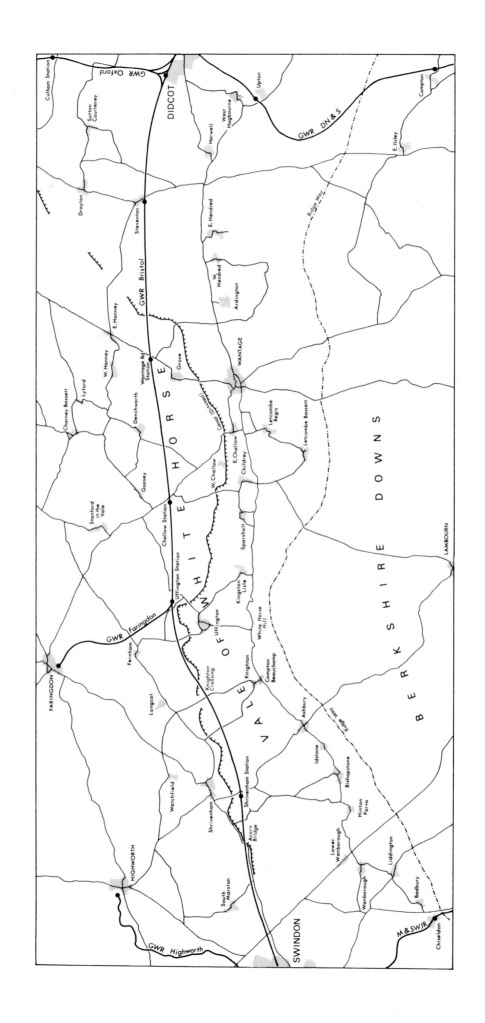

Introduction

This book tells the story of the life and work of a remarkable man. As a young man, Roye Curzon Cursham England came from his native Australia to Britain. Initially, the purpose of his visit was to patent an invention he had made for the automatic control of model railways, but that goal was soon superseded by an altogether greater ambition — to capture a portrait of a rural England that was fast disappearing and to preserve it in miniature form — in a model village of hitherto unimagined accuracy and detail, complete within a landscape of fields and woodlands and with a representation of the main line of the Great Western Railway running through the scene. The inspiration for this dream-like project was the once-beautiful Vale of White Horse, which Roye first visited soon after his arrival in England, and which he subsequently made both his physical and spiritual home. Out of this enterprise grew the world-famous Pendon Museum of Miniature Landscape and Transport that Roye established at Long Wittenham, Oxfordshire from 1954.

The story that is told in this book is semi-autobiographical and it weaves together several parallel strands. Much of the later part of the story is intimately concerned with the struggles to create Pendon, although it is not a history of Pendon *per se*, since many have contributed to that project and this account is an individual story, albeit that of the Museum's founder. Secondly, the book also presents one man's reflections upon the changing world in which he lived; of the despoilation of the countryside (as Roye saw it) in the name of 'progress'; of the heyday of steam railways and the eventual demise of steam-hauled services; of greater matters too — not least the Second World War, which left a profound mark upon Roye, as it did for so many of his generation. Then, thirdly, it is an account of Roye's life — the places that he went, the people that he met, the things that he did and just occasionally, some insights into the way he thought.

This latter aspect is, however, perhaps the most frustrating element, for whilst Roye left many thousands of words in diaries, correspondence and, not least, his monumental 'Saga of Pendon' (from which much of the text of this book is drawn), he tells us relatively little about himself as a person. To help the reader better understand the subject of the book, therefore, I am setting out in this introduction some additional notes that throw particular light upon Roye, as a man, elements that might not be too apparent from the main story but which are important to understanding this unusual and, at times, most complex of persons.

ROYE'S CHARACTER

I first met Roye in April 1978. As a keen modeller myself, I had beaten a path to the doors of Pendon Museum and, like so many before and since, had gone away captivated

Roye, photographed during the earliest days of the Pendon project, coupling some of the rolling stock on the Dartmoor model railway.   L. KENT

by the quality of the work and the sheer vision of the project. Determined to do more than simply marvel, I offered help and, in accordance with normal Pendon custom, assembled a demonstration model to show what I could do. Thus, one afternoon, I found myself approaching the door of a rather anonymous bungalow in Steventon, anxious yet eager with anticipation at meeting this great modeller, whose work I had so admired over many years.

Roye was not what I expected. Tall, remarkably young-looking for his age (then 71), he greeted me politely, if a little formally, and with just a hint of shyness. He spoke quietly and I sensed immediately that here was a gentleman in every sense of the word. Then I showed him my model and I felt an immediate change. He relaxed, his gentle sense of humour gradually surfaced, and in no time we were 'talking modelling'! His enthusiasm for the finer points of my work and the polite, but firm, manner in which he pointed out the areas that were not so convincing, seemed to confirm that he knew exactly what he wanted and how to encourage others to meet that goal. He showed me the model on which he was then working (Packer's smithy from Childrey) and I can still recall the thrill of actually handling a Roye England masterpiece. He explained how I could improve the demonstration model I had brought and, as we talked, I found his effect was genuinely inspirational. I left the house that afternoon wanting to model for Pendon and, especially, to model for Roye. I also experienced another of his great qualities that same afternoon, for after he had satisfied himself that my

1

work was sufficiently competent and I had accepted his invitation to model the almshouses from Lyford, his gratitude at my willingness to help him further his dream was both sincere and overwhelming. The uncanny ability to inspire people to help the Museum and his genuine sincerity were two of his greatest strengths.

For the next eight years, we corresponded (or spoke by phone) often and met frequently at the Museum where (amongst many things) Roye taught me to drive and comment upon the trains on the Dartmoor layout. I also read for the first time his 'Saga of Pendon', through which I came to appreciate some of his other qualities. He was, throughout almost all of his long life, a tremendously active and hard-working man, quite dedicated to his project and firm in his commitment to those things in which he believed. He was meticulous (probably to a fault) in virtually everything he did, with a passion for detail that sometimes meant the broader picture became blurred. He was also extremely loyal towards those whom he felt deserved his support and it is clear that he valued friendship particularly highly. At a rather difficult meeting at Pendon on one occasion, Roye was criticised by someone for too readily seeing good in people, but to expect anything else would have been to misunderstand completely one of Roye's most basic beliefs.

For a man in the public eye (and known to many people both through Pendon and outside), Roye remained throughout his life a rather private person. There were many aspects of his life that he kept to himself, even from people he knew well and who no doubt thought they knew Roye well! He disclosed much within his diaries and other writings that he willed to Pendon at his death and, as a result, some of his actions and beliefs have become better understood. But in many situations where he may have held strong views, he often remained silent. In some respects this was a weakness, for in later years especially, many things at Pendon went against Roye's preferred wishes, but he seems often to have been reluctant to make an issue of it. I never saw him visibly angry, nor heard him raise his voice, even when it might have been better for the outcome had he done so.

Roye never married, even though many of his attributes as a person would have made him a good and caring husband. He occasionally spoke to close friends about a girl he had once known in Australia to whom he felt some attachment, but there is no reference anywhere within his 'Saga' to romantic attachments, except to an unfortunate incident when a secretary he had employed began to show amorous intentions that Roye felt unable to reciprocate. Her advances cost the poor woman her job, yet Roye didn't shun the company of women and was quick to acknowledge feminine beauty when he saw it. There is one brief reference to marriage in some private reminiscences that Roye wrote in 1948 that perhaps gives a clue

to how he felt and which suggest that a failure to find a partner in life may at some times have been a disappointment. He wrote:

'It is difficult to see oneself — but I do know that I have [an] artesian well of affection which is simply bursting to be freed and to inundate someone for the rest of one's life. I might make a difficult husband in some ways, but given the right companion, I know I should make a loving one.'

The opportunity, however, seems never to have arisen and perhaps therefore of necessity, Roye was obviously someone who could be content with his own company.

ROYE'S PARENTS
Roye's character owed a great deal to two particularly strong influences in his life. The first of these was his relationship with his parents, whilst the second (which we shall consider in a moment) was his deep Christian faith.

The circumstances of his upbringing and his relationship with his parents were unusual (though not unique, especially in that era — *circa* 1900). As Roye himself recounts (see Chapter 1), his mother was his father's second wife and although Roye had half-brothers, they were already adults when Roye was born, such was the difference in age between his father and mother. Consequently, although Roye had a family around him, he was effectively brought up as an only child and after his father died, when Roye was fifteen, his relationship with his mother was especially close. Indeed, without the many subsequent years of sacrifices and the material and emotional support that she gave, Roye would never have been able to create Pendon.

In later life, Roye expressed some regrets that as his father had been so much older, he never really had a chance to know him well. But he appreciated the strong influence that his father had exerted upon his own development. Another passage written by Roye just after the Second World War is worth quoting at length, because it tells us almost as much about Roye as it reveals about his father, who was the actual subject of the piece.

'Father's character was intensely stable. He was sure and thorough in all he did, tirelessly painstaking and persevering, with a quick perception, a clear and ever-ready brain, and a grasp both of detail and of fundamental principles. He had a strong will and always knew his own mind and in following his conscience he was inflexible. In adversity or suffering of any kind he was patient and uncomplaining: in work he was unflagging. Mother and I sometimes called him "The Bulldog" because of the way in which he would never let go. But in spite of his dogged patience with annoying things, he found it difficult not to be irritated by annoying people. When he was with people he did not care for, he tended to say very little, but would open up unexpectedly with those he liked. But above everything he had a heart and was deeply affectionate and full of sentiment — a man full of contrasts, with his business acumen, his unwavering Christian principles and his strangely sensitive nature.

'Comparisons are odious, but I think there are ways in which I have taken after Father — his care for detail and his compelling urge to do things and always do them as well as they can be done (in my case, sometimes to a fault); perhaps something of his patience, a touch of his diffidence, and I think much more than a touch of his hidden warmth, but often as hidden as his was. Besides this, I hope I have something of Father's common sense and at least a reflection of his innate sense of rightness.

'Of course, there were differences too. I have many faults that were not his — ups and downs and ways and kinks that were not in his character. I have not taken after his business ability, nor his powers to think quickly and intuitively, particularly in creative work. I have just spent three days writing a letter, albeit an important and difficult one. Father used to write important letters straight off, so surely that he never read them through. I could do twice as much with my life if I had that gift.'

The passage is also instructive in as much as it tells us about some of the qualities that Roye valued in others as well as pointing to one of the sources of Roye's own character.

Part of the reason for Roye's rather fulsome and, in some ways, untypically open recollections of his father at this time, may have been the recent death of his mother which prompted a spell of quite profound introspection and retrospection on Roye's part. Although for much of his life they were separated, he in England and she in Australia, there is no doubting the strong emotional bond that lay between the mother and her only son. This is reflected in lots of ways; her unflinching support for Roye and the firm belief that his schemes should at least be given a fair chance; the readiness with which Roye set aside all that he was doing when the chances arose to be with his mother — especially when she was able to visit England; and the manner in which, in moments of doubt about where his life was leading, thoughts of what his mother hoped he might achieve were often powerful forces of mediation. They wrote often and Roye kept many of his mother's letters until his own death. (As private correspondence, these letters were returned to the family and have not formed any part of the content of this book, except where reported by Roye in other sources that were intended for others to read.)

Violet England was apparently great fun to be with and game for most things. Elsewhere in this volume, readers will find a delightful photograph of Roye and his mother on the motorcycle that he purchased in 1926. She poses on the driving seat (although she never actually took the controls for real), whilst Roye — peaked-cap worn in reverse — smiles from the sidecar. Together that year they toured much of England and Scotland on this uncomfortable-looking machine, with Roye driving and his mother riding in the sidecar. Later, they spent a winter travelling in Europe (though not by motorcycle!) and amongst the souvenirs of that trip which Roye kept (and a rather intriguing one, given the serious side to his character that he so often projected), was a pair of tickets to a casino in France!

It was possibly from his mother that Roye inherited the spirit of adventure that led him to come to Britain in the first place and once here, to travel so widely across (particularly) its southern counties. He kept Ordnance Survey maps of the Vale of White Horse and adjacent areas such as Salisbury Plain, on which he marked where he had been. By the end of all his travels, scarcely a lane remained unexplored.

Roye also attributed much of his sense of artistry and his sensibilities, to his mother's influence. His father had been a keen hobbyist, but it was his mother whom he said had the artistic flair that was so central to his modelling work. His instinctive kindness and concerns for others were partly his mother's too. One of Roye's earliest recollections was of a butterfly trapped in a spider's web in the garden of his home in Perth and the care with which (when called by a distraught Roye) his mother freed the creature. The image stayed with him throughout his life.

ROYE'S FAITH

The second (and even more powerful) influence in Roye's life and work was his deep Christian faith. This seems to have been present from his youth. He was brought up in a strongly Christian household, several of his relations worked in the Church and for much of his life he shared the homes of clergymen; first at Wanborough, then in Bristol, Somerset, Bristol (again), Swindon and, towards the end of his life, at Steventon. Throughout his adult life he not only sustained, but also developed his faith and his beliefs. He read widely amongst Christian literature — although not within academic theology, of which he was suspicious, and although he trained for ordination (but did not proceed), he possessed an unshakeable belief in the value of prayer and of seeking guidance when difficult decisions had to be faced. Christianity also underpinned his belief in the sanctity of life and the pacifism that saw him register as a conscientious objector during the Second World War and sustained him through the years of toil on the land that was the penalty of his conscience.

His faith shaped his whole approach to life and to his life's work, his attitude towards other people and it also helps to explain his remarkable capacity to withstand the many reverses and hardships that his chosen route through life placed in the way. After one particular disappointment, Roye wrote:

'I saw it as a test of faith. God did not ignore prayers made in full trust and He never let one down without good cause: but He did sometimes delay an answer to prove us, and in the end strengthen our character.'

However, although his Christian beliefs provided great comfort, they also created recurring difficulties of conscience. These Roye himself summarised, writing in 1979, where he appears (at last) to resolve in his own mind the basic dilemma of how best to express his faith, a dilemma that had troubled him throughout his life. He wrote :

'Most of my life till Pendon got on its feet, I had questioned whether I was right to be giving my time and energy to models rather than to evangelism or some other kind of welfare work. In 1932, when at Woodridge for a test of vocation, I promised God to give up modelling if He wished me to do so and I offered myself for missionary work in Africa. I was turned down. Later, I was accepted for ordination and on the last day was given a direct answer at the Communion rail that this, too, was not God's work for me. Having a bent for writing, I then, concurrently with the modelling, put in years, on both prose and poetry with the hope not only of earning but largely of getting a message across: yet this led nowhere. I made a definite attempt in the Guild of St. Aidan (*see Chapter 4*) to link the models with missionary work, which came to nothing. Yet Pendon grew out of the Guild, though to my later regret I had not formed it on a spiritual basis. Meanwhile I did, for the first time, real social work in the Youth Hostel, but though successful, after several years it proved too much for me. The one thing that went ahead, despite the most testing times, was the models — an unbroken thread running through the whole of my life, in which I had really succeeded. Now there came to me, a direct message — to model was the gift that God had given to me, it was the appointed job that He wanted me to do, and if I didn't I should be failing Him.'

The comment upon the failure to establish Pendon on a spiritual basis is telling. Some of his writings made at the end of his life have a pervasive sense of disillusion. Part of this unhappiness stemmed from a realisation that, rather like a child that outgrows the care of its parents, Pendon outgrew Roye. It became too large, too complex an organisation for him to continue to be involved in all aspects of its development and management as he had once been, and although Roye realised this, he never quite came to terms with the fact. But perhaps more importantly, he realised that Pendon was unlikely to become the (Christian) fellowship that perhaps he once envisaged. In 1976 he had expressed the hope that Pendon could be a medium through which the Christian message might be spread — the potential was great, if only it could be used. Yet, ten years later, on almost the last page of his 'Saga' he wrote:

'Pendon was a fellowship of people, young and old, who helped it for no financial reward because they believed in it and enjoyed helping.'

For the people who continue to develop Pendon, the Museum remains a fellowship that enjoys and believes in the work that is being done, but Roye's use of the past tense in that extract is not, I believe, accidental and reflects a feeling that things had not quite worked out as he had once intended.

ROYE'S LIFESTYLE

To many people, Roye would have appeared mildly eccentric, as those who are preoccupied or driven by a particular purpose so readily seem to appear. In some ways, there were elements of eccentricity in the way he lived, but, equally, his lifestyle was also as simple and as down-to-earth as it is possible to be.

Reading Roye's papers and his 'Saga', it is also striking that his life had two very distinct phases to it. Initially he was born into, and grew up within, a family where there was wealth. His accounts of his early years in Australia, the relative ease with which he seems to have been able to

undertake the expensive journey to England in 1925 and the subsequent holidays he spent with his mother (including a whole winter of travel throughout Europe), points to this simple conclusion. However, in later years (and especially after the death of his mother and his decision to use all his savings to purchase what later became the site of Pendon Museum), he seems to have lived a life in which money was always short.

Perhaps as a consequence, his pleasures in life were of the simpler kind, where shortage of money was no obstacle. Outside of his modelling work, he became a prodigious writer (see below), he read a great deal, painted and sketched rather less, and still had time to enjoy music. He listened to the radio but had little inclination towards television, even to the extent that he missed at least one appearance by himself in a programme made by a television company about Pendon. He didn't cook and in the years he spent at The Three Poplars in Long Wittenham, appears to have survived on a diet of cereals, boiled eggs, black bananas and Fry's 'Crunchie' bars. When I knew him, he also enjoyed coffee that was so weak that it was hard to detect any alteration to the colouring of the milk!

For a dedicated traveller, Roye was surprisingly reticent about motor vehicles. Although he owned a motorcycle at one time, a narrow escape in a motoring accident (which he doesn't report in his 'Saga') cured him of further interest in motor bikes and cars. He never owned a car nor, for many years would he accept a lift in one, preferring instead to go most places by train or, especially, by bicycle. In keeping with his meticulous interest in detail, he recorded the mileage on each of his bicycles. His favourite machine (his Dawes lightweight) clocked an amazing 109,000 miles in a little over fourteen years, much of it when Roye was over fifty years old. Apart from a brief spell as a young man when he worked in insurance and a longer period of seven years in late middle-age when he was employed at MG cars in Abingdon, Roye never had a job. I once asked him about this, to which he replied simply that 'Pendon is my work'.

He spent much of his life sharing the homes of others. The only property that was his own was The Three Poplars at Long Wittenham, but even after this ceased to be a youth hostel, Roye continued to let out most of the rooms, not because he especially wanted companionship but more simply because he needed the money. Eventually, even this passed to Pendon and Roye returned to lodging with friends or relatives, and it is probably a testimony to the charm and gentlemanly personality of the man, that so many different people were happy to offer him a roof. However, sharing tended to mean living within just a single room that he could call his own — a difficult task at the best of times but made worse by his incurable reluctance to throw anything away. This he took to extremes — thus Pendon now has amongst its 'Roye England Archive', several car parking tickets from a motoring holiday Roye made to Cornwall in 1925! Visitors to Roye when he was living in the retirement home at Newbury at the end of his life were commonly unable to sit, as all available surfaces (including the chairs) were covered in piles of papers, photographs, books and the like. Any attempt to move these was strictly forbidden for it would, of course, make it impossible for Roye to find things again!

ROYE'S WRITINGS

The piles of papers with which Roye usually surrounded himself were often a product of his vast output of written work. This spanned the full range of prose, poetry, narrative descriptions, notes on modelling work, letters and personal diaries — even a piano sonata! The only thing he seems not to have done is written a play, although it would not be a surprise if one were uncovered, even now. These writings (which at some stages of his life were also written in Esperanto) inevitably reflected the man in all his strengths, weaknesses and idiosyncrasies. His diaries — which he called 'Outline' — for example, are highly detailed, almost literally minute-by-minute logs of what happened each day. To help him record as much detail as possible, he devised a system of what can only be described as hieroglyphics which have two effects, first to act as summaries of routine, repetitive functions, and second as a form of encodement. Hence, for example, he indicated the task of correspondence by drawing a tiny envelope and then listing below the names of those to whom he had written.

It was largely out of these diaries that he created his 'Saga of Pendon'. He started work on this in March 1966 and continued, off and on, until 1987, by which time advancing age and the frailty that comes with age was beginning to get the better of him, although he continued to tinker with it even after then. In all, the 'Saga' runs to something close to 250,000 words, about 80,000 of which survive only in the form of Roye's minute hand-writing, with lettering sometimes less than 1mm high.

The 'Saga' is essentially a narrative but it contains many delightful passages of descriptive writing that reflect the sensibilities of its author and his skills as a writer. Two extracts (which have not been retained in the main story that follows) are worth quoting as examples of Roye's ability to capture scenes in words. (The Transfer, incidentally, was part of the railway yard at Swindon which Roye frequented in the early 1950s.)

'The Transfer looked perfectly magic this evening. The air was blue-misty after rain and coloured by the setting sun — everything half-seen and half-bewitched through haze, and great masses of piling steam from every train that passed and from every engine shunting — groups of signal arms rising clear and shapely, almost silhouetted against the late sky. The railway scene is unforgettably beautiful at times like this.'

And a second example

'On a perfect night, calm and almost mild, with a full moon turning the fields and half-bare trees to silver sheen, I drifted on the bike along the Shrivenham road. Opposite Acorn Bridge was the canal up-down, set richly in its trees, where I had taken so many traffic notes twenty years earlier; the rough track, mysterious tonight in light and shade, barred by a farm gate with miles of trees and placid fields behind it, the high mainline in front, the double arches of the bridge and a vista sideways of the line sweeping eastwards and away . . .'

His poetry was more personal and he seems particularly to have resorted to verse when his life was in some turmoil, for example, during the war and following the sudden death of his mother. One lengthy work called 'The Price' sets down his deeply-felt view of events surrounding the Second World War whilst others reflect upon his Christian faith. He also wrote many poems about the countryside that he cherished, especially the Vale of White Horse. The extract from one of these 'The Passing from the Vale' quoted in Chapter 3, perhaps reveals Roye's verse at its best. It was one of his great disappointments that he failed in several attempts to have some of his verse published commercially, although he did manage to publish two small anthologies privately — *The Price* and *The Vale that inspired Pendon* — a few years before he died.

The achievements of Roye England — his models, the work of others whom he inspired, the Museum that he created, his prose and poetry, his diaries, train records and modelling notes, his thousands of photographs that are now kept at Pendon — all add up to a life that was full and rich in many senses. As I drew together the final strands of this introduction, I decided I wanted a phrase or couplet that might distil and embody what Roye's life and work had been about and which might stand at the beginning as a suitable epitome for the book as a whole. As I sat idly thumbing through Shakespeare and other likely sources in search of a suitable phrase, my eyes wandered onto the music collection that shares the same shelves and I remembered something from Elgar's great oratorio 'The Kingdom'. At one point the composer gives to the voice of the apostle Peter a line from the Book of Joel, although interestingly I found on checking the original that Elgar transposed the Biblical phrase to produce an alternative which seemed even more effective, especially in the context that I was seeking.

'Your young men shall see visions and your old men shall dream dreams.'

This is the story of how the vision of one young man created a dream that was to last a lifetime.

Stephen Williams

The National Bank, Perth. Roye was born in the first-floor living quarters. The unmade road surface and the general absence of street lighting reminds us how undeveloped many colonial cities were at this time.

CTY. BATTYE LIBRARY, WESTERN AUSTRALIA

Left: *Roye, aged about two years, with his mother Violet.* Right: *Henry England, photographed in Perth at about the time of Roye's birth.*

PENDON MUSEUM COLLECTION

CHAPTER ONE
1906–1925
EMBRYO: THE AUSTRALIAN CENTRAL RAILWAY

I was born on 11th September 1906, in the living quarters which were then over the National Bank in St. George's Terrace, Perth, Western Australia. My father, Henry Robert England, was Manager of the bank for that State — an outstandingly successful manager whose business genius, I humbly confess, left no impression whatsoever on his son.

Henry England (who was the third of eight children) was born in Westbury, Wiltshire, on 13th June, 1841. He came from a Quaker family, his mother, formerly Anne Fry Sansom, being related to the famous Quaker family which included the prison reformer Elizabeth Fry and the chocolate manufacturers of Bristol. His father, William England, was a cloth manufacturer but disagreements within the family firm (principally with his father) prompted William to emigrate with his young family to America. Unfortunately, on the voyage across the Atlantic, an epidemic of cholera broke out on the ship and before New York was reached, it had claimed William, his eldest son Philip and the youngest daughter, Edith May. My father was also nearly lost, although not to cholera. He fell overboard in New York harbour and but for the prompt actions of a sailor who spotted his straw hat, he would have drowned. Now widowed and with six children, my grandmother decided then and there that America was not for them and promptly returned to England.

My father was then sent to a Quaker boarding school at Sibford, near Banbury, and on leaving (in the early 1860s), joined a bank in Bristol. But at about that time he began to have trouble with his chest. In 1984 he became seriously ill with congestion of the lungs and was advised that he would benefit from living in a warmer climate. He chose Australia and at the age of 23, leaving his mother, whom he never saw again, he emigrated from England in a sailing ship — the 'Highflyer', a crack wind-jammer which took three months to make the voyage! In Melbourne he joined the National Bank of Australia and began to work his way up.

My mother was his second wife and although he was 65 when I was born, he was still most vigorous and full of hobbies. By his first wife, whose maiden name was Kate McKee, he had four sons, the first of whom was born in 1874, the same year as my mother! One of the sons — Arthur — died in infancy but the others, Harry, Frank and Fred, were in their teens at the time they lost their mother in 1894. Their father remained a widower for some eight years or so whilst the boys grew up. They had reached their mid-twenties when a most attractive girl of about their own age, Violet Guillaume, came to Perth from Melbourne. She and the Englands became close friends.

In those affluent days the Englands did boating on the Swan River in a fairly big way, and on river jaunts, Vi (as she was known) soon became an essential member of the party. The boys were very taken with her. In fact, they had definite ideas about her and it must have shaken them when she married their father instead! The marriage took place on October 7th 1902, at St. George's Cathedral, Perth — he was 61 and she was 28. *(The marriage certificate survives amongst the papers that Roye bequeathed to Pendon at his death.)* Of French and Irish extraction, Vi was unusually gifted. With a truly French flair for colour, she was essentially artistic, besides being well-balanced and sensible. She loved people, was quite exceptionally understanding and her sunny, responsive way made her liked by everyone.

By the time I was three we had moved from the bank to a house which was then named 'Cranmore' at 3 Ventnor Avenue in West Perth. It had a fairly large garden with a croquet lawn beside the house and flowering creepers, chiefly tecoma of various kinds, covering the trellised fence. We also possessed one of those rare contraptions called a motor car. It was a Humber and its registration was P1 — not the first car in Perth, but the first to be registered there. I have no memory, however, of taking much interest in it, which seems strange, particularly in view of its novelty at the time. Yet it was in keeping for at no point in my life — and this despite working seven years in a car factory — have I been the least bit car-minded. At the age of three or so I was far more attracted to the great carthorse that used to deliver wood for fuel. One day I was left unattended for a few minutes and Vi came out to find me standing squarely between its hind legs, stroking them happily and saying 'nice horsie! . . . '

My earliest clear memories of events, begin when I was four. It was in 1910 that Halley's comet returned and it made a tremendous impression on my young mind. The first time I remember seeing it, I was with my mother in Outram Street, when it was an interesting but insignificant object in the evening sky, just before dusk. But the climax came a week or so later, when my parents woke me at night and took me out of doors to gaze at it. The brilliant, star-like head hung low above the northern horizon and the luminous tail, like a huge sword, swept upward, directly overhead, bisecting the whole heaven. I could never have imagined anything like it.

At about the same age, I owned a vast collection of toy animals — there must have been about thirty of them, all told — and one day I arranged them in a great procession in a single file.

'Look at my *aminals*!' said I.

'Where are they going?' asked Mother.

'They're going to church.'

'What are they going to do there?'

'They're going to eat cake.'

'But you don't eat cake in church!'

'You do in the *aminals*' church.'

I don't know what up-and-coming characteristic that showed — except perhaps an unconventional mind!

Certainly I've always been unconventional. A lifelong tendency, for instance, to use nicknames in preference to anything more proper seems to have shown itself early, for I christened my nurse 'Dooshio' (goodness knows why) and refused to call her anything else . As I grew older, perhaps through an increasing dislike of the prosaic and the formal, I gave names of my own concoction to almost all my closer friends. Without this habit, the name of Pendon itself would never have come into being.

At the age of about five, my father gave me a set of Gauge 1 tinplate trains. He might have given me anything else under the sun and no doubt did, but it was the trains that took possession of me. They were clockwork, of course, but for those days quite realistic in their own primitive way. Although made in Germany — like almost all toys at that time — they were English in outline and livery, if practically nothing else. The London and South Western 'express', for instance, consisted of three 4-wheelers hauled by a not-very-dashing 0-4-0 tender engine — which was hardly prototype practice. But despite their shortcomings, my joy in them knew no bounds.

My father used to spend hours on his knees laying a great oblong of track on the floor of the 32-foot dining room at 'Cranmore' — a wonderful place to run them — and then, like all fathers who have never quite grown up, played trains no less enthusiastically than his insatiable son.

Some time after this we went to Melbourne for a couple of years and when we came home it was to a smaller house — at 7 Richardson Street, again in West Perth. The trains were awaiting me but my awakening dedication to the railway cause was reinforced by a gift of *The Wonder Book of Railways* and later, *The Boy's Own Railway Book*. Almost every boy is given toy trains and books on trains and their later life is quite unaffected by them. So was mine by similar gifts of *The Wonder Book of Ships* and its companion on aircraft. They interested me greatly, yet left me unmoved.

But railways were different and over the years, these two books became the focal point of my young life. There was a magnificent picture of the only GWR Pacific — *The Great Bear* — at that time the last word in locomotive splendour and enough to fire a boy's imagination as to the glories of England. Compare this giant with the small-wheeled, unpretentious engines of Western Australia! Other foreign lines were also depicted in plenty, but they made no impact on me. English railways had a beauty, a symmetry, a pride, which gradually grew into my soul. Without the *Wonder Book* and its companion, I would never have gained a passion for an English mecca that I had never seen.

The model trains were now being run as energetically as ever in their new home. While we were in Melbourne some more had been bought and our tinplate reflection of England had come to include some reproductions of American stock. But after a time, as England gradually became my ideal, these 'outsiders' were tolerated rather than approved.

By now it was 1915 and the First World War was raging, but I was too young to enter into its horror. The chief ways it affected me were that English books were not gen-

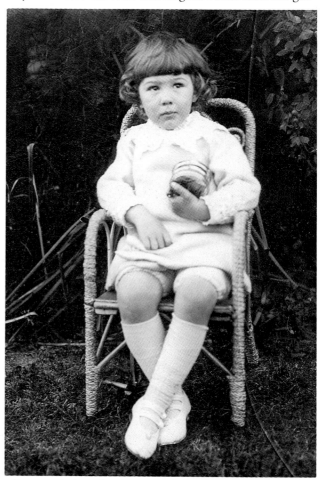

Roye, aged about four years, probably in the garden at Ventnor Avenue. (The use of feminine clothing for small children of either gender was an Edwardian habit from which Roye seems not to have escaped.)
PENDON MUSEUM COLLECTION

erally obtainable and it was quite impossible to order any of the wonderful things in the abridged Bassett-Lowke catalogue of the war years, one issue of which did reach us. Apart from that, the only privation that I remember was that potatoes became short and we had normal dinner with boiled rice instead. But men went out and often never came back and I failed completely to realise the misery that surrounded us, or the balance in which our way of life hung.

In the same year I entered the Perth High School and on my first day, we were set some long-division sums — a mysterious stage of arithmetic of which, at the age of eight, I had never even heard. So I asked the master how to do them and received the baffling reply, 'Go and find out'!

My favourite teacher was a Mr. McLarty. Unlike so many of the staff, he was both instructive and helpful — no side, no thunder, just a very likeable man who kept

Roye (centre), Violet and a friend of Roye's named Eric Tymms, playing croquet at Richardson Street. PENDON MUSEUM COLLECTION

Henry and Violet England with Roye and Jackie in the garden at 7 Richardson Street. PENDON MUSEUM COLLECTION

Violet England playing the harmonium. The photo was taken by Roye in about 1916, when he was 10. ROYE ENGLAND

order in the class by gaining its interest. It was he who nurtured my love of Shakespeare. He spent the holidays on an area of bushland near Kalamunda, where he was building a house for himself with his own hands, even quarrying his own stone from the site. His design for it was unusual, for it contained a sitting-cum-music room whose proportions would probably have satisfied Bach as the acoustic ideal! I was intrigued by the whole venture and spent many happy hours with him there.

My own constructional urges were also moving forward at this time. Meccano came to the fore as a parallel interest to the railway and gave my chronically ambitious ideas plenty of scope. One day, when everyone was out, I built a replica of the Forth Bridge, 16 feet long, in the now not-so-large dining room, leaving just enough space to squeeze in through the door. It spoke volumes for the understanding of my parents that when they returned, finding me bursting with the pride of achievement, and met my bridge face-to-face, they swallowed their dismay and appeared as thrilled as was I.

But bridges 16 feet long, the Eiffel Tower 10 feet high and so on, were not the ideal thing for indoors, any more than was a labyrinth of railway lines over the floor. I was encouraged to transfer my enthusiasm to the out-of-doors. My father fixed the tinplate track onto portable boards which gave good running on the back lawn. But a railway must have earthworks to make it really real and the lawn of couch grass was very flat indeed. As always, my parents understood my feelings, and paradise became mine when they gave me a strip alongside one side of the lawn, about 40 feet in length and 3 feet wide, to do with as I pleased. Before long it had grown into grassy hills, cuttings, a tunnel, a lake and a bridge. To my mind, it improved the appearance of the garden beyond words.

Roye, aged about 10, with Jackie.

PENDON MUSEUM COLLECTION

Some of Roye's tinplate trains in the garden at Richardson Street. To the left stands his 2–4–0 LSWR engine (without tender) and its 'express' train of four-wheeled coaches. The New York & Hudson River Railroad models, including the engine that would not run, stand alongside whilst posed at the front of the group is his first engine (also minus tender).   PENDON MUSEUM COLLECTION

It seems that even the serious young enthusiast could not resist an occasional pile-up!   PENDON MUSEUM COLLECTION

By this time the London and North Western Railway had become my dream line — its engines and its signals were so neat, its coaching livery of 'plum and spilt milk' so attractive. It ran almost the whole length and much of the breadth of England and was it not called (albeit by the genius of its own publicity department) the Premier Line? So London and North Western my line had to be, and I designed our layout to conform exactly to the shape of the original on the other side of the world.

Yet despite such unusual care, I remained quite unabashed by the fact that the layout boasted not a single piece of LNWR stock! There was the 4-wheeled salmon and brown express of the LSWR, a 2-4-0 tender engine (without a tender) in Great Northern apple green, a 2-coach express of the New York Central & Hudson River Railroad (the engine was electric but refused to run), sundry goods wagons of English outline and a bogie composite coach of the Midland Railway of Western Australia. Quite a catholic start for a model of the LNWR! But of course there was always the hope that when the war was over, some genuine North Western trains would be forthcoming. In point of fact they never came, but their constant anticipation shed a lustre which went a long way to make up for the lack.

For about five years, from eight to thirteen, the trains were a tireless delight and the delight also of selected school friends. Each of us had his own official status — Stationmaster of Euston, Crewe and so on, whilst I was

```
                                        Head Office of the L.N.W.R.
                                        22 December 1919.
MR & MRS ENGLAND,

        Dear Sir and Madam,
                    The Manager of the London and North West-
        ern Railway Company, (Roy C England) beggs you to attend a
        private meeting of the said company at 7.30 P.M. to-night.
            The subject he wishes to discuss concerns the whole future
        existence of the Company, and also the Meccano works.
            If unable to attend, please warn the Manager as soon as poss-
        ible; however, as the matter is urgent he sincerely hopes you
        will not be prevented from being in the dining room of 7 Rich-
        ardson Street, West Perth, at the time stated, sharp.

                                        Roy England
                                            (Manager)
```

This lovely piece of juvenilia was found in Roye's papers after his death, a remarkable survivor even allowing for Roye's reluctance to throw things away. Note the original spelling of Roye's name. He added the 'e', together with a family name — 'Curzon' — by deed poll in 1937.

automatically General Manager. I had an antiquated Yost typewriter and I typed out the rules for running the line. They ended with a dreadful warning 'If any member disobeys these rules, an *inquest* will be held'. It was not intended to be quite so drastic but the word 'inquiry' had somehow been altered. The company's seal was cut with a penknife from the end of a cotton reel and Vi was rude enough to say the resulting impression looked more like a caricature of Little Willie, the Kaiser's son. We were insulted but we used it just the same.

The years were slipping by and, at thirteen, I began to see the trains through more critical eyes. They had been great companions but their limitations became more and more apparent. I gradually made up my mind that they must go. One day I would replace them with a really wonderful layout. What it would be like I had no idea. It would be big and ambitious in every way — the last word in railway modelling — and it would take years and years to build. I didn't talk much about it, but we had a rough-and-ready gardener from Yorkshire, Fletcher by name, and I did confide some of my hopes to him. Surprisingly, he took them seriously. 'Well, me lad', he said, 'if yer wants a thing bad enough, an' if yer works fer it 'ard enough, sure enough you'll get it.' Those simple words have remained in my mind with encouragement ever since.

So, having made the decision, I divided the trains into three sets and sold them, lock, stock and barrel, for £3 a set. The one thing of them all that outlived the purge was the coach of the Midland Railway of Western Australia. This had been hand-built for me as a surprise by one of my three half-brothers. They now owned a farm a hundred miles from Perth on the Midland, so Harry had measured the local stock and made a very good copy of it. It was a pity that for the requirements of the layout he had to shorten it to four compartments and widen the bogies considerably from the 3' 6" gauge to make it fit the standard Gauge 1 track — but apart from this he caught all the atmosphere of the original. It was too personal and too individual to part with and I never did.

The war was over but it was followed by an epidemic of pneumonic 'flu which swept the world. I went down with it. I was quite seriously ill — thousands died of it — but I was one of the luckier ones. After getting about again I was taken away from school for a year — to be out in the sun, go up to the farm, do as I pleased — and as a result it was one of the most blissfully happy years of my life. Revelling in the complete freedom that only 2000 acres of the farm could give, between swimming, riding and walking, I spent days picturing wonderful model railways running through the wilds of the River Paddock, with great bridges spanning the stream itself. But when I mentioned models to my brothers they laughed and said 'Pooh — your railways are dead and gone. When you are a little older you'll have no time for them. You wait and see.' I knew, with perfect conviction, how wrong they were.

Time was now passing too quickly. My father, nearly 80, had suffered a stroke and felt the heat badly. Having endured one very hot summer, we decided to avoid the heat of the next and go for several months to Albany, a beautiful spot a few hundred miles from Perth on the south coast.

Christmas 1921 came, in mid summer of course, during our stay there and I went to the shops to see what I could find as a present for myself. Among many other delights I discovered a book, fat and inviting, *The Handy Boy's Book*, which described everything from carpentry to chemistry, from photography to butterfly collecting, almost from repairing the kitchen kettle to building a boat. But as it happened I was anything but a 'handy boy'. I hated odd jobs and never felt tempted to use tools. Most of the constructional things the book invited me to do left me somewhere between lukewarm and very cold indeed, and though there was a great variety of other things that were quite interesting, I was on the point of putting it down when I caught sight of one short and unexpected article in its midst.

The article was by Henry Greenly on 'How to make a Cardboard Model Locomotive' and included an outline drawing of a neat little LSWR 0-4-4 tank. All my pent-up enthusiasm for railways, starved for the last year and a half, rushed back in an overwhelming desire to start work on the promised layout. I possessed no tools and hadn't a clue how to work in metal, but here, it seemed, was a heaven-sent way out of such an ordeal. Card was a very different proposition from metal and I felt I could cope with that. Scissors and glue, after all, were always on hand.

Before the book was mine, my plans were underway and they took a most unexpected turn. In my fallow eighteen months, my allegiance to the railways of England suffered a temporary eclipse as I had become interested by the local trains of Western Australia. In Australia, drawings of English prototypes were still few and far between, but if I modelled our own Australian lines, I could measure their vehicles and make my own drawings. The proposed line would therefore be an Australian one, freelance, but based upon local practice. With that decision made, Christmas came and the book was formally presented to me in the morning.

The same day the Australian Central Railway Company was formed — very officially. It had a capital of 100 six-penny shares, which I sold to any relatives or friends who could be badgered into buying them! How I expected to build the layout of my dreams on a capital of £2 10s has not been explained but the Australian Central Railway

was the actual starting point of Pendon. Since then its every concept has fundamentally changed, but from that day to this, the project that in the end became Pendon has been one and the same undertaking — evolving, transforming, even hibernating, but never broken or discontinued.

On the first day of 1922 I started plans, not for the LSWR 0-4-4T — this would obviously not do for an Australian line — but for an experimental 4-4-2 tender engine. For five weeks construction went ahead, until the engine was about half-built. But I was not proud of it. I had already discovered that card for wheels, bearings and moving parts was just not on. I tried using some large Meccano wheels instead, which looked like anything but engine wheels. Cardboard construction — and the engine — were abandoned in mid February.

Indecision followed. Towards the end of May I started an experimental low-loader wagon — bending the body out of *roofing gauge* galvanised iron! This time construction, or an attempt at it, lasted one week, at the end of which I again decided that metalwork was not for me. Had I possessed even the rudiments of metal sense, I might have guessed what was wrong.

By now we were back in Perth, but not long after our return, my father, who had been gradually failing, took a turn for the worse and died on the 25th July, at the age of 81. Looking back, it is one of my greatest regrets that I only knew him when he was past his zenith. That never gave me a chance really to know and understand him and to ask all the questions that I now wish I had. I remember him as a deeply affectionate man, brimming over with loving care and tenderness — a man full of contrasts, with his business acumen, his unwavering Christian principles, his sensitive nature and his great gift of being able to play with his young son at a moment's notice. He was a lion in his physical and spiritual strength and a wonderful father.

Despite the sadness of the loss, the weeks ran on and by the time October came, I was thinking of the railway again. This time I began studying electricity. As yet I knew practically nothing about it, but it seemed capable of doing most things and I must sound out its possibilities. Before long, new worlds opened. Was there anything that electricity *didn't* do? My layout must definitely be an electric one. It was the only way that trains could be run without man-handling them. Surely, it might even be possible to work a layout entirely automatically, perhaps with a perforated belt like a pianola roll placed over electric contacts to make and break circuits to the train's requirements? Here was something terrific — revolutionary even for 1922. It would need a huge amount of working out, but one day . . . .

In December, with my father's affairs now settled, Vi decided we must have a break and get away from it all. By then I was just 16, growing up comparatively quickly and

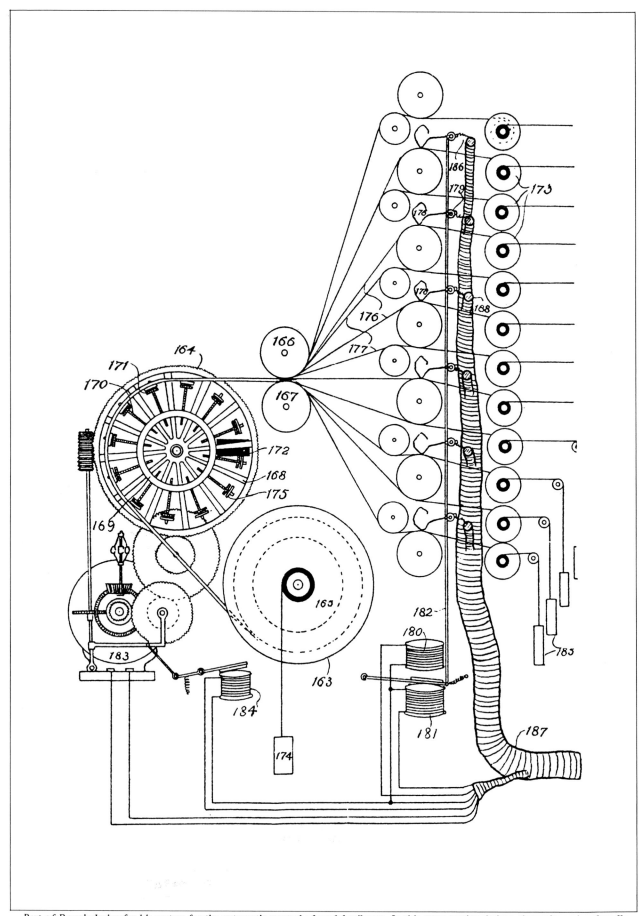

Part of Roye's design for his system for the automatic control of model railways. In this cross-sectional view, the various pianola rolls that would control the different systems (points, signals, engines, etc.) are shown feeding from the right and passing to a rotating drum (left) in which are located sets of electrical contacts.

studying at a business college. But the course, to my intense joy, was interrupted so that we could go together for a trip to Melbourne. This rather unlikely decision was typical of Vi, whose sense of the fitness of unexpected pleasures was a most endearing trait.

The 2000 mile train journey through bush, desert and pasture, was an unforgettable delight. So, too, was Melbourne itself, with a population then nearing the million, yet still served for miles by the most quaint cable trams and electric trains over the whole great suburban network. The electric trains, in contrast to the antiquated trams, seemed the last word in modern achievement. In a very short time I had made friends with the men who drove them, was being shown how they worked and — thrill of thrills — being taken for runs with the driver at the front end. It was fascinating to feel the train nosing its way over a maze of lines and points, picking its course with unfailing rightness and returning its signals to danger as it passed them. I was entranced. The ACR must include suburban electrics and it would do all they did automatically.

My railwaymen friends gave me the wiring diagram of a multiple-unit motor coach and, with this labyrinth of complexity before me as inspiration, I took the first step toward my great electrified system by designing for it the innards of a similar vehicle — very much simplified, yet not at all simple. I had set my heart on putting in every workable item possible and, when in due course it was finished, it made provision (by remote control) not only for driving and reversing the train, but for lighting it, coupling and uncoupling, raising or lowering the pantograph, setting the destination indicators, and even displaying a tail disc on what might become the last vehicle! To achieve what I envisaged, a great deal more would be required — on track, at the control centre and elsewhere. I little realised the size of the monster with which I had chosen to do battle. But the duel was on and there would be no turning back.

In Perth again, life resumed its outwardly normal ways, but after that vision of Melbourne, nothing was the same. When the business course finished, I allowed myself to be lured into a job with an insurance company — the AMP Society in St. George's Terrace. Their new office was a palatial one of polished mahogany, clear glass, white pillars and rubber floors — quite the most beautiful office I had ever imagined. But I was not in the least cut out for that sort of work and though, up to a point, quite happy, my head was far more full of plans for the electric control of the Australian Central Railway. Insurance seemed such a waste of time in comparison. In the office, out of the office, in every spare minute I worked out my wiring diagrams. When it was finally built, all one would have to do would be to sit elatedly and watch the trains going by —

starting, stopping, shunting — as they did in the real thing. It would be magnificent.

'Automotive Control' was the name I gave to the fantastic system which slowly but surely emerged. Difficulties arose, only to be disposed of one by one as more drawings and diagrams took shape. The pianola-roll principle was still the basis for it all, but I was now getting into my stride and decided to take things a step further still. Instead of one roll, a number of rolls must be used, each with its own timetable representing a different time of the day or night — the business rush to town in the morning — holiday traffic — the homeward surge in the evening — newspaper and mail trains in the small hours . . . By preparing a series of linked timetables, it should be possible to change from one to another without break and this could be set in operation by the hands of a control clock.

Such a system, it seemed to me in my enthusiasm, would revolutionise model railways. At that time there were practically none in Australia to be revolutionised, but in England there were hundreds and surely many would jump at a scheme such as this? I thought, too, of its possibilities as a shop-window display, for advertising, or for trade fairs and exhibitions! Somehow I must put it on the market. But before doing that it must be protected, or others might copy the idea and get in first. This, I was convinced, was urgent.

Fortunately, a patent agent worked on one of the floors above our office. Mr. Bonnerup was young, pleasant and very helpful. To take out a patent in England would cost about £50 to start with, followed by further payments later when the invention should be earning. But a fully detailed specification would have to be drawn up, all of which would take time for the complicated affair I was designing. Meanwhile a provisional patent could be taken out for £5 to cover the idea for nine months until the complete specification could be filed. *(Bonnerup's initial advice to Roye — contained in a letter that has survived from 1924 — was not to proceed with the patent. He saw no prospect of the invention being taken up in Australia and although he conceded its commercial viability might be stronger in Britain, his basic judgement was that Roye would 'find it very hard to make money out of it'. Roye, however, evidently did not take the advice.)*

I set to work with a will and before long, Mr. Bonnerup sent off the provisional application to England. It was a relief to feel secure. But this was only the start of the Chinese puzzle. To work out the system in full detail and then to describe it in words, covering all its ramifications and leaving nothing to the imagination, was a huge task in itself. However, in order to save money, of which I had very little, I undertook to do all the drawings as well. The further I went the more involved it became. The whole of my spare time was going into it but progress was slow and the nine month time limit was a constant threat. A certain amount could be done in the office if no one was looking — concocting paragraphs and sketches under a blotter when I should have been writing Overdue Notices. But this labour-of-desire was vital. Everything depended upon getting it done in time.

I was now 17 and the year was 1924. Months went by, I turned 18, and there was still a mountain of writing, typing, drawing and even actual inventing to get through. There was a vast difference between the final script and the rather sketchy fundamentals that had been knocked out before and new ideas as well as unforeseen difficulties kept cropping up. Vi, as usual, backed me to the hilt and her understanding and encouragement helped enormously. Yet it was beginning to look like a losing battle and before long there was no doubt of it. In desperation I went back to Mr. Bonnerup. Yes, an extension of time was possible, but no more than one month.

A week of that month went by — two — three — till only one week was left. The whole work, drawings and all, must be in the post for England by the following Monday morning. I still did my day's work in the office but everything else was set aside as I struggled on every evening into the small hours. The weekend came and I worked the whole of my available time on Saturday, almost the whole of Sunday and right through Sunday night. How I kept awake and with my mind clear I don't know — but I did it. Monday morning, very early, found me still in the midst of it, but by eight o'clock, I knew the end was within my grasp. I typed the last words of the 51 foolscap pages, arranged the many drawings and sealed the completed package for registration. A bite of breakfast, then off to the office with just enough time to get there. But I put my *magnum opus* in the post on the way.

At roughly this time — possibly a little earlier — some miniature toy trains, of a smallness unheard of until then, had reached Western Australia. Made by the German firm of Bing, they were of English outline with the colouring of the new railway companies, their size corresponding roughly to a 4mm scale, but on a gauge of 16.5mm — the very first beginnings of OO gauge. The engines were 2-4-0 tanks (of one pattern only) and the carriages were no more than 4-wheelers. But it was their diminutive scale that mattered. I bought a couple of sets and was intrigued by their daintiness. True, I had looked ahead in the patent to scales that were even smaller, but they had been more in theory while these before me were reality. They had a fascination quite beyond anything I had seen in bigger models and could offer great possibilities for my future line.

For the time being, though, the Australian Central Railway had retired to the background. One day it would come into its own but meanwhile the patent, once it was through, must be pushed. To interest others in it I should

Roye, aged 18. According to a note on the reverse of this photo in Roye's own hand, the intense expression was prompted by his being told to wear a starched collar that he disliked.
PENDON MUSEUM COLLECTION

probably need to demonstrate the system, or at any rate a part of it, and that would mean making models. They must be better than anything that had been on the market before. 'Scale Perfect' would be a good trade name. Ideas ran away with me, but they always led back to the same starting point. To do all that I envisaged I must learn to use metal working tools.

A lathe would be essential. My brother Harry, who had built the MRWA coach for me, was a skilled metal worker. He even repaired all the farm machinery when it broke down. So I enlisted his help and asked him to choose a good lathe for me.

I have never understood how his mind worked — or failed to work — on that epic occasion, but for the building of small-scale trains he recommended a lathe no less in size than the giant ones he used on the farm — and its price was £60 (a lot in those days). I was taken aback, but he assured me that if I wanted a really fine tool this was it — it would do everything one could wish and would last a lifetime.

I put the whole case to Vi, stressing, as I firmly believed, that a genuinely good lathe was the foundation of all I hoped to do and she, after demurring a little, but ready as always to make any sacrifice to help me, bowed to superior judgment and put up the bulk of the money. Pathetic as the choice was, I almost think it was worth it for the knowledge of her unfailing belief in me. To her my schemes must have seemed more than fantastic (as, of course, they were), but she agreed I must be given my chance. Without that faith in me and her unwavering support on many successive occasions, Pendon would never have come into being.

My father's workshop was still intact in the back garden — on the other side of the hedge from where the tinplate mainline of the LNWR had once run — and there the lathe was installed. I surveyed it with a mixture of pride and misgiving — but made no attempt to use it. My old aversion to metal work still defied me. Week after week the great machine stood waiting for me to make the move that never came, to learn the secrets it never yielded — a monument of hope and frustration.

Meanwhile I was feeling increasingly uneasy with the way that my employment seemed to place obstacles in the way of my plans. With its unremitting demands on my time, it would be impossible to do the study, the experimenting, the construction and then the canvassing which would be essential to the success of the modelling firm that I now pictured at the centre of my plans to promote 'Automotive Control'. Vi, fortunately, realised that I was a misfit there and since there would be other jobs going if my big ideas came to nothing, she agreed to let me have my head. I handed in my notice.

This was February 1925. A fortnight after leaving the office I began to think seriously about going to England. The difficulty — almost the impossibility — of pushing an English patent from Australia was beginning to dawn. I must be on the spot. There was now no point in delaying and I have never been more thankful of dealing with a parent who had the gift of seeing the other side. Again Vi agreed. At the time, bursting with enthusiasm to be off, I quite failed to realise how great was the sacrifice, in companionship and much else, that she was making. It must have been a heart-searching decision, but she made it without a waver and without the least hint of what it was costing her. Once the decision was made, however, preparations went ahead swiftly. In the last week of March I

booked a third-class passage on the new Orient liner *Oronsay*, 20,000 tons, due to sail from Fremantle to London three weeks later.

The day of my sailing arrived. I wanted to make the 12 mile journey to Fremantle with Vi alone, but her uncle and several too-kind friends insisted on seeing me off, so we had no more than a few poignant minutes together in my cabin. She was dry-eyed and sensible. So was I — just. But adventure called and my pangs were softened by her promise to follow after a time, if I wanted to remain in England.

So our parting was somehow made. The bell rang for visitors to leave the ship, after which Vi and the others stood waving from the wharf, while I hung over the rail, looking down with a lump in my throat, already alone. Coloured streamers were thrown between the decks and the throng below — hundreds of them — and very slowly the gap between the ship and the wharf began to widen. The streamers stretched out between us and them, Vi holding the other end of the one I gripped so tightly. Still the gap widened. One or two trains passed behind the wharf — the little trains of Western Australia that in recent years I had come to love, which so soon would be mine no more. Now some of the streamers were beginning to snap, falling limply into the water, or tangling with each other. Mine still held. More and more fell — then mine went. I saw Vi wave and laugh at me — but I couldn't see the effort of will behind her show of gaiety.

Further, further we drew apart. Our friends by now had left, but Vi stood waving, her uncle beside her. It was soon too far to see clearly and dusk, too, was beginning to fall. Yet as long as sight of any kind could persist she was there, waving something pale which showed even when her form was lost. I never saw her stop waving — she and the wharf just faded out as lights began twinkling on the shore beyond.

The Oronsay *alongside at Tilbury on 24th January 1925, about to embark on her maiden voyage to Australia. Roye came to England on the return sailing.*
NATIONAL MARITIME MUSEUM

Plymouth Millbay in about 1925. The upper photograph provides a general view of the GWR Millbay facilities, with the dock itself in the foreground and Plymouth Sound (where the ocean liners anchored) in the background. In the lower view a 'Castle' class locomotive is seen waiting as hundreds of mail bags were loaded by conveyor belt from the decks of one of the tender boats, Sir Walter Raleigh.

CHAPTER TWO

1925–1931
FOUNDATIONS: THE GREAT BRITISH RAILWAY

GWR 'Star' class No. 4004 Morning Star *tracing part of the route of Roye's first journey as it approached Parson's Tunnel between Teignmouth and Dawlish with an up local service.*

THE morning of 13th May broke dull and drizzly. When I went on deck fairly early, we were already lying in Plymouth Sound. Grey sea, dull-green hilly shores through the mist of rain. But my heart beat fast. This was England. I had seen it! And having been warned about the atrocious climate, I took this kind of weather for granted. No doubt it would usually be like this over here. I went below to pack and have breakfast. When I came up again, the clouds had broken, the sun streamed radiantly on a glittering sea, the hills had become rich and verdant. What a transformation and for the next six weeks, I saw nothing but sunny skies.

Chafing to be on English soil at the first possible moment and, above all else to see the railways, I had arranged to leave the ship at Plymouth and go by train to London. A tender took passengers ashore, then there was the passage through customs, followed by a brief walk to the boat train. There it was — no engine yet, but long primrose-panelled coaches gleaming shapely in the bright morning light — Great Western coaches, seventy feet in length, more beautiful than even I had dared to picture. It's great when dreams come true at the age of eighteen.

I found a corner seat, facing, and leant back to drink it all in. Presently there was a hissing, and a majestic engine, polished brass and copper against its green livery, passed alongside on its way to the head of the train, its crescent nameplate resplendent in the sunshine, *Westminster Abbey* — a Star class locomotive — the first English engine I ever saw.

At last we started — a slow double-headed climb from sea level with a Mogul piloting, giving plenty of time to revel in the riot of springtime foliage beside the line and, by a freak of memory, I can still see a particularly exquisite, sticky chestnut bud, just bursting, that caught my glance as it slid by. It was all so new, so fresh, so splendid.

The whole run was superb, with a stop only at Exeter and not a check all the way. Beneath a cloudless sky the fields were so green, and, after the railways of Western Australia, the speed was breathtaking. I tried in vain to see station nameboards as they flashed past and I remember just glimpsing 'Savernake'. There was no slackening and, from somewhere nearer to London, a vivid impression still remains of slated house tops, seemingly far below the line, careering past and away. Finally the long train eased, care-

Serried ranks of London taxis waiting alongside the main arrival platforms at Paddington. These views are typical of the scene that greeted Roye on his arrival in the capital. The train standing at Platform 10 in the upper view is typical of the long-distance expresses on which Roye travelled from Plymouth.

NATIONAL RAILWAY MUSEUM

fully slowing between the backs of crowded tenements — signals, engines, other trains — into Paddington.

Feeling rather small among the hurrying throngs beneath the huge roof, yet full of a sense of achievement, I collected my luggage from the van and found a taxi. As it drove from the great station into the great city outside, I caught sight once more of *Westminster Abbey* against the buffer stops, still breathing heavily, it seemed, from her run, but still looking magnificent at the head of that beautiful train.

London was just as I expected it to be — almost famil-.iar, exactly like its pictures. The taxi driver, seeing 'Orient Line' written large on my possessions, proceeded to sting me by charging about double the correct fare, on top of which he had the nerve to inform me that in this country it was usual to give a 50% tip! I knew nothing of taxi meters and had no basis to challenge his statements, so paid the fare meekly but reduced the tip by half, which must still have given him cause to rub his hands in glee.

That evening, staying in South Kensington, I wanted to see the sights, but having as yet no time to get my bearings, I was afraid to venture far. Once I was able to study a map all would be well, but meanwhile, safety first! So I took the only course that seemed really safe. I went to the Underground, took a ticket to the next station and then happily sat through a complete round of the Circle line. At least I couldn't fail to get back!

Early next morning I looked out of my window, two or three storeys up, to a kind of mews below — a wide cobbled alley where barrow men were arranging and selling their wares in the mists of a lingering dawn, calling their cries or singing their greetings to the coming day. It was a magical old-time scene and this, too, was England — quite a different England.

Very soon I mastered London's geography and was really seeing the sights — first and foremost Euston, Paddington (again), Victoria, Waterloo . . . Everything else took second place. But after a few days I had to leave London for Birmingham. Mr. Bonnerup's English counterpart wanted to see me about the patent.

Delighted with the prospect of travelling by the railway of my childhood's loyalty, the old North Western, I went again to Euston to find how the trains ran. At the enquiry office my mind must have been back in Australia for, to the amazement of the young man behind the counter, I began, 'Can you tell me what day I can get a train to Birmingham?' When he spluttered I came to with a jerk and tried to explain that until I came to England I had been used to a 'Monday and Friday only' sort of thing. I was not sure whether he believed me and felt a proper idiot. On the Underground I put my foot in it again. After dropping some pennies into the automatic machine, I took out the ticket and politely said 'Thank you' — at which the rest of the queue tittered audibly.

The two hour journey to Birmingham by the LNWR mainline was an enormous satisfaction — even despite the disappointment that it was in the process of being 'Midlandised' after becoming part of the LMS. However, the unwelcome change had overtaken my favourite only a couple of years before and there were more coaches in plum and spilt-milk livery than in the encroaching crimson lake. Most LNWR engines remained in their original blackberry black, and signals and the lineside were quite unchanged. All the dignity of the old line was there still and I was grateful beyond words to be seeing it almost, if not quite, in time.

At New Street station I lingered as long as I dared before going in search of lodgings and it was there, a day or so later, that I saw the sight — once only — which I have remembered with joy for the rest of my life, a Johnson Single of the Midland Railway, one of the most graceful engines ever built. At the time, in spite of its beauty, it looked so old-fashioned that I almost felt compassion for it and it was only in later years that I realised the extent of my privilege in having seen it, especially in normal service. It was one of the last singles still running and was withdrawn not very long after.

Consultations over the patent went satisfactorily. I was soon back in London staying with a family named Beale who lived near the Crystal Palace, but before I could begin to explore the model world as I intended, a letter arrived from a distant relative in Cornwall, asking me to spend a fortnight there. The weather was still perfect, so off I went, this time by the mainline of the former London & South Western Railway.

My relative lived in Week St. Mary, a village a few miles from Bude which considered itself rather remote. It was the shape of a piece of string — a long straggle down a single road — and the nearest pub was three miles away. On the second day I disgraced myself. Someone asked how I liked being in the wilds? My thoughts went back to Australia — to the real wilds of the farm, where kangaroos hopped in their scores, where the horse-drawn mailman drove by, half a mile from the house, once a week, except when the river was high when he wouldn't come at all. Here the post came to the door like clockwork every morning, there was a doctor in the village, a church, a shop, even a temperance hotel! 'Wilds?', I echoed, 'I thought it was suburban', which wasn't at all the thing to say. But the high-banked lanes were covered in purple foxglove and I loved every minute of my fortnight in that windswept, magic spot.

I worked my way back gradually, and whilst staying in Bristol with another relative (an Aunt Annie), to my surprise, another letter came. This one was from a married cousin living near Swindon, May French, asking me to meet them for the day in Bath. I vaguely knew of their existence — no more than that — but Aunt Annie had

A distant view of Wanborough church with its unusual arrangement of a tower and a spire, photographed in the 1920s.

PENDON MUSEUM COLLECTION

told them of my visit and they hastened to greet me. The most far-reaching crossroads may come to us unsensed and I little thought that in accepting May's apparently casual invitation, I was on the way to setting not only my own future course in this country, but the character of the whole model venture as well.

I went to Bath by the little Midland line as a variant to the Great Western and made my way in good time to the Abbey, outside which we had arranged to meet. I had been told to look out for a blue Model-T Ford with an English saloon body — whatever that hybrid might look like — but when it came it was the peering faces from inside that gave it away. May and her husband Hubert came straight over to me.

May was a pale and delicate-looking woman, though with a will a good deal stronger than her frail looks foretold. Hubert was a Church of England clergyman in dog collar and dark grey suit. May's mother, to be called Aunt Lucy — an old lady of 77 years — struck me as kindly, Victorian and very vivacious. There were two small boys, Basil and Michael, dressed all in white, with golden hair and faces shining like apples. Their nurse, Mrs. Vokes, was a dear old lady, all in black, who still wore a bonnet with ostrich feathers perched on top, although most old ladies' bonnets had gone out, like so much else, with the 1914–18 war.

After tea, when saying our farewells, there was a hesitance and Aunt Lucy, never at a loss for words, stepped in by explaining that May wanted to say something but was afraid I might feel under an obligation. May then said 'We should like you to come and stay for a couple of weeks, but its only a vicarage, a pauper's home you know, so please don't come unless you really want to put up with it.' I glanced at the Ford, at the immaculately dressed children complete with nurse-in-waiting and decided that May was probably exaggerating, to say the least. So I allayed her fears, said I should be delighted to come and, in so doing, took the road which was to become the road to Pendon.

It was 23rd July when I left Bristol by Great Western express, in a slip coach for Swindon. To be slipped would be quite a new kind of thrill. The run was a good one and at Swindon we sped past the length of the famous Works till the great moment came . . . but we tore through the

Lower Wanborough with the Harrow Inn that was also to be modelled for Pendon on the left. Notice the ornate telephone kiosk on the verge opposite the inn.
PENDON MUSEUM COLLECTION

station, slip coach and all, having failed to slip. A fierce application of brakes brought us eventually to a stand somewhere between long lines of goods sidings. There followed a conference between guard and slip guard — much banging and clanging — and after about ten minutes they got the coupling apart. The express went off slowly on its chastened way and a Pannier tank puffed importantly out and towed us back to civilisation. Hubert awaited me on the platform, brimming over with pointed remarks about the inefficiency of the railways — with which I heartily disagreed, but was too wary at this stage to say so!

All was new and sparkling. A car drive of four or five miles brought us to Wanborough, a village set partly on the hills and partly in the meadows below. The church was a couple of hundred feet up on the top of the first rise, a landmark among its trees for several miles, and Hubert proudly pointed out its tower and separate spire. It was one of only three churches in England which possessed both.

The Vicarage was not far from it, a square and rather prosaic house. It had a couple of attic windows in its slate roof, but its brick front was so obliterated by ivy that the whole became almost beautiful. As soon as I went in I saw that May's assessment of it as a 'pauper's home' was quite unmerited. Certainly, there was nothing elaborate about

it, but the furniture was mostly antique and it was comfortable. Lighting was entirely by oil lamp. In 1925, despite my first impressions of Cornwall, rural areas were still very countrified.

So the family welcomed me for a couple of weeks and it had happened, quite beyond any foresight of my own, that I had come to the hills bordering the Vale of White Horse.

A pleasant fortnight passed, everyone was kindness itself and my stay was extended to three weeks. I was then on the point of returning to the Beales in London, when Mrs. Beale wrote saying her son Jack had contracted scarlet fever and as they were nursing him at home, it would be at least six weeks before they could have me back. It was that stroke of fate which clinched my connection with the Vale of White Horse. Hubert and May said that, of course, I must remain with them, which I gladly did. Some cousins in Ireland invited me for a fortnight to Sligo — golden oak foliage, blue distances and shimmering loughs (for autumn was early there), but I returned to Wanborough as to home and began to take root.

I was not sorry for this enforced delay. After getting used to the wonder of the country, now on the brink of its autumn pageantry in the wake of that in Ireland, London was promising to look a little drab. Even then I might have gone back, but Vi cabled the joyful news that she had let the house for a year — she was coming to join me at Christmas and proposed our wintering together on the Continent. So I continued at Wanborough for the time that was left, being made to feel that I was now part of the family.

Five magic months followed, in which models and everything connected with them seemed very far away. In the middle of Italy, even England itself appeared almost unreal. We spent nearly three months in France and Italy — visiting Nice, Florence, Rome, Sorrento, Genoa and Venice. From Italy we moved on to Switzerland, staying in Lucerne. Then, travelling alone, I struck out through Eastern and Central Europe, visiting Vienna, Budapest, Prague, Dresden, Berlin, Copenhagen and Hamburg, before rejoining Vi in Paris for two weeks. It was unforgettable!

That winter and spring, inspired by the beauty on every hand, I had become involved in writing verse — a new departure — but which at that moment became uppermost in my mind. Models, when I thought of them at all, would get their due in good time. So it came almost as a shock, when, in Florence, notification reached me that the patent had been granted. Its number was 228550, but, as I was under age, it had been taken out in the name of

Cottages at the top of Kite Hill, Wanborough, just a few yards from the Wanborough Vicarage.   **PENDON MUSEUM COLLECTION**

The centre of Wanborough with 'The Old Calley Arms' (right), the subject of Roye's first model.
PENDON MUSEUM COLLECTION

The Vale of White Horse in the 1930s, seen from the White Horse Hill itself, with the road to Uffington disappearing into the distance. The GWR main line is lost amidst the trees, beyond the village of Uffington.

H. O. VAUGHAN

A shepherd gathering his flock on the slopes of the White Horse Hill, with the White Horse itself and the outer ramparts of Uffington Castle in the background.

H. O. VAUGHAN

PATENT SPECIFICATION

Convention Date (Australia): Jan. 29, 1924.

228,550

Application Date (in United Kingdom): Jan. 28, 1925. No. 2505/25.

Complete Accepted; Oct. 22, 1925.

COMPLETE SPECIFICATION.

Improvements in and relating to the Working of Model Railways.

I, FLORENCE VIOLET ENGLAND, of 7, Richardson Street, West Perth, in the State of Western Australia, Commonwealth of Australia, British subject, do
5 hereby declare the nature of this invention and in what manner the same is to be performed, to be particularly described and ascertained in and by the following statement:—
10 This invention relates to improvements in model railways and in their working and control.

Model railways are a popular hobby, and are also of advertising and educa-
15 tional value. The motive power usually employed is clockwork, steam or electricity. Up to the present time clockwork and steam models have been controlled almost entirely by hand, whilst
20 the control of electric trains, although somewhat more advanced, has been based on a system which precluded the introduction of more controls than speed regulation (including starting and stop-
25 ping) and reversing. These controls have been effected by manipulating the current supply, speed control being obtained by varying the strength of the supply, stopping by disconnecting it, and
30 reversing by changing the polarity of the supply of that section. Power has been supplied from a track conductor, the running rails acting as the return. Thus the train could only be controlled
35 by the variation of this one current in strength or polarity.

The object of the present invention is to provide a reliable and comprehensive system of control which will dispense
40 with hand operation of the trains and equipment, these being controlled exclusively by the connexion of contacts at a control station; to introduce a greater number of controls and actions into the
45 models than has heretofore been possible; and to provide, when desired, for the working of the system personally with the control levers, or automatically and completely without attention.

These requirements are accomplished 50 by the system herein described called multiple-automatic control.

Multiple-automatic control consists of the introduction into model trains of a number of controls and the working of 55 these solely by the connexion of control contacts at the control station. Real trains are operated from control levers in the motor vehicles or locomotives, these being moved by the motormen on 60 the trains. For model railways, as the levers cannot be operated from within the train, by the multiple control system electromagnets are substituted in the cars and connected electrically by means of 65 track conductors to contacts at the control station. By the connection of these contacts by control levers, buttons or stops, the electro-magnets cause the controls on the train to be operated, as if 70 by a driver in the vehicle.

The present invention comprises the combination with trains or vehicles carrying a number of different controlling or actuating devices, some or all of 75 which are operated by solenoids or electro-magnets and each included in a different branch lead, or circuit, of a continuous supply conductor or conductors giving a common supply to the 80 branch controlling circuits of the vehicle at all points of the system, and a plurality of insulated return conductors of constant polarity extending the full length of the track and respectively 85 maintained continually in electrical connexion with the different controlling circuits of the vehicles by means of depositors (except, if desired, at points, crossings and the like), said plurality of 90 return conductors being all divided throughout the length of the track into independent sections and each conductor of each section connected by a transmis-

[Price 1/-]

my mother. I tried to picture the impression it would give of the woman allegedly responsible for that electrical fantasy! With the patent grant came a list of progressive payments which would become due from year to year, but they didn't start yet, so could be shelved for the time being.

We left the Continent in the late spring of 1926, when the General Strike had come and gone. We reached England very early in the morning, so early that even Victoria Station was incapable of producing a cup of tea. We were making for Wanborough, to spend the summer there which proved, if proof were needed, that it had become my English home. In August, I purchased a

motor cycle with sidecar and, with Vi as a passenger, we were off on our travels again, this time exploring the Lake District, the Border Country and Scotland, as far north as Perth, returning through Durham and York.

It was a happy year — too happy to get much done. But being in London sometime, I did establish contact with the Wimbledon Model Railway Club and learnt a lot there. Unlike some of the more weighty engineering societies, this group was concerned chiefly with the smaller scales and I found it as helpful as it was friendly.

Though no actual progress was being made with the model scheme, I was at last trying to be realistic about it, and the more I faced up to it, the more I came to see that

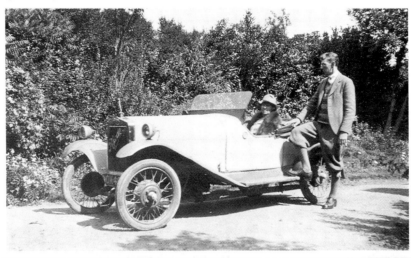

Roye posed alongside a car (which Roye nicknamed 'Cleopatra') that his mother (who is seated in the car) purchased for a holiday to Cornwall in 1926. On their return the car was sold and replaced by 'Anthony' — a motor cycle and sidecar combination.
PENDON MUSEUM
COLLECTION

Violet England, apparently at the control of 'Anthony' with Roye, cap worn in reverse, squeezed into the sidecar. The pillion passenger — a family friend named Miss Farquarson — seems less at ease with the joke.
PENDON MUSEUM COLLECTION

Roye, with May French (centre) and a friend of the family named Miss Winchcombe, photographed on the road from Frome to Shepton Mallett, en route to Weston-super-Mare in 1925. PENDON MUSEUM
COLLECTION

Although not recorded in his 'Saga', Roye began making photographic expeditions to railway locations beyond Swindon and the Vale of White Horse, soon after his arrival in Britain. The first of these views shows 'Bulldog' class engine No. 3363 Alfred Baldwin waiting to leave Swansea (High Street) in September 1925. The grim industrial landscape of the Lower Swansea Valley (background) must have provided Roye with a stark contrast to the beauty of the Vale of White Horse.
ROYE ENGLAND

the patent was a white elephant. Modellers, I found, made railways that they wanted to run, not that they wanted run for them. Furthermore, the cost, when I tried to assess it with a level head, would be so exorbitant, that few could afford it, even if they wanted to. A further contingency, that it might not work efficiently, had still not occurred to me and it remained my hope to use it on my own great layout one day. But by now I had seen the impracticality of making models commercially, so from that point of view, the patent was valueless. As soon as the first payment became due it would lapse, but I had no regrets. As a result of it, Automotive Control was fully worked out, recorded in drawings and print for my own future use and, above all, it had brought me to England.

In November, Vi had to return to Perth, and the way that could lead to Pendon was in the balance. After 18

Roye's cousins Basil (left) and Michael French, alongside the GWR main line at Savernake, sometime in the summer of 1927.
ROYE ENGLAND

'Saint' class engine No. 2907 Lady Distain *with a local train near Weston-super-Mare, September 1927.* ROYE ENGLAND

Roye, aged 21, on a motor-cycling tour of Scotland in 1927. PENDON MUSEUM COLLECTION

'Flower' class engine No. 4162 Marguerite *entering Bath on an up train, including an NER parcels van destined for Newcastle, May 1928.*
ROYE ENGLAND

Probably on the same visit (May 1928), Roye also photographed this '517' class tank engine, No. 539, on a down local passing through Sydney Gardens, Bath.
ROYE ENGLAND

'Barnum' class engine No. 3210, near Criccieth, with a Pwllheli to Barmouth train.
ROYE ENGLAND

Another view taken on the former Cambrian Railways system in North Wales, in August and September 1928. 'Dean Goods' class engine No. 2352 entering Towyn with a train for Pwllheli.
ROYE ENGLAND

Ashbury, looking east towards Knighton.

A quiet lane at Idstone, between Bishopstone and Ashbury. The building on the left was named 'Chestnut Cottage' by Roye and later included in the Vale Scene at Pendon.
ROYE ENGLAND

months of unfettered fling in England and abroad, in which I had achieved nothing towards my big ideas, Vi could so easily have insisted that I should go back with her and settle down to a sensible, if uninspired, future. That would have been the end. But with no clue to what lay ahead, Vi accepted my constant assurance that if she kept her faith in me I would not let her down. I was as convinced as ever that modelling was a thing for which I was set apart. It was not a mere hobby, it was a vocation. So she reluctantly let me choose my own road and not only returned to Australia alone, but arranged to send me a small allowance to keep me going for a time, until I had had the chance for which I had asked. Few mothers would have gambled on such an unlikely hope.

By now, of course, the Australian Central Railway had changed its name and its proposed character and at that moment, was being called the Great British Railway. But any practical start on the GBR was delayed by uncertainties over what scale and gauge to adopt. The unpleasant fact had also begun to dawn that before long, I must find myself some sort of career. Several possibilities were sug-

gested, none of them inviting, but the most likely seemed to be the Church. There I should at least be doing something worthwhile. The things of the spirit definitely mattered to me, even though (as yet) no-one could have called me a particularly good churchman. But there would be a lot of training first and the way might open.

Vi came back to England in 1929 and in the spring of 1930 we were in Touraine. With the incredibly fascinating French railways of those days all about me, I began again to channel my ideas. A pencilled note dated 3rd March of that year and headed 'Proposed Basis of the Model System' summarises the conclusions, which were an enormous advance on anything I had had in mind before. There were six main points:

* my model must be an historical one.
* in order to give a representative picture, it must include several differing railways.
* the trains must run through imaginary but typical scenery of the lines being modelled.
* the period must be that of the steam locomotive's prime.

Roye's own caption for this photograph is 'a typical scene beside the Vale of White Horse in summer'. The exact location is Bodyhorse Lane, between Wanborough and Hinto Parva.
ROYE ENGLAND

The same scene photographed in winter.

ROYE ENGLAND

A distant view of the Berkshire Downs from the Vale. The openness of the scene is typical of the modern Vale which has been stripped of its trees by hedge clearance and Dutch Elm disease, but is less typical of the 1930s when the photo was taken.

- there must be correctness in railway practice as well as in construction.
- a certain amount of chronological licence must be allowed to give historical coverage.

So the freelance bogey had finally given way to historical accuracy; the ambitious depicting of several railways — far beyond what I could do myself — could only mean enlisting the help of others; the creating of typical scenery demanded that the layout must be an indoor one and also of a comparatively small scale; and the prime of steam could only mean those expansive years around 1930. The 'Proposed Basis' formed, in fact, a reliable charter for the future Pendon. Things were beginning to fall into shape.

But the clouds of depression were gathering on the clear skies of the past few years and though outwardly they appeared to make little difference, there was hopelessness, increasing daily, in all industrial areas. In a different way it began to affect Vi too, for the exchange rate between Australia and England went up and up, threatening to become prohibitive. The days of comparative affluence and the freedom that went with it, were very surely passing. To get a job now became a priority. But it was not as easy as that. With neither training nor experience, where should I turn?

To insurance. It was the one thing I had done — and the last thing I wanted to do again. But jobs were getting scarce and the chance to be choosy had gone. This time I was not doomed to work in an office, but was given an outdoor agency in Brighton, which I hoped would be better. In practice it was not. Acute depression had already hit the poorer parts of the town, yet I was instructed that whether people could afford it or not, new business had to be found. Never take 'no' for an answer. If they shut the door in your face, put your foot in it first. It may have been business, it may have suited some, but I vowed, business or no business, that nothing would make me a party to that way of getting it.

The other side of my area — the commercial premises and the luxury hotels — should have been an opportunity, but here business acumen was essential. These were worldly-wise, hard-headed people and they knew all the answers. Who was I, utterly unsuited to business techniques, to talk them round and convince them that white was black? So I got no business from them either.

For six months I struggled on, working from nine in the morning until ten or eleven at night, for no thanks and for very little pay. It was £3 a week — a pittance even in 1930 — plus commission which I failed to earn. As an insurance agent I was a complete failure, but as a weekly visitor to the poor, I was a great success. In many ways it was like parish work but without the time or authority to do anything for them. Perhaps, after all, the Church was the right path for me to follow? Until I took that agency,

I had no idea how the poor lived — or how poor they could be. The urge to help them was very real, but in the Church there would also be services and preaching . . . Would training take care of these? I had doubts, but they might be groundless. The personal side, the visiting, just then was uppermost in my mind and plans went ahead on the strength of it.

On 28th February, 1931, the sixth anniversary to the day of my leaving the insurance office in Perth, I walked out of the office in Brighton.

I made, as usual, for Wanborough to take stock. To matriculate would be essential — no college would accept one without that — and owing to the bout of pneumonic 'flu at the start of my teens, I had no examination passes whatsoever to my credit. The financial slide was becoming so serious that Vi had unwillingly to return to Australia, but, before she left, we arranged a correspondence course with Wolsey Hall. This would allow me to continue at the Vicarage, where I could live far more cheaply than anywhere else.

I chose the Durham matriculation and got down to work with true resolve, deciding to study morning and evening with a period of freedom in the afternoon.

Models, my conscience told me, must not be allowed to encroach on the things that now really mattered, but though I aimed to follow that conscience, I couldn't entirely believe in it. Models mattered too, quite a lot, in a different way. However, the exam was the thing of the moment and must have priority. What would follow at the end of it I felt was in the lap of the gods and, for the time-being, I was quite content to leave it there. A life of services and Church routine still didn't truly appeal but no doubt the way would open. If not, perhaps matriculation might open a way elsewhere . . . .

Which was precisely what matriculation began to do, but in a most unorthodox direction. By giving me my afternoons free, my studies opened the way once more to the Great Western, to the villages and country of the Vale. Day by day, month after month, I roamed them till they became a part of me as never before, and paradoxically it was my leisure time, the wandering hours that I allowed myself away from study, that was in fact fulfilling my appointed vocation. With the prospect of a settled year or more before me, I decided to lick my plans for the models into shape and get under way.

A winter scene along one of the many lanes of the Vale of White Horse with the distinctive line of the Berkshire Downs in the distance. Puddles in the rutted track reflect the approach of a stormy sky that also silhouettes one of the characteristic signposts of the Vale.

A steam engine driving a threshing machine on a farm near Newbury. A glimpse of the countryside of the 1930s that Roye saw slipping away. MUSEUM OF ENGLISH RURAL LIFE

CHAPTER THREE

1931—1934
THE ACTUAL BEGINNING

Bishopstone in 1932.

ROYE ENGLAND

NEARLY ten years had passed since the days of *The Handy Boy's Book* and not a thing had been built. But now I knew what I wanted. I should start with the Great Western mainline through the Vale — none was more inviting — and hope to go on to others in due course. Also, I knew at last what scale I wanted. The very small scales, as HO and OO were thought of at that time (the market as yet knew nothing of N gauge, TT or even EM), were now going ahead so well that I had no hesitation in discounting O gauge in their favour. But OO was a visibly inaccurate gauge, which was anathema to the historical modeller that I was on my way to becoming, whereas HO promised to be the scale of the future for all serious small scale modellers, and on the strength of that promise, I accepted it without further question.

To celebrate, I brought four HO scale wagons. Afterwards, of course, they proved quite unsuitable for Pendon, but they came into their own some thirty years later when they could be seen standing as visitors on the siding of John Ahern's Madder Valley layout, after it had been installed at Pendon. Although lacking brake gear, I told myself they all looked very pleasing — an LNWR open,

an LSWR van and two private owner wagons that I painted myself. Painting stock was so much easier than building it!

In fact, I was coming to see that to build stock would never be my line. Sooner or later the construction of vehicles must lead to metalwork and this, even now, was a sleeping dragon that raised a forbidding head and hissed whenever I thought of it. Even working in wood had very little appeal for me. But card — that was my medium, so a further decision was taken. The artistic side — the country, the buildings, the lineside — I should make myself. Someone else must be found to build the trains. That would be easy providing the money could also be found. However, surplus cash was anything but a strong point at the moment, and this, frustrating as it was, delayed railway construction indefinitely. It was not until HO gauge (in England, at least) was on its way out that I realised that the delay had been fortuitous.

If lack of funds held up the advance on the railway, there was nothing to prevent me starting work on its surroundings. To build an effective setting could be a brief, impressionist adventure, or it could be a life's work, mod-

Cress beds were a characteristic feature of the landscape along the spring-line at the foot of the Downs, particularly in the area around Letcombe Bassett.

elling everything with meticulous care till it became a worthy equal of the railway as a work of art and of history. No one had done that kind of thing before but I felt sure that if reproduced with sufficient skill, both railway and country could be made to took entirely real. Nothing less would do, for both (in their different ways) were equally beautiful and, as I was now being forced to see, both were on the brink of change.

On the railway, change was slow but organised. In the countryside it was insidious and went largely unnoticed. The age-long heritage of England appeared to be timeless, but to anyone who knew it well, it was already showing signs of crumbling. One by one the chalk roads of the Vale were being tarred over. Here and there a length of wire replaced a failing hedge, a sheet of galvanised iron appeared over a patch of leaky thatch, and, on farms, there

Water meadows in the Vale, near Swindon (1934).
PENDON MUSEUM
COLLECTION

An idyllic scene that captures the timeless quality of rural England before World War II. Boys fishing for minnows in a chalk stream at West Hendred (1939).
H. O. VAUGHAN

A glimpse down one of the tree-lined, gated lanes that ran from Knighton into the Vale. The cottage is now demolished.

The village shop at Wanborough, prior to rebuilding. PENDON MUSEUM COLLECTION

The same building photographed in 1982.
A. E. SMITH

were whole sheds built of it. Concrete had come as well. Occasionally the disrepair of a cottage drove out an old couple, or they died and it became a ruin. A tree beside this lane or that was cut down, or it blew down, and another small vista was marred. A hump-backed bridge with rickety wooden railings was straightened and widened because now more cars were coming on the road.

Evidence of this change lay near at hand. In Wanborough as early as 1924 — before I went there — the village shop, a half-timbered and thatched gem, had been martyred by reconstruction into a hideous example of what looked like suburban jerry-building. The next

victim was a thatched cottage adjacent to it, after which there was a lull until 1931, when the desecration of a further building coincided with my awakening sense of a mission to preserve the lingering present in miniature. This time it was a simple cottage, partly of stone, partly of brick, under shading thatch, whose successive layers of wash — pale cream, rich cream, an almost indefinable hint of duck-egg blue, fawn, buff, peach — were peeling off one by one, like the bark of a plane tree, leaving the old walls in a mellow fantasy of indescribably lovely hues. But all this was ripped off. The graceful ups and downs of the thatched eaves were levelled to a hard straight line with an iron gutter. The sloping ends of the roof were built out

The old 'Calley Arms' in the condition that Roye first saw the building.
PENDON MUSEUM
COLLECTION

square and prosaic. Roughcast was daubed over the whole of the stonework and the desolation was made complete by the addition of a roof of pink asbestos. Never had a worse defacement been perpetrated in the cause of 'progress', but the family who lived there were delighted. 'It's just like London!', they exclaimed.

It was situated facing a triangle of grass where three roads met and opposite which stood a red-brick public house, 'The New Calley Arms'. Rumour (which proved many years later to have been true) said the cottage itself had once been an inn, but that long ago it had given way to its upstart rival across the road. While the heart-breaking restoration was in progress I went inside and saw what I could, taking main measurements and making one or two rough sketches. But it was too early to foresee the importance of such work, and the particulars that I took were very far from complete.

A sense of vocation has to grow and it was doing so fairly fast now. Then the determination followed to model, for the generations to come, not merely a stretch of countryside along the railway, but combined with this an unspoilt village — a composite one, typical, in its entirety. The first building to be brought to life again — as far as was still possible — would be the mutilated former inn. This, at last, was the real Pendon.

Village modelling in the early 1930s was something entirely new. No one, so far as I was aware, had ever attempted it to any serious extent and I had to start absolutely from scratch. There was no one to ask, for no one knew. But in artistic work I was on my own ground and the prospect of working out a satisfactory technique gave me no qualms.

The same building photographed in the 1970s. ROYE ENGLAND

After some abortive experiments with pieces of match-stick to form individual stones, I came back to my time-honoured card. I reasoned that card could be notched with a penknife to suggest stones, or perhaps scored with some sort of blunt instrument. The walls of the inn, I decided fairly early, to represent in this manner, for having been washed over, no actual stonework was visible. However, where some bricks had crumbled and come through, they could be dug out of the card and paint would do the rest. It sounded hopeful and one or two experiments confirmed the method had potential.

As yet I was only feeling my way to becoming an historian-in-miniature and it didn't particularly worry me that lack of full information made it impossible to reproduce part of the building as it really had been. In fact, unbelievable as it now seems, I made no attempt to use a good deal of the information that I had noted. The front

Roye's attic/sitting room in the Vicarage at Wanborough in 1934, with the partially-completed model of the inn on the right.
ROYE ENGLAND

The model inn, showing a glimpse of some of the interior detail as well as the main walls. The holes in the roof were to allow the hair-thatch to be sewn into place.
ROYE ENGLAND

was fairly faithfully copied, though leaving out a long line of outhouse walling at one end. But the other end, of which I had some dimensions and a sketch, I perversely made freelance — as, of course, was the back where I had nothing. Since my village would be a composite one, the extent of my aim at this time was simply to make it typical. Later, of course, authenticity became the watchword,

scholar, so the building of the inn continued slowly and the exam work not much faster.

Would my great layout ever become an accomplished fact? Against all probability I firmly believed it would. If so, it must be an exhibition model — there was no point in doing all this work just for oneself. If people would pay to see the model, it might earn a surplus — in which case

Tea at Knighton Crossing in 1933, with May French (seated in the motorcycle sidecar) and her younger son, Michael. The engine is 'Star' class No. 4044 Prince George.
ROYE ENGLAND

and after that, no liberty at all was allowed unless I believed it to be fully justified,

Construction now went ahead in earnest. A floor appeared, then interior walls, and before long, appropriate furnishings. When windows posed a problem, I found I could cut frames, with good effect, from visiting card, and I glazed them with mica from the front of a blue-flame stove. Glazing bars, generally one to each casement, seemed too difficult, so I left them out. They were added years later by a member of Pendon's team.

Little by little the model inn grew. But I was a slow worker and every move had to be thought out, tried, sometimes rejected and done again. Yet what I had done so far convinced me that card was the right material to use. I now looked at the villages with a newly practical eye. How would one reproduce the varying tones of weathered stonework, make tiles and slates, thatch, grass, trees? Everything lay ahead, everything had a query attached and everything would have to be made convincing or the whole scene would fail. It was a great challenge but I had unbounded faith that I could pull it off.

Evenings came all too quickly. The morning had dragged in study but the afternoon fled as I explored the Vale. Then there was more study to be faced. When would the inn get built? Often I stole part of the evening for modelling and my cousin May, though not Hubert, encouraged me in my lapses. I was never made to be a

there were always good causes crying out for help . . . missions, for one. Would this be a way of serving the Church without getting involved in it?

So my first scene would be a landscape of the Vale for public exhibition, perhaps with others to follow, and, after paying expenses, it would work for charity. With these decisions taken on top of those that had recently gone before, the essential foundations of Pendon had virtually been laid. The date was the end of 1931.

In those years I ran a Triumph motorcycle and, often with May in the sidecar and Michael on the pillion, we used to take a picnic tea to the mainline, striking at one of two selected spots. One was an up-down over the disused canal, half lost in trees, where the line took wing high over the double skew arches of Acorn Bridge. The other was Knighton Crossing, its little signal box and gates seeming then as permanent as the fields around them. The line here swept from a cutting on to a long embankment just where a lane turned conveniently to run beside it.

For hours we used to sit watching the pageant that went by in that high noon of steam. There were Bulldogs and Flowers in plenty — occasionally Barnums and Dukes with their large domes — Prairies, Moguls, Halls and, most numerous of all, the tremendous galaxy of great engines, Saints, Stars, Castles and Kings. They hauled everything from vintage Clerestories, Dreadnoughts and Concertinas, to the sleek steel-panelled stock of the 1920s.

A corner along the lane between Knighton Level Crossing and Uffington.

ROYE ENGLAND

A Mogul 2—6—0 locomotive flashing past the box at Knighton Crossing on a down train.

ROYE ENGLAND

GNR Atlantic No. 4428 near Steventon in 1927.

M. W. EARLEY

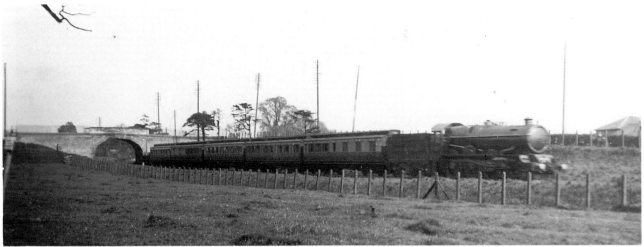

An unusual combination with 'King' class engine No. 6011 King James I *— an example of the pinnacle of GWR steam power, hauling five rather elderly clerestory coaches past Stratton Green, east of Swindon.*
                                        ROYE ENGLAND

Intermixed we saw heavy 28s at the head of anything up to 100 wagons of coal, the gleaming 'Fishguard Boat Express', the 'Cheltenham Flyer', then at the pinnacle of world fame and beautiful trains of varnished teak coaches from the LNER behind a Great Central Director or Great Northern Atlantic in apple green. Always, too, there was the thrill of the unexpected, for almost everything on wheels went to Swindon sooner or later.

Equipped with notebook and pencil and using a short-hand of my own brew, I jotted details of every train that passed — anything and everything that I could get down in its brief flight, or that I could remember after it had vanished. These were happy, carefree times, and the work I did there in that couple of years has given Pendon a unique record of Great Western traffic. In all, I recorded details of about a thousand trains.

It was the autumn of 1933 when at last I felt ready to face the exam. I had taken a long time over it but preferred to be thorough. Even so, anything could go wrong and it naturally came as a relief beyond words when I heard that I had passed. But what next?

Had I failed, my call to the Ministry would have been openly questioned. Now, instead, it was taken for granted by everyone except myself. It was not the spiritual aspect that worried me; with that I was in full accord. It was the public interpretation of it. I still couldn't see myself living a life of services amid all the petty mundanity of parish administration. The Brighton vision of the human side was fading. It was only a small part of the whole anyway and could I ever go through with the rest?

'Of course you can', said Hubert, 'you'll be given strength.'
'Of course you must', said friends, 'you'll be alright when you get into it.'

'I think you should', said May, 'remember your poor mother waiting all these years.'

Perhaps it was this latter thought more than anything else that made me steel myself to go on.

There was no money, of course, to do it with. Things were far from what they used to be. To get a grant was the only way possible, and, in the depression years, few grants were available. Then, in a cable from Vi, came the news that the Archbishop of Perth had accepted me for three years' training at no cost to myself. In all it would involve a total of seven years in Australia, working in the Outback probably, after which I would be free to leave if I wanted to.

Seven years before I could return to the Vale! Seven years and no models! That, it's no use denying, was the first thought that entered my mind. From that alone I should have realised that I had no vocation in the Church, but any better judgment that I had was being talked down all the time. Well-meaning friends were so very well-meaning — and it would be terrific to be with Vi again. I arranged to sail to Fremantle by the P & O *Moldavia* early in September.

Meanwhile, I had been doing important work in my beloved Vale. Free of the exam, I often had the whole day to explore, to note and, if only money hadn't been so short, to photograph. Here was the chance to get the priceless photos — vintage shots that would never be possible again — yet I was powerless to do so in any quantity. In seven years anything could happen and I set to work desperately to capture as much as I could. I took notes galore and every photograph I could afford, both of cottages and the railway. Rumours were afoot that the new electricity grid was approaching the Vale — pylons through the meadows and heavy wires down village

'Castle' class No. 5007 Rougemont Castle leaving Swindon in April 1933 with the up 'Cheltenham Flyer' – at the time the fastest scheduled service in the world. The engine in the distance was 'Star' class No. 4022 Belgian Monarch. ROYE ENGLAND

A lovely study of a 'Mogul' class mixed-traffic engine on an up goods, passing through Swindon on the start of its journey through the Vale of White Horse. ROYE ENGLAND

'Saint' class No. 2935 Caynham Court *leaving Swindon with a down express (May 1934).* ROYE ENGLAND

'Saint' class No. 2916 Saint Benedict *photographed at Swindon in May 1934, on a Weymouth to Birmingham train. The unique eight-wheeled tender had originally run behind No. 111* The Great Bear — *Roye's first glimpse of the GWR in a childhood book.* ROYE ENGLAND

An unidentified 'Castle' class engine threading its way through the Vale, passing the Carpenters Arms between Swindon and Shrivenham with a Paddington express.
ROYE ENGLAND

Hay ricks lining a quiet lane between Compton Beauchamp and the GWR main line, a route that Roye must have known well through his excursions to record trains around Knighton Crossing.

ROYE ENGLAND

Bodyhorse Lane looking towards Hinton Parva and Ashbury, with the Berkshire Downs receding into the distant haze. The photo was taken in September 1932.

The small tower of Hinton Parva church overlooking the barns and ricks of one of the village's farms. For many years Roye intended that Hinton Parva church would be used in the Vale Scene at Pendon, but eventually he decided that it was too small for his needs and Bishopstone was selected instead.

A stook-filled field at Hinton Parva, looking north across the Vale towards Faringdon, August 1933.

ROYE ENGLAND

A magnificent elm standing sentinel at the junction of the lane from Bishopstone and the Hinton Parva to Bourton road. ROYE ENGLAND

One of the many thatched cottages at Bishopstone photographed from the churchyard, April 1934. ROYE ENGLAND

Roye described this view as showing a 'glade' or grassy lane in fields off the Roman Ermine Street, near the old Wilts & Berks Canal.
ROYE ENGLAND

'. . . a lark-trilled peace, day long and summer through' – the Vale that Roye left in 1934.   ROYE ENGLAND

For Roye, elms were almost a symbol of the Vale and he took many photographs of them in all seasons. This group stood alongside Ermine Street near Wanborough. The photo is dated 1934.
ROYE ENGLAND

'... that sleep in mossy thatch' – Billy Goodman's cottage, Knighton.　　　ROYE ENGLAND

streets. I saw my intended model becoming more cogent, more pressingly needed, every day. And here I was, deserting my post for seven long years. There were also other rumours, and facts that were harder than rumour. Hitler had come to power and, I was told, I was lucky to be getting out of England.

The day before the actual departure, I went to London to clear up some outstanding arrangements. It was another of those superb Great Western expresses, the engine was *Carmarthen Castle*, and tomorrow I would be threading through the Vale for what might be the last time. My feelings welled up and I began to write, scribbling blank verse as best I could through the motion of the train. The Vale slipped by as I wrote, the canal up-down, Knighton Crossing with its little box and the chalk lane alongside the line.

As the train slowed into Paddington I wrote the last words. It summed up all the joys, the loves, the devotion of the past nine years. It was implicit with their highest hopes and it rang with the agony of parting before I could fulfil them.

... But this I ask — my one request of those who stay.
That sometimes in the Vale,
Beneath the vigil of the lone White Horse,
Just one or two may wander thoughtfully
And when they see those mellowed, gracious hills,
The lichened farms that sleep in mossy thatch,
Their lofty elms, lost villages unknown,
Where scarcely man, save countryman, has trod.
When they see the waggons brush the lanes,
The hedges wisped with straw, the corn lands stooked.
When distantly they glimpse, in flickered stir
And fleeting primrose-gold, these wreathed expresses
Threading quiet fields.
More, hear the very
Quietude, a lark-trilled peace, day long
And summer through.
And then I'd have them say
'He knows, he loves'
And pray that by God's grace
He may perchance, long hence, pass by again.

(This is extracted from the much longer piece that Roye wrote on his journey to London)

Roye, aged about 30, and by his own admission 'looking horribly supercilious'. The location is his mother's home at Darlington, Western Australia.

CHAPTER FOUR
1934–1948
THE GUILD OF ST. AIDAN IN THE DIFFICULT YEARS

The completed model of the old inn from Wanborough, which Roye renamed 'The Waggon & Horses' for use at Pendon. By the standards of his later work, Roye's first model captured only a part of the character of the original, but set in the context of modelling in the 1930s, it was a stunning achievement.
ROYE ENGLAND

THE Archbishop cheerfully confirmed my acceptance, but the interlude in Australia did not last seven years. Doubts increasingly assailed me, Vi began to share them, and literally the day before the final decision had to be made, I withdrew. I never had any regrets.

The next couple of years were unforgettable ones shared with Vi. During them I completed the inn, proving beyond doubt that card and watercolour could produce perfectly realistic buildings. I thatched it with human hair which turned out to be an excellent material, but I had no originals to copy and my early method of sewing the thatch into place was not the right one. So compared with later work, the results were far from convincing. For various reasons, however, it served as it stood for a great many years, in fact until a much improved method was evolved by a Pendon modeller who at that time was not yet born!

Although I had now come to appreciate Australia as never before, I knew in my heart that I was spending time whose loss I could not afford. My schemes were a life's work needing everything I had to give them, none of which would eventuate if I remained in Australia. So when an offer came from Hubert and May to go back to the Vicarage and coach Michael (their younger boy) each morning, I saw it as a great opportunity. It would leave me

short of money, yet how worthwhile to be free every afternoon and evening for my modelling and all else that my project would entail. The family had, by now, left Wanborough and gone to a semi-industrial parish at Coalpit Heath near Bristol. From there it would be forty-odd miles to the Vale. But from Australia it was ten thousand.

Vi could have begged me for once to stay with her and have nothing tangible except the inn to show for all my years in England, to be content now with Australia. But instead, for the umpteenth time, she sank her own feelings and, despite a recent vow that there must be no more partings, I accepted her sacrifice.

Was I wrong? There was no hope of her coming with me and it was a cruel decision to make. Yet a sense almost of compulsion drove me on. When one day my great work bore fruit, I should look back and know that the return to England had been right. So with optimism but not much else, I lost no time in laying plans for my return to England. A loan on an insurance policy gave me the fare and a couple of months later, I sailed via Panama. Vi would follow, when and if the exchange rate and world affairs allowed.

The England of Coalpit Heath was not the England of the Vale and I now had no means of transport. However, I settled down quite well. Basil, the elder boy, was largely away, but Michael, growing up fast, became a good companion both during study and away from it. So the weeks and the months began to fly again.

I had formed the idea that to bring my plans to fruition, I must enthuse others and gather them about me in some form of society, to achieve what I could not do alone. I toyed with the idea of forming a body to be called 'The Miniature Trust' — a kind of National Trust in miniature, but it suggested such a vast scope that I ruled it out. 'Lineside Miniatures' was another name that was considered and rejected. But, name or no name, the idea refused to let me rest. Set an ideal before people, get them interested, and it might lead anywhere. For one thing, it could solve the financial dilemma and, no less important, it could bring other modellers about me to help with both the railway and the village. Work on the latter, to judge from the inn, was threatening to be so slow that help there might prove essential before long.

Would it be forthcoming? Village modelling was still an untried art, for even now, no one else had done that kind of work, at any rate of the calibre that I envisaged. Even the pioneering achievements of John Ahern in his Madder Valley layout, started that year (1937), still lay ahead. Yet I had set a standard. The inn had been built and furnished to show what I wanted and I felt sure others could be trained in my techniques. Not till years later did I realise that every craftsman thinks his own job is easy and can't see why other people think otherwise. I learnt the lesson in the end, but at that time I saw village modellers round every hearth.

Beyond this, however, there were more than enough big questions to face and these, just then, appeared the most formidable: membership, officers, publicity, accounts, correspondence. Could I ever cope with them? If I were not careful the society might hinder more than it helped. I must have time to think.

Some time the previous year, I had begun to collect railway tickets and by now, the bug was becoming a craze. There were dealers in them even then, in the thirties. But the oldest and most fascinating tickets, with history written all over them, were above the economic borderline, so I gave up smoking for a year, after a herculean struggle, and converted the entire proceeds into tickets. It was the start, had I known it, of Pendon's Relic Room.

An ardent collector, a young man named Quartermain, had amassed a superb collection of 44,000 tickets and over a period, we made some very interesting exchanges. But only a few years later he was killed in a car crash and his tickets went to the railway museum at York. Before that tragedy happened, however, he offered me two GWR engine nameplates for which he had no space. If I wanted them they were mine for paying the carriage. One was a crescent plate from a 4-4-0 County class engine — I forget which one — and the other was the combined name

and numberplate for *Sedgemoor*, one of the early Bulldogs. I, too, was rather short of space and, believe it or not, I refused the County. But I gratefully accepted the oval plate for *Sedgemoor*. It cost me ten shillings in carriage, with some tickets thrown in and, after serving as a fire-screen for many years, it eventually became one of Pendon's most prized relics.

In the Wanborough days, a young fellow from London who had dabbled in modelling had stayed with us for a time and, one day at Coalpit Heath, he turned up unexpectedly. He was marrying — no time for playing trains now — and was having a clear-out from his shed. There were no models, but there was an old bike — one of the sit-up-and-beg kind, with a seat as comfortable as an armchair. If I wanted it I could have it, also for the cost of the carriage. I told him no, I didn't want it. After so many years on a motorbike I had a 'thing' about push-bikes. They got you nowhere fast — in fact, not even fast — and they made your legs ache. Michael pleaded with me. He cycled and would like to do more, but had no one with whom to go. So eventually, in the face of his continued protestations, I agreed, if rather ungraciously, to let it come.

It waited forlornly in the garage for a long time. It got covered in dust. Michael was exasperated. Then there shone a beautiful day when everyone else had gone out in the car. I longed for the country but had no means to get there, except for the sit-up-and-beg. Feeling a little sheepish, I dusted it off and took it out onto the drive. It ran freely, fitted me perfectly and had armchair comfort. I was surprised and ventured to the road. It did go well . . . By the time I returned, I had been through eleven miles of country lanes, like a breath of heaven after the something-and-nothingness of Coalpit Heath. From that day, however, gradually at first, I became a keen cyclist, to Pendon's lasting benefit in the times ahead.

Little by little, the ideas for my new society were falling into place and they were coloured by a re-awakened interest in the Church. Whatever might emerge would have a Christian and spiritual basis. There were many self-contained bodies within the framework of the Church of England, why not another on untrodden ground? Miniature reproductions in the service of missions. Years ago I had thought of missions as a cause to help, and with the backing of the Church, such a society should go a long way.

I envisaged the society in the form of a guild. It would encourage craftsmanship in the building of its models, educate by exhibiting them, and support missions with the surplus profits. The scene in the Vale of White Horse would remain its first concern but if much help were forthcoming, it would go on to model other scenes later. Service to the guild by its members would be in the form of anything they could offer — prayer, gifts, modelling or

This view of Britchcombe Farm, taken in the early 1950s, shows the farmhouse in the distance, set against a magnificent backdrop of mature elms on the scarp slope of the Berkshire Downs. ROYE ENGLAND

help in a variety of other ways. There would be no fixed subscription and it would rely for its fulfilment on the keenness and co-operation of its supporters.

I named it 'The Guild of St. Aidan' after one of the most lovable of the early missionaries. His symbol was a lighted torch — the light of the Gospel — and when designing a badge for the Guild, I found that this emblem would combine effectively with the letters GSA. It also formed the basis of a Collect which I wrote as the Guild's official prayer. In St. Saviour's Church, Coalpit Heath, at the early celebration of Communion on St. Aidan's Day, 31st August, 1939, Hubert read the new Collect before the few who were present. It was the signal that the Guild of St. Aidan had come into being.

Germany invaded Poland the following day.

A black-out was imposed at once, and white lines, in paint to begin with, appeared on main roads for the first time. We heard that two sisters in Wanborough had been knocked down by a car in the dark and one of them killed. But our lives had to go on while they could and I did my best to keep my mind on the new Guild. It had been inaugurated with two members — Michael and myself — and with funds in hand amounting to 3s 5d. It was a less auspicious start even than had been the £2 10s capital of the Australian Central Railway. I enrolled Vi as

the third member by proxy. After having done so much for the cause, she must be in on it from the start. The elder boy, Basil, also came in, as did a kindly neighbour whom we called 'Auntie Vic', and Hubert and May in due course. Despite their joining, neither of the latter professed the least expectation that it would get anywhere and had no hesitation in saying so.

Meanwhile, after a long initial pause, the war flared into action and France fell. More and more men were being called up, but for the time being, as a tutor, I was in a reserved occupation. I wanted to continue modelling but everything was difficult now and I never felt less in the mood for it. However, I still looked ahead to future needs and, fortunately, realised that card would get short, besides almost certainly losing its quality. I took no chances and bought from a shop in Bristol £10 worth in varying thicknesses. It was a providential thought.

Another urgent need was to get photos and measurements in the Vale before any war damage was done there, or even normal changes unrelated to the war. So one day, Michael and I went by train to Swindon with our bikes and cycled to Britchcombe Farm, an especially beautiful spot on the hills just below the White Horse — tall elms, two magnificent thatched barns, other buildings including a little granary with dovecote — the whole set in a great

One of the magnificent thatched barns at Britchcombe Farm. This photograph, which dates from 1932, also shows part of the stable block in the background and to the right. This entire group is now being faithfully recreated in miniature for the Vale Scene at Pendon.
PENDON MUSEUM COLLECTION

semi-circular coombe of the downs, richly wooded from top to bottom in great trees festooned with wild clematis. It was a must for my model village but, as yet, we had only two or three photographs and no dimensions at all.

The weather deteriorated and by the time we reached the farm it had become dark and threatening. But we went up the drive to the house, explained why we had come, and were given permission to start work with the camera. Ten minutes later a large car drove up and two policeman came over to us. What were we up to? Didn't we know there was a war on and that photographing was prohibited? How were we going to prove we weren't spies? After a good deal of questioning, we did prove it and they went away. But it took the gilt off things and a downpour of rain did the rest. To cap it all, the photos we had taken turned out to be hopelessly under-exposed. It was the last excursion to the Vale for a very long time.

Amid wailing sirens, air raids started and we went everywhere carrying gas masks. Destruction came near at hand when Bristol was bombed — dog fights over the city and the billowing glare of huge, consuming fires at night. Bombs were also dropped in our parish and invasion was expected nightly. But even so, we were a thousand times better off than the people in Bristol, and when a request came that we should accommodate a married couple who wanted to evacuate from the city, we prepared the drawing room for their use as a bed-sitter.

They arrived, in time for tea, when I was upstairs finishing some work for the Guild, which delayed me a little. In those days, when I was chilly, I used to wear a brightly-coloured towelling beach gown on top of everything else, which in winter became virtually part of me. I never took it off except to go out or to bed.

Lewis and Mary Ramell had been welcomed and by the time I came down, they had started tea with the family, not yet knowing of my existence. There was a lull in the conversation and Mary Ramell looked up to see a brilliantly-clad apparition in the doorway — crimson and blue and green. Her eyebrows lifted eloquently. Even in that moment, I knew a friendship had been struck.

Lewis Ramell (who was generally known to his friends by a contracted form of his name as 'Ram') was a quiet, thoughtful man, very musical, with an engaging smile and a beautiful tenor voice. At the time he worked in a Bristol bank, although not through choice. Mary was small, with red hair and compelling brown eyes. Though lame in one foot, this was completely outweighed by the force of her dominant personality and vivacious manner. She was a complete individualist, very outspoken, but once one knew her, she was the staunchest of friends. She joined the Guild the same day.

Mary's arrival gave my plans the biggest fillip for years. She was nothing if not energetic and very soon she had the wheels turning. For the first time in twenty years I had active support in my striving. She recruited her friends as new members and encouraged me in everything, including the writing of a brief illustrated account of the Guild for various Church magazines. That brought in some scattered enquiries, followed by a limited number of supporters. The furthest afield was in Norfolk — we were already (just) on the map.

Mary next set herself to raise some funds, which was probably our greatest need. Ram could give a song recital in Bristol in aid of the new Guild (and over a long period he gave a considerable number) and Mary began making things for sale to friends and supporters. Things were beginning to move, but a serious check was very near. My reservation as a tutor had been cancelled. Call-up was imminent.

I had, of course, seen it coming and had been thinking out my position for a long time. In this, Michael, Ram and I saw completely eye to eye and there was only one course. If we were shot as a result (as could well happen if invasion came), that was the price we would pay. Our names went forward as conscientious objectors and, in due course, but at different times, we went before the Tribunal. Ram, doing essential work, was ordered to stay in his job, but Michael and I were both given exemption conditional on our doing landwork or some other form of manual labour. For me, the prospect of manual work was a nightmare, not because I thought it in any way degrading, but because I knew that as yet, I had not the strength for it. However, I was fortunate in finding a farm locally where my misgivings were understood and I was able to get into harness comparatively gradually. Even so, I never forgot the blisters and the backache of the first few weeks. Later, Michael and I both went to a market garden in Somerset, going home on weekends, and with Mary's help, the Guild continued to go ahead, even if slowly.

The garden work, though seldom heavy, was boring in the extreme, and to relieve the day-long monotony, I decided to take up a language with the idea of practising it while I worked. I chose Esperanto. It had been created years before by a young Pole to by-pass the world's barriers of speech and was a straightforward language, a beautiful one, logical, efficient and easy to learn. My first sen-

Although change came rapidly to the Vale in the 1940s, Roye knew that many corners still remained untouched. This wheelwright's shop at East Hendred (photographed in 1940) was typical of the scenes that Roye wanted to record, but was powerless to reach.

H. O. VAUGHAN

The war effort led to extensive ploughing of former grazing land on the Berkshire Downs and in the Vale of White Horse, but even before the war the landscape was beginning to change as farming modernised. This view was taken at Uffington Castle in 1939.

H. O. VAUGHAN

tence was appropriate 'Mi estas laca' — I am tired. But though my back may still have ached, I was no longer tired of mind. So Esperanto satisfied a need at the time; it had not yet occurred that it might also serve the Guild.

During that year (1942), Hubert made another exchange of livings, going to the tiny but utterly delightful parish of Chilton Cantelo, near Yeovil, a beautiful church, an ivy-covered Rectory, thatch and trees everywhere. By sheer luck, Michael and I were moved soon after to Vale Farm, only seven miles from Chilton Cantelo, so we were able to live at home, cycling each day to work. The farm was a large one, unspeakably beautiful,

and though the long chapter there was often difficult and, from the point of view of the Guild, always frustrating, it was seldom really unhappy.

By now I was calling Mary by the Esperanto form of her name — 'Mario'. She had remained in Coalpit Heath but was battling for the Guild as ardently as ever. Quite early she started a working circle which made an astonishing variety of wares for an annual Sale of Work, bringing in, as time went on, as much as £100 for a one-day sale. This was a lot of money at that time and it gave the Guild new power to go ahead.

The Rectory at Chilton Cantelo.
ROYE ENGLAND

A family gathering at the Rectory, Chilton Cantelo, during the 1940s with (from left to right) Hubert, Michael and May French, Grace (Basil French's wife), Sarah Partridge (a family servant) and Roye.
BASIL FRENCH

Harvesting with a horse-drawn reaper on the Berkshire Downs, during, or just after the Second World War.

To begin some modelling was the next greatest need, though time to get down to it had never yet become available. Being now cut off from the White Horse country, I began to wonder whether we should set aside the Vale Scene until after the war and try to model a village closer to hand, perhaps an actual one, reproduced intact. After Michael and I had cycled on weekends through something like a hundred villages, we chose Lillington, near Sherborne — a dream of a place with a towered church, a tithe barn and much thatch, set among elms and apple orchards in a deep, grassy valley. Dorset at its loveliest. The one lack from the modelling point of view was that there was no railway and I was greatly tempted to introduce a section of the nearby Southern Railway mainline!

The model of the inn, of course, had been built to HO scale — 3.5mm to the foot. But by 1943, serious modellers were beginning to adopt 4mm scale with EM gauge (18mm) track for the railway, all but correct at that scale. I decided the Guild could not remain in a scale which (in this country, though not abroad) was becoming obsolete, and in any case, a slight increase in size would be a very real advantage. Although the inn had been built to the smaller scale, there are no standards in country cottages. A doorway may be five feet high just as likely as six — and any inexactitude in the inn's dimensions would be negligible. So EM gauge track and the 4mm scale were officially adopted by the Guild, a decision which was to carry on, without question, into Pendon.

Peace came to Europe in 1945 but, at Vale Farm, work continued unabated, for peace didn't mean release. An initial drainage project was long ago finished but wheat growing, done on a large scale, took its place. Harvest lasted for weeks and was carried on entirely with reaper and binder, huge fields being stooked by hand, loaded by hand and built into stacks, often thirty feet high. Then the thrashing took further arduous weeks to complete.

Esperanto had by now become a major factor in the Guild's plans, and through it a foreign membership had begun to trickle in. I thought that if we started branches in other countries, they could model their own countryside and exhibit their scenes. The Guild could become a truly international organisation and raise miniature artist-craftsmanship to a recognised art form. My old over-ambition, my unbounded faith that anything was possible, were back in full force.

It was terribly exciting, but also very wearing. I used to come home tired at night, to be faced by piles of letters to be read and answered. Sometimes I almost fell asleep at the typewriter while doing it. Eventually some relief did come through a part-time secretary who offered help for very little remuneration and over a period of months, her help was a godsend. Then, without the least warning, she became amorous and, not feeling at all the same, I had to terminate her services as abruptly as they had started.

By the spring of 1947, the membership stretched from Tanganyika to New Zealand, from Finland to Argentina, from the Canaries to China, from Nigeria to Brazil. Released, at last, from work on the land, I set about preparing the first Esperanto edition of the Guild's occasional magazine *Aidania*. But even though I now had the full day at my disposal, the time this consumed, on top of all the other work of the Guild, I found crippling. Although no one saw it coming, the crash was very near. But it came in a most unexpected way.

For ten long years, Vi and I had been held apart, by the war for so much of the time, and then, when she would have joined me, by the impossibility of getting a passage. There were waiting lists of thousands. At last she succeeded, enduring a dreadful voyage around the Cape which left her far from well. For the whole six weeks I had worried about her, and now, when the ship berthed, the agents failed in their promise to advise me. The liner sailed again almost immediately and Vi, with no one to meet her, was left sitting on her luggage on the wharf. For six hours she waited there while I, in desperation when I

Part of the Guild of St. Aidan room at the Rectory, Chilton Cantelo, with the engine nameplate from Sedgemoor *serving as a firescreen.*
ROYE ENGLAND

Roye, photographed in 1949, whilst attending an International Congress of Esperanto at Bournemouth.

GRAHAMS LTD.

found out, did the only thing now possible to reach her and took a taxi from Somerset to Liverpool.

So we met in the end, a wonderful moment, promising ourselves all kinds of times ahead. But even before our meeting, I too had begun to feel off colour and we were hardly back in Chilton Cantelo when I went down with a high fever which nothing would reduce. Vi sat often by my bed, but I was generally past talking.

Then, only a week later, the blow fell. While I was still good for nothing, Vi had a stroke. She became paralysed on the whole of her right side and lost the power of speech. As I gradually pulled round, Vi became worse, and for four agonizing weeks, we could look at each other and she could make sounds, but I was the only one who could convey any thought. I dared not voice the anguish I was feeling.

One day she was able to say a word or two and raised my hopes. But after that she sank slowly into a coma. Her last message to me was a single warm squeeze of the left hand, which still had use. She always had such warm, comforting hands. And so one Sunday evening, Vi slipped silently away and at the moment she left us, the church bells suddenly struck up what seemed, even then, a joyous peal. For a moment I almost heard the hosts of heaven singing her their welcome.

But the bottom had fallen out of my world. Ten years of hope and anxiety, momentary fulfilment with the whole bright future before us, and now — nothing. At least we had been together at the end, but we had been nowhere, done nothing together. The Guild had been getting out of hand before Vi died. Now I simply let it go. In my still weak and heart-broken state I could cope no longer. Letters came and lay on the table unanswered, even unopened. One day I might pick it up again, but for the present, I no longer cared.

I turned again to writing poetry and gradually my sense of proportion returned. I had left the Guild to collapse as it might, but now I felt concern at my own default and I started wondering whether it could be salvaged. Ram and Mario discussed its possible future with me and we decided that if it were to go on, all unnecessary work must be

Violet England in later life.　　**LAFAYETTE LTD.**

cut out and modelling commenced instead. Ram offered to take over the burden of a reduced correspondence if I modelled, and in April, I started work on the Old Rectory at Lillington — a charming thatched cottage that had been destroyed by fire a year or so before. For a time everything went well, but after a couple of months, the inevitable crop of Guild work that Ram was unable to do had piled so high that I had to stop modelling to catch up. In point of fact, I never succeeded in catching up. The inspiration of the Guild of St. Aidan had gone. It was never wound up, but was left in abeyance in case one day it might stir again. When eventually it did so, it was no longer in the form of a guild. But the intention had not changed and its aims were to live on, dormant awhile, to fight another day.

West Hendred in the 1930s.　　　　　　　　　　　H. O. VAUGHAN

Although the Vale of White Horse of the early 1950s showed many changes from the countryside that Roye had known twenty years earlier, to his relief much of the atmosphere and detail remained. Apart from the intrusion of the motor car, this threshing scene photographed near Theale shows remarkably few changes. MUSEUM OF ENGLISH RURAL LIFE

CHAPTER FIVE
1949–1953
THE NEW APPROACH

WITH Vi's affairs settled, I had enough to live on in a quiet way, and poetry (and the countryside that inspired it) held me for a long spell. The original sit-up-and-beg bicycle had been replaced by a new lightweight Dawes which became the joy of my every day, a lovely thing in chrome and forget-me-not, that was to remain my chosen companion for more than 25 years. By this time, also, Michael and I had become keen youth hostellers, touring the country far and wide whenever we were able.

These were energetic and satisfying days, but intensely as I enjoyed the isolation of the country, life at the Rectory was rather circumscribed. I was in a rut and for some time had been aware that I ought to be nearer civilisation. In answer to this, Ram suggested my joining him and Mario in a cottage they had bought at Frampton Cotterell, the next village to Coalpit Heath, and though at first I hesitated to cut the ties with the past, when Michael married and left home, I knew a turning point had come. A breeze in the family tree just at that time helped me make the break, and the following day, 31st December 1950, I cycled to Frampton Cotterell, taking with me what I could carry on the bike and my back.

Although, modelwise, nothing was moving at all, my interest was rekindled in the April of 1951, when I was given the address of the Bristol '7-4-2 Club' which, as its name implied, catered for modelling in the smaller scales. 'Outline' (my diary) records, 'shall probably join. Wish I could do some model railway work in spare time'.

Early the following month I went for a 140 mile cycling weekend to Malvern, going by train to Gloucester to get a good start. On the station bookstall were three magazines, *Trains Illustrated*, *Model Railway News* and *Model Railway Constructor*. I bought them all and soon found myself actively contemplating a new approach to my long-held ambitions. The Guild had foundered because it had been all administration and no models. Now it must be models before anything else — no organisation to start with, no sidetracking. I reasoned that if I got some models underway, other modellers might join in as they saw the project shaping. But I must concentrate, to begin with, on the railway side. It was there that most modellers' interests lay, there that I was most likely to recruit others. After much deliberation (in which I relied greatly upon the good advice of Mario), I resolved to have an engine built to order that would establish the standard of modelling that I was aiming to reach and which might prove an incentive to others to join me. A Saint — perhaps the most elegant of all the Great Western engines.

I discovered a small model shop in Bristol run by a man named Steve Ryan, who offered to build a fully detailed Saint for about £20. This, he said (and I believed him) was his price for the love of the work, rather than as a purely business proposition He let me see catalogues where similar jobs were listed for two or three times this amount. The samples of work he showed were definitely good and I came away thrilled.

I became a regular visitor at Steve's shop and life began to take on a new urgency. There was much now that had to be decided, for the more Steve and I went into the building of the Saint, the more problems emerged that must be resolved before work could start. I had, for exam-

Roye, photographed somewhere in the Vale, during the late 1940s or early 1950s. **PENDON MUSEUM COLLECTION**

75

ple, taken finescale wheel standards for granted, but Steve thought them impractical for an intended exhibition layout. I stood firm, even though this was a critical issue and I had no experience whatsoever to support my position. When we couldn't agree I wrote to three of the EM Finescale experts in Manchester, including the renowned Alex Jackson, and was still left guessing, not by their doubts of the efficiency of finescale, but by their conflicting views of what was possible with neither elaborate equipment nor a limitless pocket.

I joined the '7-4-2 Club' hoping for enlightenment and made the casual acquaintance of a builder of engines in EM Standard. I walked part-way home with him afterwards to discuss my problems. He was very definitely against finescale, especially for an exhibition layout. It was quite a matter-of-fact contact and gave no clue whatever to all that the future held for both of us. His name was Guy Williams.

'Outline' noted the historic event most prosaically: 'A chap named Williams was at the Club who has done loco-building in EM Standard and we had a long chat.' In the light of what we subsequently know of him as a superlative craftsman and a pillar of Pendon, Guy's negation of finescale comes as a shock. But this was a long time ago. He had only recently turned from aero-modelling to loco work and his achievements and fame in this field still lay ahead.

At Steve's suggestion, I discussed my problems with a young fellow who had a working layout in EM Standard, Paul Counsell. He was not aiming so high as I was and seemed a little overcome by my insistence on such exactitude. But he warmed to the picture I gave him and I knew I had gained his interest. After this meeting, however, he soon moved abroad for nearly fifteen years, so was out of the picture. He was then to return and dramatically make up for his absence by playing a trump card that saved Pendon from defeat. But in his Bristol home in 1951, when everything lay ahead, no thought greater than that of wheel standards filled my mind.

In the end I managed to convince Steve that a finescale exhibition layout could be done. Then a further problem loomed. I found he was without a lathe, so was unable to turn down our wheels as I now required. However, I overcame this by rubbing them down myself with a file. It was primitive, but it answered.

During these months I began taking photos and notes of rolling stock, particularly coaches and private owners wagons, an urgent job that must be done before everything began to change. The other main activity was the purchase of all the model supplies I could still lay my hands on, and I broke into my limited capital reserves to do it. In some cases this proved a saver and was absolutely right, but inevitably on others I bought things which

were never used, spending money I could have used more effectively later.

One purchase, however, was much more exciting than a stocking-up of mere parts. While the building of the Saint (now to be No. 2921 *St. Dunstan*) was being delayed by the difficulty of getting the right wheels, Steve showed me a detailed Collett 0-6-2T, No. 5624, newly and beautifully made. It was built to OO gauge, but Steve offered to convert it if I liked to have it. There was no question about that, so I went home to work on quite a different set of wheels from those I had expected.

As autumn approached, the delightful times at Ram and Mario's cottage were already drawing to a close. Ram, who had left the bank, had been reading for ordination. Now he had been offered his first curacy. Bristol diocese ran from the Bristol Channel to north Wiltshire, with the mass of its larger parishes (where a curate would most likely be needed) centred on Bristol itself. Somewhere in that hub was where Ram had seemed certain to be sent. But fate (or Providence, as I firmly believed it to have been) was with me, for instead of a parish in Bristol, Ram was called to St. Mark's, Swindon! So at the beginning of October, I moved with him and Mario to the very heart of the old Great Western and to the doorstep of the Vale of White Horse.

It was incredibly fortunate. The focus of my modelling switched back overnight from Lillington in Dorset, to the villages of the White Horse and the Great Western mainline. It was the second time I had been brought to the Vale beyond any scheming of my own. Since last I saw it — on the abortive expedition to Britchcombe when Michael and I were suspected of spying — a decade had passed. Changes were there in plenty — and almost always for the worse — but to my relief, the overall atmosphere (and very much of the detail) as yet remained. It was not too late.

On the railway side of the project, to live in Swindon was to live in the focal point of my universe. Every day there was an endless flow of stock, old and new, passing to it, or through it, a constant feast of information to record, which I did increasingly and systematically as time went on.

Nine days after coming to Swindon I went back to Bristol to collect 5624, not entirely finished after conversion to EM, but ready to test. Next day I cycled home with it in high delight. The diary observes, 'Steve, or whoever built it for him, has made a most beautiful job of it. Raised it on tins and boxes on the table while having supper and gazed at it for an hour. While there are models like that, the Great Western will always live — especially if I can create a Wessex countryside for it to live in'. The opening sentence of that entry is interesting. I had been told that Steve was not actually doing the work him-

Roye's second engine, a model of the Collett 4800 class of 0—4—2 tank, No. 4837. The model was built by Guy Williams but came as a gift from Steve Ryan of Bristol.

L. KENT

self. Who it might be, no one knew, but whoever he was, he was a fine craftsman.

I had been making a length of track on a six foot board, using some Peco 'sub-standard' rail (which meant it was almost exactly to scale), fixed with Bostik into adapted chairs. I thought it looked not at all bad, though of course it was anything but strong. At first, 5624 refused to run on it, but when teething troubles were put right, she took the reverse curve without a hesitation. My finescale standards seemed to be vindicated, for if they worked on that track, they would work anywhere. So now I proudly possessed one engine — 5624 — the firstborn of the Pendon family.

Railwaymen at Swindon still knew their goods yard as the 'Transfer' — a relic from mixed-gauge days when goods of every kind had to be transferred from one wagon to another before they could continue their journey. It was interesting to find that such names survived. If only the Transfer hadn't been forbidden territory, it would have been an ideal hunting ground for my collecting of wagon photographs and data, for even from the approach road there was a lot to see. This road was not open to the public (except on business), though I found I could measure and photograph there without getting in anyone's way. But one day I looked up from my notebook to see a large policeman bearing down on me. He confronted me sternly and inquired by what authority I was on the site. I admitted that it was by no authority and explained what I was doing. He became reasonably understanding but said I was trespassing and would have to keep out. I asked if I could get a permit. He thought not but suggested that I write to the Chief Operating Superintendent in Bristol. I came away crestfallen, but wrote the most tactful letter I could put together. Then I had to wait.

The day after this encounter, I was trying to find an address in Old Town and stopped a passer-by to inquire.

He could not tell me, but as he lived close by, if I cared to accompany him to his home, he had a street directory. On the way, never able to keep off my pet subject for long, I started a conversation about the railway, which soon turned to coaching stock, about which he seemed to speak with unexpected knowledge. It was no wonder, for I'd stumbled upon Mr. Crooke, the Assistant Carriage and Wagon Engineer of the Western Region. I told him all my hopes and he invited me to ask for him at his office at the Works at any time I needed to check up on anything. He afterwards gave me some most valuable help.

The new year, 1952, turned to February and still there was no word about my permit. Every day I was missing so much. Then one evening, the doorbell rang and Mario called up to me, 'The stationmaster from Swindon Junction is here to see you'. The stationmaster, I thought, what could the stationmaster want with me? On tenterhooks, I came downstairs. 'I've been sent your letter', he began, 'Where exactly is it you want to go?' I explained. I outlined all my plans. I showed him 5624 and the model of the inn and stressed how urgently I needed to get photographs and data to do justice to the GWR, before it was too late. 'Oh, we can fix that alright. Once you get the permit for the Transfer, I'll see the Goods Agent and if there's anywhere else you want to go, come and ask me and I'll send someone with you.' I could have shouted for joy.

Then another bonus came my way. One day in Bristol, Steve showed me an EM gauge engine — a little Collett 0-4-2 tank, No. 4837; a gleaming thing, as yet unpainted, of nickel silver and polished brass. Whose was it? It made my mouth water. Then the answer came. 'You've spent a lot of money with me', he said. 'You've almost kept me going for the past year and I've never given you any discount. This is a little present instead.' It was a magnificent gesture and I could hardly believe it.

During one of my trips to Bristol I cycled out to Coalpit Heath and saw Auntie Vic again. She was now in poor health, but she gave me, as always, the warmest of welcomes. Before I left she said that since there was no longer a Guild to help, she wanted to buy me something for my present scheme, to remember her by, as she put it. She gave me a pound.

A piece of rolling stock was the obvious choice and I asked Steve to make two Macaws (GWR bogie bolster wagons) one of which was covered by Auntie Vic's pound. There had been a drawing and photograph of one in the *Model Railway News* about twenty years before, and for Auntie Vic's wagon, we retained its number, 84773. In my photographing of wagons I had not yet taken a Macaw and in Swindon, a little after this, one came along in a favourable position. It was No. 84773! Later our model was given a load of two signal posts and thereafter entered into regular service on Pendon's Dartmoor layout, but at the time it was the first of the wagon stock and a permanent memorial to Auntie Vic. She passed on not very long after.

Then came another of those important turning points and it hung on no greater a thread than that Ram was out and I happened, for once, to answer the front door. The caller was the Priest-in-Charge of our church. He was taking some boys on a private tour of the Works and it occurred to him that Fr. Ramell might care to join them. They would be seeing parts of the factory where the public were not taken. I promised to give the message and whether a touch of envy crept into my voice I don't know, but as he turned away he looked back and asked, as an afterthought, whether I would like to come too?

We had a fascinating time but the real significance was that the visit introduced me to Mr. E.G. Lomas of the Estimating Office, who (unusually) was our guide. He was a big-built man with an enthusiastic manner, who was obviously keenly interested in all he showed us — so much so that I began to tell him of my own plans to re-create a glimpse of the Great Western and its countryside. He seemed taken with the idea and invited me to go and see him any evening, if difficulties arose.

I was not just then needing any information in particular, but here was a contact that was too good to lose, so after about a week, I thought up a couple of useful queries and went to see him. He was not only very helpful, but he and his wife made me so welcome that it became the start of a firm friendship.

'Macaw' No. 84773, the prototype for Pendon's first railway wagon, photographed at Swindon in 1951.
ROYE ENGLAND

The model of the GWR 'Macaw' bogie bolster wagon — Pendon's first goods wagon, built by Steve Ryan.
ROYE ENGLAND

The view from Swindon East signal box. The Transfer sidings lay to the left in this view, adjacent to the houses in the background.
CTY. GEOFF COOPER

Part of 'the Transfer' at Swindon, with 0-6-0 pannier tank No. 1371 shunting and 2-8-0 No. 2825 alongside one of the yard's water cranes.
ROYE ENGLAND

Above: *One of hundreds of photographs that Roye obtained in Swindon carriage sidings. This is a 57ft composite built to Diagram E132 in 1928 and photographed in June 1952.*
ROYE ENGLAND

The end of the line. After more than fifty years of service a venerable clerestory coach awaiting its final destruction in the scrap yard at Swindon.
ROYE ENGLAND

Before I left, their son Peter came in from nightschool, a cheery looking young man of nineteen years. There was no chance to speak to him then but as he went through to the next room for a late supper, he beamed across at me and I felt an affinity was somehow there already. His parents said they told him what they could about my models and that he was keen to see them. Two evenings later he came round and stayed three hours. He had plenty to talk about, was interested in everything, and I learned that he cycled and hostelled. We seemed to have almost everything in common.

Meanwhile, with my permit from Paddington and the approval of the Goods Agent, I had begun my exploration of the Transfer. All that year, with camera, steel tape and notebook, I was constantly at the yards or the station. True to his promise to help, the stationmaster gave me permission to leave the platforms and walk by the lines where I would. This opened to me, among much else, the carriage sidings. Then I discovered that the Transfer merged imperceptibly on its further side into the repair sidings and then into the condemned sidings and the wagon scrap yard. So without quite knowing where I was beginning to exceed the limits of my permission (and without trying to find out), I encroached further and further, eventually even into the heart of the Works.

No one there ever accosted me. The police now knew me and asked no further questions, any senior of the factory who saw me took it for granted that to have penetrated so far, I must be officially sponsored, and the men soon began to look out for me until I had a greeting wherever I went. I took photos of them at work and gave them copies and sometimes I brought a model down to show them at first hand what it was all about. The '56', the '48' and sometimes the new Pannier (when it arrived from Bristol), went into everything; loco cabs, signal boxes, grounded coach bodies where shunters and engine crews had tea, goods offices, even the guarded inner sanctuaries of the Works proper, to be shown to the heads there.

When recording near the mainline, there were always splendid sights to see. But there were sad sights too, even in those days, the saddest of all being the scrap yard. Beautiful coaches were there, still in primrose and chocolate, having their insides ripped out as a first stage to demolition. The whole body was then rolled sideways off its underframe, lying helplessly upside down, to be burnt at leisure. One that I particularly remember was a 'Dreadnought' composite, which Mike Longridge of the Wimbledon Club had described as 'one of those rare vehicles'. No matter how rare, everything came to Swindon, though too often never to leave again. At least I now had every chance to preserve a record first.

In other ways as well, I was getting closely in touch with things. At the Model Railway Club Exhibition in London, I met Mike Longridge again, after a break of a great many years. He had been doing prolonged and invaluable research concerning Great Western rolling stock and had also founded the Great Western Circle. I had known for some time of the Circle's existence, but believed that with a long list of potential members, I had very little hope of getting into its restricted membership. However, when I told Mike of the work I was doing at Swindon, he replied that this was the very work of the Circle itself. A month later, I had jumped the queue and was a fully-fledged member. It was another avenue that

Roye also took the opportunity to take photographs of wagons. Sometimes he went to the trouble of chalking-in the outlines of the faded lettering on former private owner coal wagons, as in these two examples.   ROYE ENGLAND

The beginnings of Pendon's model railways with, from right to left, No. 4837, No. 5624, the first two 'Macaw' wagons, and the Pannier (still unpainted). The date was 1952. The models are shown upon the short length of test track that Roye built to prove his finescale standards would work.

ROYE ENGLAND

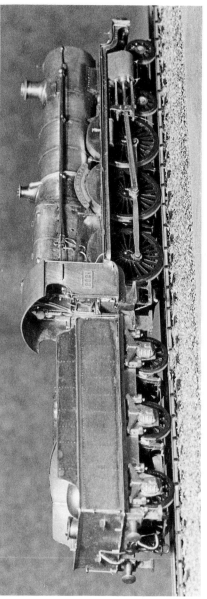

The model of GWR 'Saint' class No. 2921 Saint Dunstan, the first engine Roye commissioned for Pendon, although the fourth engine to be delivered. This picture of the unpainted model dates from 1954.

L. KENT

proved not only most interesting, but exceedingly helpful.

Modelling via Steve, apart from the two Macaws, was as yet confined to the production of engines. In the spring, the Pannier, No. 5724, in unpainted nickel silver, had been ready for testing and by the middle of August, *St. Dunstan* had at last appeared. The next on order was *Broome Hall* at the head of a long and hopeful list.

Amid the excitement of so much progress on the railway, the village side of the work had been taking a back seat. But it was not forgotten and on the few occasions when Peter Lomas was free to go with me to the Vale, we were always on the look-out for cottage prototypes to record. By now, true to my habit of finding nicknames for my friends, I was calling him 'Petro' — Esperanto for Peter.

One day in June we happened to cycle through Badbury, a hamlet on the hills between Liddington and Chiseldon. There we came upon a particularly attractive group of thatched cottages. They ran down a sloping lane and boasted a disused Primitive Methodist chapel in one of the back yards. It was a picturesque cluster that cried out to be modelled, even to the chapel. 'Which cottage

Roye, with Michael French (centre) and Peter Lomas (left) on one of their many cycle trips. The location is not recorded but appears to be on the Berkshire Downs with the Vale of White Horse as a background.
PENDON MUSEUM COLLECTION

Peter Lomas and Michael French at Knighton Crossing with an express en route to Paddington.   ROYE ENGLAND

will you model?', asked Petro. 'I'll model the whole group', I replied, without any suspicion of the thousands of hours it would take.

On 17th September 1952, I started to build the group, beginning with a small detached cottage beside the chapel, 'Little Chapel Cottage'. I had finished measuring this in detail only the same day. The following day I went back to Badbury for further photos, taking not only the chapel group but as well, a pretty little cottage in a garden between a fork in the lanes, which we knew later as 'Jessamine Cottage'. I also took what had been a fairly large farm, the house still beautiful with old tiles and thatch, but with stables, sheds of all kinds and a considerable barn, all now sheeted with galvanised iron. I

The buildings that were to become the corner-stone of the Vale Scene at Pendon – the Chapel group at Badbury.

Peter Lomas with one of the occupants of 'High Thatch'.
ROYE ENGLAND

Top left: *Readers familiar with the model version will note that Roye turned 'Little Chapel Cottage' (far right) through 90 degrees to face the path that ran alongside the group.* Top right: *A closer view of 'Little Chapel'.* Left: *The rear of the Chapel group with the disused Primitive Methodist chapel on the right.* ROYE ENGLAND

The rear of White Cottage and the Primitive Methodist Chapel. In viewing the subtle textures, the range of materials in the buildings, as well as the weathering and decay, it is easy to appreciate why Roye was captivated by this group.

ROYE ENGLAND

Badbury Farm photographed in the early 1950s and showing the rear of the house, much as the model itself is now seen at Pendon.
ROYE ENGLAND

A rare view of the front of Badbury Farmhouse (with 'The Baker's Arms' public house beyond), photographed in 1948.
PENDON MUSEUM COLLECTION

promised myself to restore them by modelling the complete farm in its heyday. This was Badbury Farm. All three groups lay within a few hundred yards of each other and it gradually came to me that if I brought them a little closer together, they would make an ideal upper corner in the model village. This early intention to create a 'Badbury Corner' has remained through all the subsequent iterations of the plans for the Vale model.

As I explored the Vale more thoroughly, I came to realise that the villages of the White Horse were unique in the whole of England. Set at the meeting point of four counties, they borrowed the characteristics of each and produced a variety of types and a composite charm that was all their own. Stone walls and deep thatch from Wiltshire and Oxfordshire; red tiles, mellow brick, weatherboarding, flint and half-timbering from what was then Berkshire; Cotswold stone from Gloucestershire. As a backdrop were the beautiful white chalkstone hills in which the villages clustered. Mix these ingredients as haphazardly as you would, weather them with mosses and lichens, give them gay gardens and set them at random on winding chalk lanes in the shadow of towering elms, and you had a paradise that was breathtaking. Yet it was one that was systematically being destroyed because no one would put themselves out to save it. Except, I told myself, in miniature.

The GWR Circle showcase at the MRC exhibitions in London was a meeting-place, it seemed, for all the elite of the small-scale model world. There were always groups gathered about it in earnest discussion. At the 1953 exhibition, Dennis Birse (the Secretary of the Circle) beckoned me over. 'Roye', he said, 'I've discovered who has been building your locomotives. A chap had been gazing for some time at *St. Dunstan* (which was on display in the showcase) and I remarked 'A beautiful engine, isn't she?' He replied, 'I'm glad you like it — I built it. My name is Guy Williams.'

So, the cat was out of the bag at last, but after thinking it over, I decided not to act on the discovery for the present. If Guy Williams was building engines for Steve, it was not for me to upset the applecart. No doubt they would tell me in their own good time, if they wanted to.

After finishing 'Little Chapel Cottage' (apart from its thatch, for which I was unable to obtain hair locally), I started on the chapel. But hair had to be found, so I enquired at a ladies' hairdresser in Swindon which gave me an introduction to Osbourne Garrett's, the large wholesale firm in London. I went up for a chat and some advice. In all their respectability, they were a little taken aback by the unorthodox idea of using their hair to make a roof on a model building and also, perhaps, by my unprecedented cycling get-up in their heavily carpeted showrooms. At first they were a trifle stand-offish. What

'High Thatch', Badbury, in June 1952. The old couple who lived in this cottage died not long after this photograph was taken and within a year the cottage was demolished. ROYE ENGLAND

organisation did I represent? I had to explain that, as yet, it was not an organisation, but that it would become one in due course. It was obviously a bad mistake that the project had no recognisable name★. However, name or no name, my reasoning prevailed and they advised Chinese hair for the task, it being straighter, duller and much less expensive than English hair. They produced 16 ounces of it, bleached and dyed, for £6.

My choice now, with the chapel practically finished, would of course have been to thatch 'Little Chapel Cottage'. (It had not yet occurred to me that the hair should be moth-proofed.) But instead I started to model 'High Thatch', for the old couple living there had died and the cottage itself was doomed, the loveliest of the whole group. A home broken up, another perfect corner of the countryside to be wiped out.

I was still building the model when the original came down.

★ *The question of a name for the project was resolved very soon after the visit to Osbourne Garrett's. A little earlier, Roye and Petro (Peter Lomas) had agreed to form a partnership to secure the development of the project. During a casual discussion one evening, they were toying with alternative nicknames for each other. Petro was a keen draughtsman and Roye suggested 'Pen' as his epithet. For himself, the name 'Den' was chosen, Roye being (as he seems to have been throughout his life) the guardian of a room in which he lived, worked and modelled that was so cluttered with books, papers, photographs and the like, that a den seemed the only possible description. The partnership never materialised as Petro opted to train for the Church instead, but Roye took the name they created from their pseudonyms, 'Penden Models', as the name for his project.*

'The Three Poplars' at Long Wittenham.

CHAPTER SIX
1953–1954
PENDEN–WHITHER?

IT was not long before the new name became attached to the model village. Since the church, rectory and school that I hoped to model were to be taken from Hinton Parva ('Parva', very aptly, meaning 'small'), it was a short step to put the two together and make 'Penden Parva'. This identified the village with the work as a whole and though, in fact, the name 'Penden' was not yet quite in its final form and with the meaning it was to acquire, at that time it seemed that no further thought was required.

At the start of the year, Steve had been having trouble with one of his hands (which culminated in an operation) and for some time he had been making no secret of the fact that he was passing my work elsewhere. So it came as no surprise when he suggested that since Guy Williams was doing the building of my engines, it would be better if I now dealt with him directly. I went to Bristol and we talked 'shop' for seven hours. He told me that he preferred building engines to coaches and wagons and hoped I might find someone else to deal with these. I asked Steve if he could suggest a coach builder and after a short pause, he suggested Ken Budd. Soon after, when I was spending a day with Steve in his shop, Ken came in and showed me some of his work. It was not then up to the standard that I required, but Ken thought he could reach it and offered to make a trial coach on a sale or return basis. Though at the time I could do no more than hope, Penden had in fact found another member of its future team.

Very soon after this, Mrs. Lomas became critically ill and was rushed into hospital for a major operation with only a fifty-fifty chance of success. She pulled through but the doctors advised that she must not come home to an empty house all day and, with both the others at work, there was no one but myself to step in. I put their predicament to Ram and Mario and, with their agreement, moved to live with the Lomases, a couple of streets away. My regrets in leaving were balanced by now being in even closer touch with Petro, but as his interest in the project waned as his dedication to the Church grew, the greatest impact of my move was to come through his father.

As a business man, Mr. Lomas looked ahead in a very different way from my own tendency to take the future on trust and now I saw more of him, he began to stir me up about it. It was no use, he told me, having models to show if there would be no money left to house them, and at the rate I was going — living out of necessity partly on my dwindling capital reserves — he foresaw this as proving their downfall. By now I had no more than £2,000 all told and, unless I did something about it quite soon, the picture looked gloomy. I couldn't help admitting that he was right.

The only course seemed to be to set modelling largely on one side and get a job. Enquiries after work, however, seemed only to confirm my fears that few would want a man of nearly 50, with no particular skills and experience. I began to think of alternative approaches — something that would bring in some money, yet leave me with more than the dregs of the day in which to model and gather information. Suppose I bought a cottage while I still had some capital, furnished it and let part of it? This would provide some income and, besides modelling, I could begin to show the models in a very unpretentious way. It would help the funds if I did teas as well. Once again, I completely failed to realise the headache I was proposing to indulge. Fools rush in where angels fear to tread, but it was fortunate in the end for Pendon that I was fool enough to imagine I could pull off something of the kind.

As so often, I turned to Mario for advice and she unexpectedly favoured the cottage idea in some form or other. That was encouraging. It would need to be in a tourist area, or at least within reach of big cities by car and for modelling, it must be within reach of the Vale. In many ways, Oxford appeared to be the best bet. So on 3rd May, 1954, I went to Oxford armed with a list of every major estate agent in the city and called on most of them. Cottage property was far more expensive than I had hoped and after spending a day and a half there, I was forced to the conclusion that Oxford had nothing to offer me. My money wouldn't even run to the cheapest property.

I went through the sheaf of leaflets again. There was one possibility — an old house fronting directly onto the main A34 at Enstone. I went to see it and found the house to be in reasonable repair and at £1,250 all in, I might just afford it with the help of a mortgage. A day of concentrated thinking followed, but suppressed misgivings over the suitability of the property left me hesitating. Mr. Lomas was as far as ever from thinking the scheme practical, but at breakfast, two days later, he suddenly remarked, 'If you find you can't make a go of it, you can always turn it into a youth hostel.'

It came like an electric shock. Why hadn't *I* thought of it? It was the one job that I knew from the inside, that I could enter into spontaneously and enjoy. It would cut out the need for letting rooms, it should leave reasonable modelling time, at the very least all winter, and would give an automatic introduction of Penden to a public drawn from the whole land. On the adverse side, apart

A rear view of 'The Three Poplars' with the overgrown garden and profusion of wild flowers that Roye so enjoyed.   ROYE ENGLAND

from the possible difficulty of raising a mortgage, there appeared to be one hurdle — Enstone was only three miles from the hostel at Charlbury.

Anxiously I contacted the secretary, Miss Simkins, at the regional office of the Youth Hostel Association in Oxford, but she immediately said Enstone was quite out of the question. Charlbury was already having a struggle and another hostel so close would break Charlbury and ruin the new one as well. The only areas in the Oxford region where there was scope for anything further, apart from Oxford itself, were Wantage or the escarpment of the Chilterns. Wantage proved impossible for the same reason as Oxford, the escarpment of the Chilterns even more so. 'Yes', said an agent in Thame, 'we've the very place for a hostel — magnificent views — and it's only £9,000.' After two days of searching I returned, frustrated, to Swindon.

At home a further collection of agents' leaflets awaited me. I glanced at them without any real expectation until I turned up one at Long Wittenham. Brick built, tiled house and good outbuildings — an acre and a half of land — price £1,850. Would the house be big enough to make a hostel? It was excellently placed — ten miles from the Oxford hostel, eleven from Streatley. It would complete a chain between the two and it had the attraction of the river. The Thames lay only one field away. But dare I go to that price? Would they perhaps come down?

I caught the 9 o'clock train to Oxford next morning, Saturday, 15th May, and having seen the agents, cycled to Long Wittenham. Last time I had ridden through the village, rounding the corner by the old stone cross and its twin lime trees, I spared not so much as a glance towards the 'No Through Road' that ran off to the south-west, but today, nearly at the end of the lane, I found my goal: 'The Three Poplars', until a few months ago a public house, with one or two trees opposite and its rather nice sign of three poplars standing in front.

The brick squareness of the house was not alluring, but it was relieved by having the front and a further side hung with tiles. There was no fence, but a slope led from the road to a gravelled yard and outbuildings. Beyond was a large, overgrown garden with half a dozen apple trees, and beyond that lay an empty field of about one acre that was also included in the property. One pair of houses lay between the Three Poplars and a mile or more of meadows.

Inside, the bar was just as it had always been — no counter, since drinks were served from the cellar, but darts were left sticking in their board, a notice offered 'Mild Ale — 1s.1d. in the Public Bar' and another proposed 'Health unto Her Majesty' for the coronation of the previous year. The grained wall-seats and a couple of tables remained, not to mention, pervading everything, a very strong smell of beer!

There were two other rooms downstairs and three up, with the kitchen perched halfway between floors to give headroom in the cellar beneath, There was no bathroom, no water in the house and no sewerage. Sanitation was across the yard by latrine and two earth closets. On the other hand, mains water immediately outside the back door could be brought in and sewerage was coming to the village 'sometime'. Electricity was installed downstairs and, after a fashion, upstairs, and I noted that there was a telephone line in the road. Outbuildings, all in brick, were plentiful and good.

Though accommodation was not as great as I should have chosen, I estimated it might be stretched to put up thirty or forty hostellers at a pinch, and if it bordered on the primitive, I knew, and liked, many hostels that were worse.

I spent a long time there picturing all that could be made of it and all the future could hold for me there, if the way opened up. While standing in the road gazing at the building, a man in working clothes passed me, making for one of the pair of houses beyond. We nodded at each other and then realising that this stranger might one day be a neighbour, I remarked, perhaps rather naively, 'I'm thinking of buying the Poplars.' 'Good', he said, 'then come in and have a chat about it.'

This was a happy and most unexpected turn and as we walked to the nearer house of the pair, I felt I had a potential friend already. Very soon after going inside, I knew I had. His wife, a charming woman, fair and very attractive, with four small daughters, gave me an immediate welcome. Roy and Wynne Morris were to become staunch supporters of the fledgling hostel. We talked at length of my ambitions and plans, and by the time I left, I was increasingly sure that I should buy the Poplars. Whether I could get it was a very different matter. But my hopes were raised because that very day, the price was reduced by £200 to £1,650. (A copy of the agent's leaflet with the reduced price was found in Roye's papers after his death. It was entirely typical that he should keep such a document.)

When the Lomases saw the Poplars the next morning, they were very taken with both the house and the land and pressed me to lose no time in trying to get it. So as soon as they left, I went across to Roy and Wynne's house and wrote a letter to the agents asking for an option. This, it turned out, they could not give as they were not the sole agents, but they would tell the owner I was prepared to go ahead if I could get the blessing of the YHA.

On seeing the Secretary again, she said my proposal seemed quite a hopeful one, if only the Committee could be persuaded to give a firm decision in time which, to my dismay, she thought was doubtful. But they would certainly discuss it when they met in two days time.

The delay was exasperating, for several parties had already been out to look at the property at its reduced price and any of them might take it at any moment. I lived those two days at boiling point. But on the morning after the meeting, the suspense was broken by a phone call from the Chairman. He admitted that they did have misgivings over whether a hostel could be financially viable, but if I wished to go ahead, they could provide the basic equipment to permit the hostel to open for the summer rush — in six weeks time!

At home again, the Lomases and Mario were unanimously in favour of my taking the plunge, and, although there were still big questions to face, I paid the agents a 10% deposit, subject to contract and mortgage. Could it be true that only a week before this, I had not so much as heard of 'The Three Poplars'?

But now, after a flying start, the wind changed. Three building societies turned down the mortgage. The bank had already refused and there was nowhere else to go. Without a mortgage, I was defeated. On top of this reversal, the Rural District Council advised that it might be mid July before they could approve a change of use for a hostel. Despair, fortunately, proved short-lived. I was gloomily thinking over the whole confrontation of troubles when the phone rang. 'We've good news for you', said the agents, 'the owner of the Poplars is offering you a private mortgage'. I could hardly wait to hear the terms, Then, only a few days later, the RDC gave their consent for change of use.

The opening date of the hostel was fixed for Thursday, 8th July, only three weeks ahead. It would be announced in the YHA Bulletin for that month and I designed a small poster to be printed and distributed to all hostels in the region. This included a paragraph in Esperanto and a note saying that models of a thatched village under construction and some GWR rolling stock would be on exhibition at the hostel, admission 6d, juveniles 3d. It was the first public announcement of Penden.

An initial weekend at Long Wittenham showed how much work there was to be done in the conversion of the pub to a hostel, but Roy gave me his energetic and unflagging help, not to mention the 'help' of his four small, but very enthusiastic daughters. Among other things, Roy offered to take over a good deal of the overgrown vegetable garden. I agreed, but it broke my heart to see him let loose on the exquisite wilderness that had grown up everywhere. From the house to the edge of the wheatfield that ran to the river, the long grasses were sprinkled with white campion, gilded with charlock and fired with great sweeps of dazzling poppies. But they all fell to the scythes of Roy and Wynne's father, Mr. Collett.

Day by day, the transformation of the house and its outbuildings went on, with Roy often working alone when I had to be in Swindon, so by the time the YHA Committee came to see it, the site was vastly adapted, renovated and tidied, as far as had been possible in the short

Although not in the Vale of White Horse, the countryside around Long Wittenham enjoyed much of the charm and solitude that Roye valued in the Vale itself. A deserted lane, near the village, photographed in 1974.

ROYE ENGLAND

'The Three Poplars' after the Long Wittenham Youth Hostel had opened.
ROYE ENGLAND

time. Wynne had also agreed to cook suppers, amounting to full dinners, each night for hostellers. Any profit would, of course, be hers, but it made the hostel infinitely more attractive. All the help so lavishly given by my new neighbours to put the new hostel on its feet was for friendship's sake alone, unasked for and unpaid. It was a great experience.

To cap it all, I bought, of all things, a luxurious carpet for the Common Room — rich copper-rust figured with green and cream. Usually hostel common rooms were made up of bare boards or similar and often of dreary furniture, but Long Wittenham was going to be different — a Sheraton chest-of-drawers, a Chippendale cupboard, green Lloyd Loom chairs, all my hundreds of bright books and the cosy carpet to complete the picture. I was told I was mad, but over the years I proved my point. It made the hostel, and all the thousands of hostellers who used the carpet over the years never wore it out.

Though the move of my many possessions was now impending in only two day's time, I had to leave unexpectedly for Bristol to see Guy on a matter that would not wait. Guy was also on the point of moving (to a different part of the city) and his unfinished EM gauge layout was being dismantled, there being no room for it in the new house. It included a fine Brunel timber viaduct of four piers, its structure being that of the Walkham Viaduct near Tavistock, which Guy had built from scale drawings published in the *Railway Modeller*. Inspiration came in a flash and I asked whether I could buy it, with its length increased, as a centrepiece for the running of my trains before the village was finished. It would give something spectacular to draw the hostellers and having only a

handrail and no parapet, it would show off the rolling stock as few other types of viaduct would do. Guy agreed enthusiastically and promised that as soon as he had settled down, he would begin extending it. The Vale scene was still to be the core of Penden, but the setting of the first layout had veered in a single evening from the White Horse country to the start of the Dartmoor scene.

The day of the move (30th June) dawned clear and bright. It was actually a double move, for beside a mass of things in Swindon, I had left almost as many possessions with Hubert and May, who now lived in Theale. The van started early at Theale, took the whole morning to be loaded there, before proceeding to Swindon where it spent the rest of the afternoon. It was nearly seven in the evening before we were finally ready to leave for Long Wittenham. Then, amid a host of goodbyes and good wishes, I was driven away, sitting in the front seat of the van, with the unfinished Chapel Group in a large Puffed Wheat box, for safety, on my knee.

As the van arrived at the Poplars, the whole family of Morrises and Colletts were waiting to greet me and to help unload. We did it in record time, piling everything everywhere, inside the house and out, to let the belated van return. After cups of tea all round, it left just before ten, having started out at 5.30 that morning. I had never known two more willing or more cheerful workers than the removals men who took me to Long Wittenham.

Then, at last, when everything was stacked safely indoors, and with a great feeling of contentment, I took a final look around my new territory and went across to Roy's house for supper and a ready bed.

Y.H.A.
A NEW HOSTEL
NEAR THE THAMES, at
LONG WITTENHAM
OPENING DATE 8th JULY

THIS HOSTEL was until recently the Three Poplars public house. It is situated in an old village near the river and forms an ideal centre for exploring this attractive part of the country, including the Wittenham Clumps (marked on maps as the Sinodun Hills).

Oxford is only 10 miles away ; Abingdon and Wallingford (both on the river) 5 miles, and Dorchester (with its ancient Abbey) 4 miles.

Details.

LONG WITTENHAM (Wed., Closing Scheme B)
   The Warden Y.H.A., The Three Poplars, Long Wittenham, Abingdon, Berks.
POSITION AND MAP : In village at end of 'No Through Road.'
   O S. 158. G.R. 543945. Bart. 14.
HOSTEL DETAILS : M & W 34. SJP. Store at Hostel. KFS.
   Esperanto spoken. Camping. River Thames 10 mins. Bathing 15 mins.
   Model of Thatched Village (under construction) and G.W.R. rollingstock on exhibition at Hostel. Admission 6d. Juveniles 3d.
STATIONS : Didcot 3½ m. Culham 2½ m.
BUS : Reading—Abingdon 2 hourly service to Clifton Hampden (1½ m.)
STEAMERS : 20th May to 19th Sept., daily incl. Sundays. Oxford 9.30 a.m. or Reading 10 a.m. to Clifton Lock (1 mile).
NEXT HOSTELS : Oxford 10, Streatley 11, Henley 16, Speen 26, Inglesham 26.

AL ESPERANTISTOJ

ONI KORE INVITAS AL LONG WITTENHAM SAMIDEANOJN EL ALIAJ LANDOJ. LA JUNULGASTEJO, KIU ESTAS EKSTRINKEJO. SITUAS EN MALNOVA VILAGO PROKSIMA DE LA RIVERO TAMIZO DEK MEJLOJN SUDEN DE OKSFORDO, EN TRE ALLOGA KAMPARO.

   VENU AL AMIKECA GASTEJO, KIE VI POVOS UZI ESPERANTON !

A copy of the leaflet that Roye prepared to announce the opening of Long Wittenham Youth Hostel and containing the first public reference to what was to become Pendon.

CHAPTER SEVEN
1954–1958
PENDEN MODELS AND THE HOSTEL

ON Thursday afternoon, 8th July 1954, the warden (myself) and helpers of Long Wittenham hostel were gathered on tiptoe in the little office, waiting to open officially at five o'clock. Would anyone come? It was such an out-of-the-way spot and the weather was dull and cold, drizzling on and off. Two minutes before the appointed hour there were footsteps and a hosteller walked in, very determined to be our first. Then another and, before long, another. To our surprise and delight they continued coming, spaced out widely in ones and twos, until almost ten at night. With our very limited bed-power it was almost a full house — every bed in the men's dormitory taken and three in the women's — and they included a New Zealander, two Americans and three Dutch.

Despite all we had done, the hostel remained a shambles in many directions — floors still up for wiring, nothing working efficiently and the only water still at the tap

in the yard. But the atmosphere was great with everyone happy and most helping. Wynne's supper went down with acclamation and the Common Room was cosy in the extreme, with its rich carpet, a bright wood fire reflecting on the gay backs of its many books and every chair filled. One thing was certain from the start — we should have to get more beds and find somewhere to put them. If this was a week night, what would it be like on August Bank Holiday?

Two days later, on the morning of 11th July, Penden gave its first public showing. In the former bar, which had become the hostel dining room, I placed the only movable bench on top of a table, with my few feet of test track on the bench. On this stood four engines, the two Macaws and a coach and one or two items of goods stock that I had recently bought from a member of the GW Circle. After describing them, I showed in their place the inn and the various uncompleted parts of the Chapel

The first public showing of Pendon (then called Penden) in the former bar of 'The Three Poplars'. Perched on the old bench are (from left to right) the models of the 'Waggon & Horses', 'Little Chapel Cottage', the Primitive Methodist chapel, parts of 'High Thatch' and the remaining cottages in the Chapel group.
ROYE ENGLAND

Members of the 'Silverwing Cycling Club' erecting the first sections of the ex-RAF hut that was to become Pendon's home for the next eighteen years.
ROYE ENGLAND

'Marilyn' takes shape.   ROYE ENGLAND

Roye at work on the construction of 'Marilyn'.
PENDON MUSEUM COLLECTION

Group, telling my hopes and my plans for the future. One hosteller asked how big the finished scene would be and I replied, 'At least twenty feet long'. When one had nothing, twenty feet seemed quite a lot. *(The Vale Scene at Pendon turned out to be some seventy feet in length.)* It was a small enough beginning, but five hostellers paid sixpence each to see it and they thoroughly entered into the spirit of it. The start had been made.

Five days after the opening, Roy came to me bursting with the news that he had found the very thing to increase our accommodation, both as a dormitory for the men and to make a home for Penden — a large RAF hut, several of which were being offered at a bargain price. Measuring sixty by eighteen feet, they were a really practical size, and at £45 each, about one third the usual cost. They were presently erected at the RAF camp in the grounds of Medmenham Abbey, near Marlow, but the Queen was going there in a few days and as they lay in the path of her tour, they had to be disposed of in a hurry. We chose one in an excellent condition that had been lived in until a day or so before — a timber-framed structure covered in felt and lined with plasterboard.

It was delivered in sections on a day when I was alone in the hostel and unloading was a fearsome task. However, we accomplished it without damaging either the hut or ourselves. The heavy sections comprising walls, windows and doors (and also the purlins and trusses) were deposited in great heaps in the garden, with a large pile of asbestos roofing sheets beside them. Only then did it fully come home to me that it was one thing to see a hut standing happily assembled on a concrete base and quite another to be left with a mountain of parts stacked forlornly in an overgrown orchard awaiting whatever attention might, or might not, be forthcoming.

It was at about this time that the fourth member of the Pendon team came forward. The first YHA group to book at the new hostel was the 'Silverwing Cycling Club' and they soon became regulars. One of their leaders, Paul King, offered his help to Penden. His work was locomotive engineering with British Railways, initially with steam and later with both diesels and electrics, but his special contribution to Penden became technical plan drawing, the construction of track and pointwork and the design and installation of electrical control — although as yet, most of these were a good way ahead.

Meanwhile, hostel attendances still soared — boiled egg breakfasts in the crammed bar, the office, anywhere — the self cookers often overflowed, But one weekend, as the crowd began to thin out, work started in earnest on the site for the hut. A couple of volunteers had come specially from Birmingham and, by the greatest luck, two student architects happened to be in the hostel. They stayed most of the day pegging out the line of the foundations and, a day or so later, work started on their digging.

However, to dig 160 feet of foundations and floor over a 1000 square feet with concrete proved a bigger job than we had foreseen, but, fortunately, a hosteller from Yorkshire, Ken Tolson, came to the hostel and, at my invitation, became a permanent for several months. He set to with a will to dig those endless foundations, assisted by working parties and by Roy and eventually the site was levelled.

One Sunday morning early in October, a hired cement mixer arrived. All was now ready to put in the foundations proper, until the mixer refused to start. By the time we had it going it was afternoon, but the whole perimeter of the hut had to be laid before the mixer was returned next morning, and by sunset we had only reached the half-way point. Yet finish we must, so Roy began switching on lights — outside the back door, in the kitchen, in the office, in the girl's wash. To crown it all, a magnificent moon rose, almost full. So the scene of work fairly glittered with light, and a couple of hours after dark the foundations were complete.

Before going to bed in the now empty hostel, I wandered out again into the perfect night to gaze over the scene of so much effort — the ringed rectangle of concrete that now held all my hopes. With the Brunel viaduct coming to make a separate scene, would the models in the future demand the whole of the hut instead of half of it? My ambitions already looked like being doubled. I pictured these untended surroundings, glistening now in the moonlight, changed one day to form a car park for those who came from afar to visit Penden. Would even the hut at last become inadequate and, on its site, a new building arise, incorporating a tea-room and with a garden set with coloured umbrellas . . . ? Far, far dreams, yet not impossible.

Autumn that year ended in streaming rains and screaming gales. But all through this wild weather, the sections of the hut were stacked in the garden. No one had thought how long it would take to make the base and no one had thought of buying a tarpaulin to cover the sections. So the rain seeped in, the gales drove the water in further and, slowly but surely, the plasterboard lining of each section was turning, unnoticed, into a creamy, slimy pulp.

The New Year, 1955, found a gathering of the 'Silverwing' and others around the Common Room fire having a party, but, spurred on by Paul King, they decided to stay on for a day to start work on the erection of the hut. It was then that the damage to the linings was discovered, but, with their enthusiasm undiminished, the volunteers worked on the main shell, and by dusk the whole 60 ft structure was standing. We had to confess that it lacked an architect's precision, for some picturesque curves had appeared in the sides of the building. To the 'Silverwing', curves meant nothing less than glamour —

Marilyn Monroe in those days — so the hut was forthwith named 'Marilyn'.

The following morning was cold and louring, with an angry, blustering wind — and disaster nearly overtook Marilyn before anyone realised it might happen. The hostel was empty and, almost by chance, I went out to gaze at the work of the previous day. To my dismay, I found the near end of the hut sagging dangerously inward, its sections swaying and creaking with every gust, the whole end hingeing on a single nail which threatened to give way at any moment.

I dashed next door to give Roy a desperate call — heard him answer that he was coming — then ran back and braced myself, spread-eagle fashion, against the col-

The back of 'The Three Poplars' in January 1955, with the partially finished hut on the left.
ROYE ENGLAND

January snow arrived before the new building was roofed, delaying work for several weeks.   ROYE ENGLAND

A rare view of the early stages in the construction of Pendon's 'Dartmoor' layout, with Guy installing his model of the Walkham Viaduct from the Tavistock line. ROYE ENGLAND

Another early photograph of the completed viaduct, standing on its base of secondhand canteen tables. In the background, three volunteers from the scores of helpers that Roye recruited are seen at work on painting the walls. ROYE ENGLAND

lapsing end. The wind drew it backwards and forwards in spite of me, but I held on, praying for Roy to be quick. The minutes dragged by, the wind buffeted relentlessly on. My arms were aching. I couldn't hold out indefinitely, but there was still no sign of Roy. Ten minutes passed before he came, having been interrupted at the crucial moment by a business phone call, and somehow, I held on for another quarter of an hour whilst he found and nailed up some temporary supports. Had the end fallen in that wind, there would soon have been nothing left standing.

Among our other troubles, Marilyn was also costing much more than had been expected. I had to buy £40 worth of hardboard to replace the pulped plasterboard, and large areas of exterior felt had to be renewed. A financial crisis developed and I reluctantly asked the Oxford Region of YHA to lend me £150 to complete the hut and tide me over. Maeve Simkins said that they had had so many letters of appreciation of the hostel and National Office was so pleased with it, that they could not afford to let it fail. That quarter, apart from the large Oxford hostel, Long Wittenham topped the regional bednight figures — and that at a time before it was in the Handbook. The loan was made.

Work on Marilyn continued doggedly and by the end of January the roof was on and attention had turned to the inside. How big the enclosed space looked and amid hectic preparations for Easter, Wynne and the rest of us sandpapered and painted the ceiling, trusses and walls, in the nick of time to move in the beds.

Showings continued in the former bar and, on 20th March, Pendon's first showing to the public (as distinct from hostellers) was made when eight members of the Mounthill Rambling Club from Oxford turned up and asked to see the models. They went away intent on mak-

ing the models known, and, since a start had been made, I decided from then on to set aside every Saturday and Sunday from 3 o'clock for public exhibiting.

Guy announced that on Easter Tuesday he hoped to bring the viaduct up from Bristol by train. I imagined all thirteen feet of it stretching majestically down a corridor, but it arrived, without drama or ceremony, dismembered in a suitcase. Roy had bought me 36 stout wooden canteen tables from his work for the absurd sum of 5s. each, and, after a day's planning, we brought in 22 of them to form a ready-made staging for the layout. By placing them in pairs one on top of each other, they gave a rail height of five feet, and since stock of Pendon's calibre must be seen at eye level, they seemed, both for height and the saving of labour and expense, exactly what we needed.

The date of this beginning of Pendon's first layout was 13th April, 1955. It was on that night, thirty years before, that I had sailed from Fremantle by the *Oronsay*, bound for England. Delays, setbacks and frustrations had been endless, but the purpose had been unchanging and it was a strange coincidence that that anniversary, to the day, should have seen one of the layouts for which I had planned for so long, started.

Work on the baseboards then took a further day. Guy then began putting up the viaduct and continued with it until four in the morning, by which time half of it was in place. The following day it was completed with all its sixteen piers standing stark with nothing round them, but looking most imposing nevertheless. Guy told me that the whole structure was made up of 2,686 pieces.

A view of the site with the completed 'Marilyn' on the left and 'The Three Poplars' largely obscured by trees. The two buildings next to 'Marilyn' were the former stable block and the old skittle alley that belonged to the pub.
ROYE ENGLAND

On the morning of Sunday, 17th April, in the presence of hostellers and friends, the inaugural run was made over the viaduct by the '56', running light. For those of us who had been counting the years, then the months and the weeks, for the first run on Penden's first layout, it was a thrilling event. Later, the '56' took a train of borrowed goods stock across, looking wonderfully real, as did *Broome Hall*, but the '28' refused to budge. However, Guy soon had her going and she took 25 wagons, most of them on loan from Guy, with the greatest ease. When one thinks

of what she handled in later years this was no achievement at all, but on this morning, at the outset of our hopes, it delighted us.

The design of the Vale layout was now evolving, first in my mind, then on paper. Branching main lines were decided upon — the Oxford one as well as the line to Swindon — and there must be a station near where they met. Penden Parva village on the hills, Penden Parva station in the Vale below.

Roye posing in front of the model of the Walkham Viaduct with the 'Waggon and Horses' and two engines, No. 5624 and No. 4837. The photo is dated 1955.   ALFRED CARPENTER

After Saint Dunstan *was completed, Guy Williams's next model was 'Hall' class No. 4908* Broome Hall, *also finished in 1954.*   L. KENT

Culham Station (the chosen prototype for the main station in Pendon's Vale Scene) photographed in about 1930. Culham, of course, is not in the Vale of White Horse but Roye felt this delightful station — which was designed by Brunel — was too good to disregard.
C. L. MOWAT

Culham goods shed, which was also to be included in the Vale Scene.
ROYE ENGLAND

The choice of a prototype for the station needed no thought. Culham, on the Oxford line, only 2 miles or so from the hostel, made an unusually beautiful little group. Built by Brunel in 1844, it was still in almost original condition and looked very contented in its Great Western shades of 'light and dark stone' — so called, although in fact these were pleasing tones of biscuit and pinkish buff.

But not long after this, the spoilers moved in and these soft colours, weathered warm and mellow, tawny and smoky, were exchanged for a coat of uncompromising British Railways cream.

Until now, the name 'Penden' had proved a good title for the models, as 'Penden Parva' was doing for the village. But there was one fault and a hosteller had already

The platform side of the main (up side) building at Culham Station — one of the best examples of Brunel's 'cottage-style' of small station. ROYE ENGLAND

The road side of the main building at Culham.

ROYE ENGLAND

*A working party shapes
the basic landscape for
Dartmoor.*
ROYE ENGLAND

pointed this out. If I were taking such pains to make the village typical and historically correct, surely similar care should be taken in choosing its name? For 'Parva' there was the local precedent of Hinton Parva, but 'Penden' didn't ring true in that part of the country. There were no villages within miles ending in '-den'. In the Vale and on the downs one found '-stone', '-bury', '-ford', '-ham', '-ton', and '-don and of these, the last would fit easily into the scheme of things if 'Penden' became 'Pendon' and the village 'Pendon Parva'.

Beyond this, we suddenly realised the village name would gain a very appropriate local meaning, 'Pen' standing for high ground, a bold eminence, 'don', the village and 'Parva' small — the name as a whole, in free translation, giving 'little hill village', which was just what we planned to make it. So from 16th June 1955, the name was changed to 'Pendon Models' — or more often, of course, just 'Pendon'.

It was August when Guy came to create scenery round the viaduct. The whole day on his first visit went in putting up the dry bones of the valley — dozens of timber struts to shape the moorland terrain, though when he had to leave it, still unfinished, it looked more like the framework of a prehistoric ship than part of the West Country. However, he came back soon after and put in a concentrated week's work. Spreading roofing felt over the timber and dyed surgical lint over the felt, he turned the whole into very presentable moors, especially when clumps of spray-painted moss were placed at strategic points on the hills and in the valley below. There was still no sky and a lot of surface modelling and colouring

remained to be done, but Pendon now had a simple landscape across whose viaduct three trains ran.

It was shortly after this that Guy made a gesture which was to be the forerunner of the new spirit of Pendon. "I shall be delighted", he wrote, "to give my services to the project until the exhibition is on its feet" and since by 'giving' he meant no longer accepting payment, in that sentence the whole nature of our relationship changed. Pendon had become a cause, an adventure, a labour of love, for him as it had always been for me. In due course, Ken Budd followed suit with the coaches he built for us and so was established the convention by which members of the Pendon team take no payment.

With the onset of winter there was time for modelling and I turned once more to the Chapel Group. Thatching still lay some way ahead, but I was already planning for it and just at this time, a hosteller pointed out that hair should be mothproofed. He put me in touch with Leeds University, where Dr. J.W. Bell of the Textile Industries Department, confirmed that moths look upon hair as a special delicacy. He most generously arranged for proofing, without charge, of all the batches that we used during the next fifteen years.

In the spring and the summer that followed, many hostellers signed the housebook. The good name of Long Wittenham was spreading far and wide. One hosteller told me he had heard a warden as far away as the Lake District remark that he was "flabbergasted at the popularity of Long Wittenham". But increasing popularity meant more and more work. This year (1956), the 40 bed hostel put up 60 on Easter Sunday and although this, in numbers, was

Uffington Station, photographed in the 1950s, looking towards Paddington. The Faringdon branch may be seen to the left, whilst the Junction Hotel (where Roye liked to stay when on visits to this part of the Vale) features behind the down platform, on the right.

P. J. GARLAND

the ultimate, it was no more than the start of the oncoming summer avalanche. Had I been married, the support of a partner might have made things easier, but single-handed it was killing.

Fortunately, the help that I needed so desperately was not many months away. A hosteller named David Morris, of stocky build, with a fairly generous beard — an amateur artist and quite a character — offered me permanent assistance for the ridiculously small payment of 10s. a week plus insurance stamp and keep. I was not sure that I could afford even that pittance but whether I could or not, Dave started as Assistant Warden at Long Wittenham in the middle of September.

This not only helped the hostel, but Pendon too, for it freed me to a certain extent to get into the Vale for photos and measurements. On these expeditions, as there was no youth hostel in the immediate area, I began staying overnight at the Junction Hotel beside Uffington station. There I was generally given a room overlooking the line and in the morning, enjoyed the unprecedented thrill, whilst still in bed, of watching expresses behind 'Castles' and 'Kings' thunder by, just below. The lulls between these passings were filled by the busy pottering of a

Pannier on a pick-up goods. It sorted itself, then trundled down the branch to Faringdon, returning after a while to puff its leisurely way up the main line to Didcot. Early doves cooed from the elms opposite, people arrived laughing and chatting in the still air, awaiting the stopping train to Swindon in time for work and the whole atmosphere was one of stability, of peace and contentment. Ten years later, the entire scene, the branch, station, signals, and steam itself was swept away and the hotel closed. Even the elms were afterwards cut down.

By now I had shown Pendon to 4,000 visitors — mostly hostellers, although there was a gradually increasing public on weekend afternoons. The collecting of railway relics had become an acknowledged part of the programme and when I heard that the 'Kings' were being given double chimneys, I asked Swindon if I could buy a single one when it came off. They replied that I could have one for the unexplained sum of £4 13s.9d. and, before long, a magnificent 3 or 4cwt of it arrived by lorry, with one man to unload it. As usual, when anything heavy arrived, there were no hostellers available to help, but a couple of neighbours came to the rescue. It was placed imposingly on a box at the end of the passage in the hostel, where it rested for the next seven years. Its only diversion during that time was when two of the cats had kittens in it!

It was now a priority to colour and detail the Dartmoor scenery, and Dave Morris, with his artistic bent, was keen to attack it. We started with the sky, then the hills, and although the work was halted on several occasions as we debated (and disagreed) over tones and hues, eventually it was done. The total effect was most convincing and made our trains look very small as they plunged into the hillside beneath its heathered heights and rearing skies. Rock making and tor formation followed and, to add to our elation, the viaduct was now crossed for the first time by a five-coach train, owing to the arrival of four new 'Toplight' coaches built by Ken. These ran behind *Broome Hall* with a slip coach built by Guy at the tail. Pendon's first glimpse of the past in miniature was now really coming to life.

My acre of field, cut once a year for hay, had other possibilities, and, for some time, I had been encouraging an occasional caravan to park there. Now, after a succession of difficulties, I had been given a licence for twelve vans. This would considerably boost my shaky finances, but first, a good deal of money (which I didn't possess) would have to be spent in preparing the site. On top of this there were other debts and the lean time of another winter looming. The only way out was to borrow — but from whom? My capital was now entirely gone and I already had a maximum overdraft at the bank.

The answer was the Guild of St. Aidan. Its moment had come. The Guild had never previously done anything to help the models for which it had existed, yet now, long after it had ceased to live, it suddenly became the means of making the life of Pendon more secure. For it still had funds — something like £150 lying dormant and as its Founder-Warden, I had been given authority to conduct

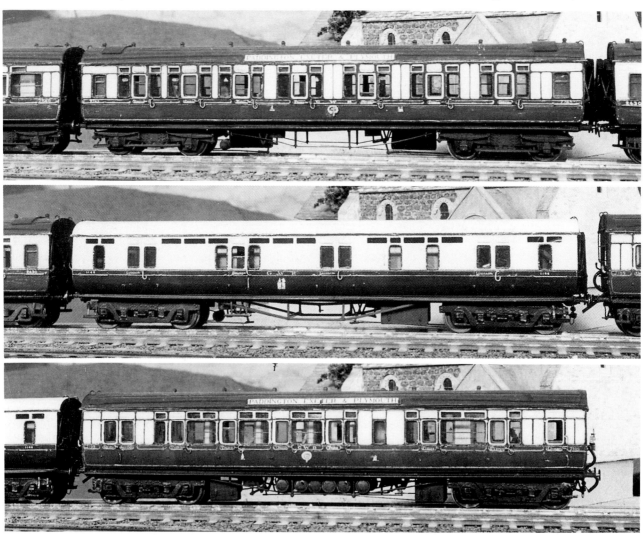

Portraits of several of the coaches built by Ken Budd and Guy Williams for the first express train used on the Dartmoor layout.

Above: *Another of the coaches built by Ken Budd for use on Dartmoor. This model is still in service at Pendon in one of the trains being used to test the track and control systems in the Vale Scene.*

Roye at the control panel of the Dartmoor layout in 1956. Broome Hall is seen pulling the express, some of the coaches of which were borrowed, although others had already been built for Pendon by Ken Budd.
PENDON MUSEUM COLLECTION

all its affairs as I thought fit. Mario, Ram and Michael all strongly advised me to turn its aid to the present crisis, arguing that the survival of the hostel at present meant the survival of Pendon. That winter, the Guild's help averted disaster.

So the caravan site was able to take shape, vans and their ground rent began coming in. But even so, money remained painfully short. I still had several debts and it was impossible to make the site as good as I should have liked. As a result, I couldn't pick my tenants and I found too many were not the types I would have chosen for myself, and too many were out of work, or ill, or said they were. Not knowing which were genuine, I tried to help them all. But I was in no position to lend food, to waive payments even temporarily, less still to lose them when I was let down. Each time any of these things happened, it was inevitably bringing the then unseen trough that lay ahead, that little bit nearer.

One Saturday in August (1957), I had an unexpected telephone call — Lord Glyn would like to see the models, would it be convenient that afternoon? The showing was a fairly crowded one. He appeared quite interested, but said very little, and, to my disappointment, excused him-

self before seeing anything at all of the village. As he left, I asked would he care to have any photos of the models and he said, "Yes, but not now. Send me a few." I felt a good chance of gaining his interest had slipped through my fingers, but, in due course, I sent off half a dozen photos, expecting to hear no more.

Nor did I from Lord Glyn. But one day I was called to the phone. "This is the General Manager's Office, Paddington. The General Manager, Mr. Grand, has been shown photographs of your models by Lord Glyn and wishes to send a personal representative to see them"!

The great day proved a delightful one. Mr. Grand sent B.Y. Williams, the Chief Statistician of the Western Region at Paddington and he brought with him J.N. Maskelyne, Editor of the *Model Railway News*, They came at ten, had a boiled-egg lunch in the Common Room, and stayed till four in the afternoon. Mr. Maskelyne, an intensely interesting man with an Edwardian charm, actually remembered my ambitious plans for Pendon from a chance meeting some six years earlier. "I thought then", he confessed, "that this chap doesn't know what he is up against. He'll be fortunate if he can do a tenth of what he thinks he can. Yet here it is being done."

Roye watching an express train cross the Walkham Viaduct on Pendon's Dartmoor layout.

What had brought Lord Glyn to Pendon? A good deal later I found that it was thanks to a teenager, Frank Griffin, who had been helping us at Pendon. He had enthused about Pendon to Mr. Hanks, later the Chairman of the British Transport Commission and it was Hanks who had remarked upon Pendon to Lord Glyn. So, thanks to a schoolboy, Pendon became known at the highest levels in Paddington and as time went on, the results of Mr. Grand's interest became very evident and much to our advantage.

Meanwhile, Ken Budd had just built Pendon two steel-panelled coaches of the mid-1920s, which were painted by Guy. But none of us could be sure what the actual shades of primrose and chocolate were correct for our period, so one day I went to Swindon to try to find out. Mr. Woodman, the foreman of the Paint Shop was a true Great Western man, not at all happy at the changes that were taking place. When I told him we were making a model of the railway in its heyday as an historical record, he was on our side. A tactful mention that the General Manager was personally interested in the work clinched it. Yes, they still had the 1930 formula and would make a special mix of it. If I called back in a fortnight, a panel painted in the two authentic colours of the period would be ready. When I saw it, it confirmed that as I had suspected, none of the cream on our coaches was of the right tone — that fresh, clear primrose that looked as though it came straight from the woods in spring. Also, the chocolate was generally not dark enough.

On the back of the panel we inscribed its date and exactly what it was, and for more than fifteen years, it remained one of our most precious records. By the end of that time (1973), the model trade was making a serious attempt to offer productions that were really authentic, and to assist one of the firms turning out paints for modellers, we lent them our panel. After using it, they failed to return it, so Guy wrote asking for its return. They replied, totally unabashed, that they never kept samples and had thrown it away. Such utterly wanton behaviour seemed hardly conceivable, for the panel was quite obviously of a permanent and valuable nature. But it had gone and our scathing comments would not bring it back.

Despite progress in so many ways, 1957 ended on a pensive note. I was again short of money and the axe fell hard and in several directions. One victim was Dave, and his going raised all the old problems of time. Modelling and measuring, once again, ground to a halt. 'Outline' records — "I am getting worried as to whether the completion of Pendon Parva will ever be possible. If many more years slip by . . . it is quite certain that life will prove too short".

An unidentified 'Castle' class engine crossing Acorn Bridge, about a mile to the east of Shrivenham, with an express for Paddington. This was one of Roye's favourite spots for watching trains. The A420 road is deserted in this late 1950s view, but today the widened road uses both arches of the bridge. The undergrowth on the left concealed the remains of the long-disused Wilts & Berks Canal which used to pass through the left-hand arch of the bridge.
ROYE ENGLAND

Wynne Morris (left) apparently cutting the hair of her daughter Sandy for use in thatching Pendon's models, while Roye looked on eagerly. The young man was a hosteller from Germany.
BERNSEN PRESS AGENCY

CHAPTER EIGHT
1958–1959
MORE UPS THAN DOWNS

A brief fragment appeared, unannounced in the *Daily Mail*, origin unknown — 'Girl hostellers at Long Wittenham youth hostel give their hair to thatch model cottages!' Insignificant in size, its impact was far-reaching. It brought the Bernsen Press Agency hot-foot to find out what it was all about and they spent five hours one afternoon and evening, photographing the complete story of Pendon's thatch. It had to begin, of course, with a shot showing the denuding of a hosteller of her locks. Sandy Morris (Roy and Wynne's eldest daughter) by now was growing up into a ravishing blonde, so the Bernsen photographer pounced on her and posed her

with Wynne in front of Dartmoor. Armed with a pair of large scissors, Wynne was shown apparently acquiring a worthwhile handful of Sandy's locks, while I stood by, avidly watching. Not quite Pendon's usual method, but it made a good story. The last shot in the sequence was of a finished building, the inn, held against Sandy's (undiminished) head of hair.

The first result of this session was a picture in *Reveille*, of all places for Pendon to appear. The circulation of *Reveille* was enormous and it inevitably brought sightseers to Pendon — who included the informed as well as the merely curious. But it also brought a representative of

Another posed view by the Bernsen Agency, with Roye supposedly preparing hair to thatch 'Little Chapel Cottage', which features alongside 'The Waggon & Horses'. In practice, the hair had to be treated by moth-proofing, before it could be used.
BERNSEN PRESS AGENCY

Pathe Pictorial, who drove from London to consider filming our story. It would be shown all over England and
abroad as well, including Australia.

The filming (for which Guy came up from Bristol) was
done on a cold, stormy day, but floodlamps and batteries
of lights, on the trusses over Dartmoor generated so much
heat that we had both doors open and a fan going most of
the day. The 'Barnum' — Guy's latest engine for Pendon,
was the principal star, with the '28' and its long goods a
worthy second. Cottage building and the shearing of
Sandy were done in the dormitory half of Marilyn, which
was rigged-up as a studio-workroom, and there were also
field-work shots of myself measuring an old cottage down
our lane, taken in short breaks of sunshine between heavy
cloud. It took seven of us 9½ hours to make a film lasting
four minutes, but the results, when they came, justified it
all.

Pathe Pictorial No. 205 was released in London and in
ten principal centres from Brighton to Edinburgh.
Consumed with curiosity, I went up to Town to see
myself as others were seeing me, found the little Eros car-
toon theatre at Piccadilly and asked the girl at the door
when the *Pictorial* would be coming on. Before replying,
she gazed at me and exclaimed, "Did you make those
beautiful models? We've enjoyed seeing them", she
purred. "But tell me", she continued, with a pert smile,

"why do you have to take that poor girl's hair when you
could have cut off your friend's beard instead?" Guy
should have been there to answer that one!

Inside I waited impatiently through the first feature of
the *Pictorial*. It seemed hardly credible that Pendon Models
would shortly take its place. But with no warning at all,
there was an abrupt change to myself in blue pullover and

*Three views of the Pathe Pictorial filming session. Guy attending
to the 'Barnum' (his latest engine) with Roye looking on.*
PENDON MUSEUM COLLECTION

Adjustments made, the engine was filmed being attached to its train.   **PENDON MUSEUM COLLECTION**

shorts measuring the little cottage near the hostel. This field-work scene came out extremely well, with no indication of the hostile weather. Then the film switched indoors. The cottages looked very attractive and my impression was that both Wynne and Sandy had more glamour than many genuine film stars! In the Dartmoor scene there was a sudden ridiculous acceleration of the

'Barnum' in starting away and a solemn announcement by the commentator that the models were built to a scale of one centimetre to one foot — 2½ times too big. But otherwise, everything went well.

In due course, the film came locally to Abingdon, Didcot and Wallingford, and, at all three, we were allowed to show photographs and distribute leaflets in the

The 'Barnum' and its train filmed crossing the Walkham Viaduct, with Guy watching progress with fatherly concern and Bob Pulfer attempting a photograph.
PENDON MUSEUM
COLLECTION

The model of 'Barnum' class No. 3222 pulling a typically mixed train across the model of Walkham Viaduct.
PENDON MUSEUM COLLECTION

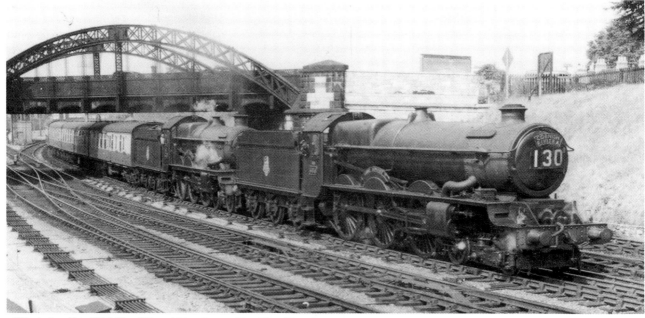

'King' class No. 6016 King Edward V *and an unidentified 'Castle' class leaving Newton Abbot with the down 'Cornish Riviera' in August 1953.*
COLLECTION R. S. CARPENTER

Collett 14XX class 0–4–2T No. 1472 drifting into Totnes down platform with a local train, possibly off the Ashburton branch.
ROYE ENGLAND

entrance. In this way, the film brought us a considerable tide of extra visitors — far more than we later had from several appearances on television.

The last week in June found me travelling by 'The Cornish Riviera' to Plymouth. Thanks to the interest of the General Manager, I had been given a Walking Permit over a number of key spots on British Railways — Old Oak Common, some local yards and several branch lines in Devon. With the hostel closed for the Warden's annual holiday, now was my chance to get colour notes of the real Dartmoor landscape and to find a prototype for the station buildings of what we proposed to called 'Pen Tor Junction' on the Dartmoor layout.

Behind *King Edward V*, in a train liveried entirely in chocolate and cream, the non-stop run of four hours was completely enjoyable, and, to stint nothing, I had lunch for an hour between Pewsey and Taunton — 11s.6d. all told — in a Great Western bow-ended dining car. At high speed, winding this way and that through a countryside that I had mostly cycled, was a thrilling time — and incidentally, a very good meal. Later, on the curves round the sea wall through Dawlish and Teignmouth and on the climbs and descents of Dainton and Rattery banks, I could see the train ahead quite clearly, the engine swaying and weaving with the effort, safety valves blowing intermittently. On the curve in Parson's Tunnel, there was one magnificent vista when light from the approaching outside world caught the engine and all the train in a glancing highlight within the darkness.

At Plymouth I bought a Runabout Ticket for myself and bike, which allowed a week's unlimited travel in the area — a wonderful feeling of plutocracy — though the six days I had allowed myself proved all too short. Armed with this ticket and my permit, I discovered Yelverton — set in tremendous country on the Launceston branch. The true atmosphere of branchline friendliness pervaded each of these little stations and, as the small train puffed away and left me on the Yelverton platform, I found myself gazing at the most enchanting of them all — a verdant tunnel mouth framed by a very attractive footbridge, charm-

ing station buildings, all in wood, with flower baskets hanging from the canopy, and everything still in Great Western colouring that I thought I should never see again. Here, beyond any doubt, was the station building for the branch platforms at Pen Tor Junction. Even its irregular shape, almost a triangle, caused by the alignment of the recently-closed Princetown branch, was just what we wanted.

Above: When Roye visited Yelverton, the branch line up to Princetown had already been closed and the track lifted, but in this view taken a few years earlier, the Princetown train — behind 45XX class 2—6—2T No. 4542 — was ready to depart on its arduous journey onto Dartmoor.

Yelverton station in 1958. The unusual polygonal shape of the main building exactly suited Roye's needs for his imaginary station — Pen Tor Road — on the Dartmoor layout.
ROYE ENGLAND

For the mainline building at Pen Tor Junction, we needed an earlier structure, probably a legacy of the South Devon Railway, and had already chosen Ivybridge — totally different from Yelverton, but just as full of character. The photographing and measuring of both of these was perhaps the most important work that the holiday made possible. Another highlight, however, was the chance to get colour notes of the great Walkham Viaduct that meant so much to Pendon — no longer, of course, in the beauty of fanned timber, but with Brunel's stone piers still doing duty beneath its steel girders. Among tall trees

in its setting of a richly wooded valley, the viaduct was difficult to see in detail, but at Pendon, long after the tremendous structure had been razed to the ground, the notes that I did manage to get that day were to become an invaluable possession.

Although there were stations in Devon still in the 'light and dark stone' of the GWR, this tended usually to be somewhat faded and I was anxious to get a colour photograph of a really fresh, 'live' example. To my joy, I found it on a single tiny building at Marytavy — a little closed station a good deal further along the Launceston branch

Ivybridge, on the main line between Totnes and Plymouth. The unusually wide platform in front of the main building was formed when the track was realigned in 1892, in association with the construction of a new double-track viaduct just to the east of the station.
ROYE ENGLAND

Roye selected this typical Brunelian building as a prototype for the main line platform at Pen Tor Road.   ROYE ENGLAND

from Yelverton. What was more, my transparency produced, on this occasion, a perfect reproduction of the
colours. We now had an authentic and accurate sample
from which to work.

At Lydford, still further along the branch, where the
Southern ran beside the GW line and even shared a
station, I took many Southern photos in the hope of
somehow including something of this in our Dartmoor
scene, too. It was not, however, to be, and the only
glimpse of the Southern that we later managed to achieve
was the Bude portion of the 'Atlantic Coast Express',
diverted (no doubt for some good reason) over Great
Western metals.

I returned to Pendon surfeited with beauty, delighted
with my finds and more content than ever with our modelling to date.

The hostel continued to flourish and, due to extra publicity, Pendon's weekend showings were now often
uncomfortably full. For a long time, an extension of some
sort to the further end of Marilyn had been projected and
discussed, but always shelved through lack of funds. That
autumn, however, Bob Pulfer, a hosteller who had
become a good friend to both Pendon and to me, stepped
in. He would advance us the greater part of the cost of the
extension as an interest-free loan over whatever period we
needed it. It was a marvellous offer that immediately set
wheels turning.

Paul drew up plans for an 18 foot extension and, after
several delays, planning permission came through. But
Bob was not able to put up the whole cost and it was a
great disappointment that by the time the work could
start, my own endless financial problems had again put it
beyond reach.

Caravans were, as usual, at the core of the trouble. In
the hope of building up my resources, I had bought, over
a long period, a total of three vans — one of which I was
still struggling to pay off. The summer of 1958 had been
a consistently wet one and the winter that followed was no
better. The site became a sea of mud. Tenants began
demanding a reduction in the ground rent and threatening to bring in the council. Seeing my straits were desperate, the bank yet again put up the overdraft. So I survived the mud on the site by sinking deeper into the mud
of debt.

During that winter of crisis, the loss of Dave's help was
unexpectedly made up by the coming of Walter — an
older man of easy-going habit, a lover of the quiet life
who gave considerable assistance in the hostel but yet,
because of my financial difficulties, agreed also to pay his
keep. For the next year, his help was to prove as fortunate
as it was unexpected. The following summer (1959)
turned out to be a brilliant one, and, thanks to Walter's

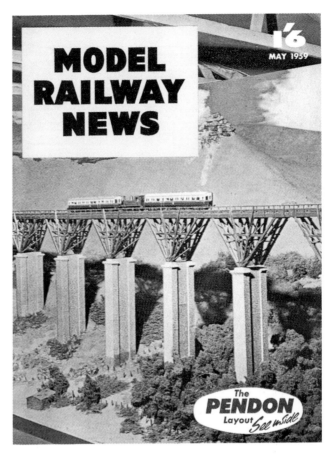

help, I was able to go often to the Vale for photographing
and measuring, sometimes for up to four days at a time.

The first mention of Pendon in the model press also
came that summer with an article in *Model Railway
Constructor* which included a magnificent picture of the
Dartmoor scene and a more comprehensive account in
the *Model Railway News*. The latter article, in particular,
was to give Pendon a wide recognition among modellers
and continued to bring them to Long Wittenham for a
number of years after.

Its most direct effect on Pendon, however, was in leading Stewart Hine into our team. He turned up on an
afternoon of the Whitsun holiday when the temperature
in Marilyn was at heatwave level and the track buckled till
not a thing would run. Although then only an interested
visitor, he immediately tackled the problem and our
dilemma soon melted away.

Stewart was a meticulous modeller in 2mm scale, half
the size of the Pendon models, but he offered to build us
an occasional coach — "to make something big, for a
change" — as he put it. Being by profession an electronic engineer, he said he would fit interior lighting —
something that had already defeated several attempts by

Highworth station, photographed in September 1959, after it had been closed to passengers but while a daily goods service still operated.
ROYE ENGLAND

The Highworth branch goods waiting at Cricklade Road crossing, while the guard worked the crossing gates.   ROYE ENGLAND

others. "It's easy", he said — and in due course proceeded to prove his point.

One hot, beautiful day in September, I went to the little station at Highworth, the end of the line set high on a hillside a few miles north of Swindon, to get branchline photos. It was already closed to passengers, but while I was there, its one tiny goods train came from Swindon, puffing up the long curving rise into the station. It consisted of no more than a Collett 0-4-2T, No. 1410 and a goods brake.

After picking up a few wagons to go back, the men had some tea on the platform — all delightfully rural and unhurried. By the time they were ready to leave, they had put my bike in the van and I was there with it — getting a wonderful view of the line and of the really lovely countryside, the trees often almost touching the train. At Cricklade Road crossing, true to the atmosphere of the whole branch, the train waited happily while the guard strolled out to open the gates. It ambled through, then waited while he closed them. The original gates had only just been replaced by new ones, due to road widening, and the old ones were still standing on one side. Here was the germ of an idea and a few weeks later, the rejected gates were delivered to Pendon on a low-loader. I paid the ridiculous price of £1 for them and there was no delivery charge. Such co-operation was possible, I was told, because some time ago the General Manager had written to Swindon asking special consideration for Pendon.

Quite a number of relics came to us at about that time, perhaps the most outstanding being a leather dumb buffer of 1851 from the broad gauge engine *Lord of the Isles*. It was advertised in the *Railway Magazine* for £20 — an almost unique possession that even British Railways would be proud to own. I could not afford it, but I telegraphed for it, nevertheless.

Bob Pulfer had left to spend a couple of years in America, but his loan still stood, and work on the extension to Marilyn eventually started. Work proceeded slowly, frustrated by shortages of roof timbers and other materials, but, at the end of the year and quite unexpectedly, the builder went into liquidation. This posed an immediate problem as we had negotiated an agreement for an extended period of payment. In the end, Roy finished the job, and, although a number of other clients of the firm were sued for payment, Pendon was treated with great lenience. Needless to say, it was several years before the debt was wiped out.

During the previous winter I had begun, for a change, to model the house from the Badbury Farm Group, but the usual interruptions came, and when I was able to start modelling again, I turned back to the Chapel Group. Hollyhocks were already in bloom in front of Middlecot, and, after adding some cornflowers, I faced up to the big (but tiny) work of the Jackmanii clematis over the porch, with its 51 four-petalled flowers, 201 trifoliate leaves and 31 stems — the whole plant about an inch high. This was followed by lavender, a giant sunflower, alyssum, lobelia, snapdragons, pansies, a rose, fern, Russian vine over the hedge, valerian, gladioli, nasturtiums, forget-me-nots and scabious — in that order. And 103 daisies on the lawn! The gladioli had had a particularly long history, for I had started them in 1939 to go behind the inn. But they were interrupted by the founding of the Guild and the outbreak of war. Now, twenty years later, in November 1959, I used the original leaves and some of the flowers that had been waiting patiently all that time.

Pendon's visitors were up by over 700 on the previous year, an increase of about 33%. Yet the increased takings were not much more than a drop in the ocean of our needs. Would a grant be possible? On making inquiries, I found that a body called the Pilgrim Trust gave grants to schemes dealing with historical work and the preservation of beauty. I drafted an application most carefully, and, five days later, I received a reply from Lord Kilmaine, the Secretary. He regretted they were unable to consider our application as Pendon was legally my personal possession. The help of the Pilgrim Trust was confined to charities that were recognised in law.

Work progressing on the new extension to 'Marilyn'.   ROYE ENGLAND

For some time I had been wanting to put Pendon on a better footing, for it was not fair that the others were giving their time and skill to a scheme which I considered I shared with them, yet which was in fact entirely my own. But now there was an even stronger reason for change. I went to a solicitor in Didcot. He said the concern could probably be made into a charitable trust, but he had had no experience of such things and advised my getting in touch with the Charity Commissioners in London. They advised an exploratory return to the Pilgrim Trust who now sent me to the Inland Revenue officials in Oxford. Everything hung on what the Revenue would accept as a charity.

When I outlined my case, they said no decision on charitable status could be taken until a trust had been formed and a copy of the deed supplied to them. I enquired whether I could send them a tentative copy for their advice and was told they were not particularly interested in helping people to avoid paying tax! Their only suggestion was to put it in the hands of a competent solicitor.

The one in Didcot had admitted he was not well informed about charities, but, after a most unhelpful visit to one in Oxford, I found Norman Challenor in Abingdon. He was as active, interested and competent as the Oxford one seemed inept. Furthermore, he had already seen the models, so was with me from the start. He said a case like this was an unusual one, and, since everything must depend upon the expert drawing up of the deed, he recommended our getting specialist advice before committing ourselves.

The next day I went to Bristol and discussed the whole question with Guy and Ken, both of whom approved wholeheartedly. Paul had already done so and Stewart followed, as did another member of the team, Jim Arnold. Jim was an artist, a writer and a Pendon helper of several years standing, having helped to erect Marilyn and put finishing touches on parts of the Dartmoor scene. These five completed the Pendon team at that time, so everyone was with me. Just before Christmas I received a letter from Challenor saying he had placed our case "before a Counsel learned in Charities and Trust Deeds" who, however, could only accept it if we were prepared to wait until pressure of other work should lessen. That could be a long time and so it proved. But Pendon's future could not have been in safer hands.

INTERLUDE — The Battle of the Signal

Now, for a change, the story of Pendon's longest (or tallest) relic. It had started back in 1958 when I went to Reading Signal Works and asked if I could buy a signal. I said I couldn't afford to pay a lot and, owing to the cost of carriage, it must not be too far away. I was told that the Up Main Distant at Culham was on the point of being taken down and, since I wanted it as a collector's piece, I could have it for ten shillings. Had I wanted it for firewood, it would apparently have cost a good deal more. I should write to Swindon and they would make the arrangements. Swindon replied that since we should be having not only a 38 foot post but also all the fittings and a 28 foot wrought iron ladder, a price of sixteen shillings would be a fair price! I was intrigued by this most generous piece of logic but sent the sixteen shillings and had a receipt in due course.

A few weeks later, a letter came from Reading. They had the pleasure of informing me that the signal was now lying at Culham and would I please arrange transport? Bob Pulfer and I went to Culham station, where we were surprised to see no signal lying. So we found the station master and showed him the letter. He read it with mounting astonishment. "But you can't take our signal!" he exclaimed, "We're still using it. You can go down the line and see." So off we went down the line — beyond the sidings, into a long, deep cutting, half a mile perhaps from the station — and there it was, a beautiful thing in all the untouched pride of regular service. Yet it was mine — I

had the receipt in my pocket. I was probably the only person who owned a signal in full use by British Railways on a mainline. I thought of sending them a bill for the hire of my signal but reflected that they might send me a bill for its maintenance, which could be more.

They kept it in service for a further five months and then, in February 1959, they wrote to say it was really taken down. We found it lying in the goods yard and I was pleased to see the good condition of the post. [The post actually withstood the elements for a further 30 years before substantial remedial work became obligatory in the early 1990s.]

Two hostellers dug a six foot hole for the signal at the bottom of the garden, but the weather had broken and, with the ground now a quagmire, we judged that with the signal weighing around a ton, moving it then would have been to court disaster. More than six weeks passed until the weather (and the ground) had improved sufficiently for the low-loader and crane to collect the signal from Culham. With its ladder removed, the signal fitted the low-loader as though made-to-measure. To my surprise, the driver recognised me from the Pathe film and he cheerfully put my bike aboard and took me back on a journey that was surprisingly free of difficulty — even over the narrow bridge at Clifton Hampden. The signal was placed, for painting, on a line of benches, its butt end quite near the hole — and there it lay for nine months. It was fine to buy a 38 foot relic weighing over a ton, but how did one stand it permanently on end in the garden?

'Hall' class engine No. 4955 Plaspower Hall *heading a fitted freight towards Oxford, past Roye's signal, the Up Main Distant at Culham.*
PENDON MUSEUM COLLECTION

It was again February, but now 1960, when a party of Rover Scouts from Oxford offered to erect the signal — a mere sixteen of them, including several girlfriends. They put up a structure of scaffolding poles left by the builders of the extension to Marilyn and attached ropes and pulleys. Then, slowly but surely, the giant post slid into its hole, rose in the air and poised upright while four guy lines and its ladder were attached. When the arm, lamp, finial and the smaller fittings were added and it was in full working order, the completed signal was most beautiful. There were few signals so shapely as the family of wood-

Roye, with two friends (and his signal) in the yard at Culham station. The lady's name was Jeanne but the young man is not identified. The photograph is dated 23rd April 1959.
PENDON MUSEUM COLLECTION

The party of Rover Scouts, together with several girlfriends, manoeuvring the signal post, weighing more than a ton, into position over its hole.   ROYE ENGLAND

The post being set into position with the help of scaffolding poles and ropes.   ROYE ENGLAND

en posts of the Great Western. Being a distant, its arm was painted yellow and fishtailed, and, by night, its amber or green light (though only lit by oil) shone out far more brightly than we had expected. We hoped, in our enthusiasm, to keep it permanently alight.

That looked like the end of the story, but it was not. For five days we enjoyed our new acquisition and thought all was well. Then trouble came. Miss Mercy Ward, who lived a few doors away, could see the signal from her garden. She said it spoilt her view and stirred up the Parish Council, who took the matter to the District Council.

Some Council members came out a few mornings later to discuss it. Why hadn't I applied for permission to put it up? I said that I had asked the advice of the leader of the Council before buying it and he had told me that permission was not necessary. Then they suggested that such a thing as a signal could mar the beauty of the countryside. I pointed out that it had been part of the countryside only a couple of miles away for the past 50 years and no one had objected. They agreed that this was a good point and also admitted that it could only really be seen from a few

Another view of the post as the arm was being raised into place.
ROYE ENGLAND

neighbouring gardens. Nevertheless, it would have to be discussed at a meeting of the Council the following week.

By then the fun was starting in earnest. Articles appeared in the *Oxford Mail* and the *North Berks Herald* stating that 'a strong protest' had been sent to the District Council. *The Daily Express* immediately sent a reporter from London, seconded by their photographer from Reading, to do a full write-up, and the following day the signal was featured in headlines that crossed most of a page. Not content with this, they also made it the subject of a leading article in which they came out strongly on my side. If I wanted, they argued, I could grow a hideous monkey-puzzle tree in my garden and thus, in a free country, I should also be permitted to put up a railway signal.

The same afternoon, reporters from the *News Chronicle* appeared from nowhere to take photographs and copious notes, and, before they had gone, a BBC television team and a sound reporter for radio arrived and stayed for two hours. During the late afternoon, groups of visitors began coming to gaze and comment, without exception, I found, taking my part. Even a member of the Parish Council came by to tell me that they had been far from unanimous in their protest and that he, for one, was against it from the first.

The TV report was done very well, The signal itself looked superb, with angle shots looking up and a more distant view over the treetops, with the arm suddenly bowing to the 'clear'. Later, I went across the road to thank a retired railwayman who had appeared in the report and he remarked "I don't know whether Mercy Ward has thought about it, but she has made you a present

of publicity that would have cost hundreds of pounds if you had asked for it".

By the next day, six letters and one phone call had come to side with me in the 'Battle of the Signal' — one saying rather wittily — 'Keep it up!' Another was from an old man who had lived in Long Wittenham when a boy — at a pub called 'The Three Poplars' — and he wondered if the signal was anywhere near there . . .

The Council enquired whether I would consider lessening the height of the signal to make it less conspicuous. I replied that a thing of beauty relied upon its proportions and I asked whether they would find an architect to lower the spire of Salisbury Cathedral to make it less conspicuous. Concern was then expressed that our lighting the oil lamp at night might mislead engine crews on the mainline (over a mile away!) or lead aircraft off course.

By now, the signal had featured in nine national daily papers. Finally, the BBC sound broadcast appeared on *Town and Country*. Everyone had said their piece and there was little more left to say. The advice of the Area Planning Officer was to hold on until the storm passed over, which it fairly soon did. When the Council finally considered the matter, he advised that the signal was 'incidental to the use and enjoyment of the youth hostel.' That settled it. The signal had come to stay and despite everything, Mercy Ward and I remained good friends.

The restored signal, set somewhat incongruously amidst the rough vegetation at the rear of Roye's caravan site.
PENDON MUSEUM COLLECTION

An aerial view of the Museum site taken in 1959. 'The Three Poplars' together with its outbuildings and 'Marilyn' (with a white roof) feature in the bottom right corner. The scatter of caravans indicate the extent of the land that Roye purchased in 1954. The signal post can also be seen lying on the ground at the rear of the site, its original position.   SKYVIEWS

CHAPTER NINE
1960–1961
PENDON MUSEUM TRUST

Early in 1960, a young man whom Roye refers to as 'Jake' entered the story. Jake was clearly a forceful character with plenty of ideas. Although initially a tenant in one of Roye's caravans, Jake moved into the hostel after some domestic difficulties with his young wife, and, before long, he was suggesting a host of improvements to the hostel and the site and offering to join Roye in a partnership to run the venture. As soon as Roye had been persuaded that this was the way forward, Jake — on his own initiative and to Roye's great concern — bought several new caravans on hire purchase, expanded the hostel shop so that it could also begin to start serving the village as well as hostellers, and took on several high cost summer lets of the new vans to tourists. Despite evident misgivings, Roye (typically) kept faith with Jake, and in due course, and with Roye's support, the YHA Committee was persuaded to accept Jake as Joint Warden of Long Wittenham hostel. Then, just as the point of signing the legal documents of partnership was reached, Jake decided to withdraw from the agreement.

In the meantime, other problems with the site tenants had developed, one of whom stirred up trouble by spreading rumours and lurid stories through the village, concerning a number of site residents. Although largely groundless, the rumours were reinforced when domestic difficulties between Jake and his wife flared up again. Jake decided on a swift departure from Long Wittenham, leaving Roye not only to placate his now estranged wife but, more significantly, with the worry of the new commitments that Jake had made on their collective behalf. To compound the crisis, the government soon passed a Caravans Act that set stringent new conditions on site owners and which Roye couldn't expect to meet. Roye continues the story:

I was left with a busy shop which was on top of all the demands of the hostel, site and models. I had no money to get any kind of help and no possibility of coping with even half of it alone. Beyond that, there were not only bills, instalments, and overdrafts, but now the caravan site (which seemed the sole means of paying off my debts) was as good as doomed by a combination of its new-found 'reputation' within the village and the new legislation. My predicament — and Pendon's — had become a matter of near despair. How soon would the site be closed? Then what? It was a thousand pities that the models were not already in the hands of a trust. Bankruptcy would have no compassion.

However, the London Counsel's findings were quite hopeful over the forming of a trust, but he requested a personal visit to discuss them. So one beautiful morning at the end of April, Guy and I travelled to London to meet Mr. Bryan Clauson and Mr. Challenor at Lincoln's Inn.

His opinion was that what we wanted could be done to the satisfaction of the Inland Revenue, but he strongly advised a company limited by guarantee rather than an actual trust. While a trust was dependent on the life of its trustees, a company was an entity in itself, recognised by law and dependent upon nobody for its continuity. There would be no shares and no profits and the name 'Trust' could still be used, but with the word 'Limited' to establish its actual nature. Its members could be called upon to undertake a small guarantee, but beyond this there would be no liability. Owing to unremitting pressure of work, Mr. Clauson warned us of a further long wait before he could draw up the crucial Memorandum and Articles, but we left feeling very encouraged.

Later we spent an hour or so at King's Cross, where everything we saw, diesels as well as steam, was filthy dirty — the whole prospect was very depressing. The only exception was the Deltic in cream and blue. The glory of the LNER, with its apple-green engines heading magnificent expresses of varnished teak, had gone out like a light, as did the different beauty of the LNWR some thirty-five years before. It was quite a relief to get back to Paddington and see at least some pride in the line and some semblance of former times.

Back at the hostel, the summer rush lay immediately ahead and I hardly dared think of it. Life somehow went on, though it was now a disturbed and difficult business. However, friends rallied to help and it was a huge relief when Sandy and a woman from the site took over the running of the shop and kept it going for me. But the work was unremitting, and in July, even before the August climax, the diary notes that I had just put in an 87 hour week, of which 70 hours were on the hostel and 17 hours showing Pendon. It also remarks that the chores and shortage of sleep were getting me down — always the same story, but now magnified out of proportion. People said I looked tired and worried. But Pendon was still different — a joy and an escape despite the effort it involved. Someone at a showing said it must be most captivating work because I looked so happy!

Although from mid-1960 I was on the edge of disaster — and Pendon with me — a very limited amount of progress on Pendon did continue to be made, including the arrival of the first lighted coach from Stewart. It was the one which contained, in a reserved First Class compartment, the Indian potentate in blue robes and, in the next compartment, the Special Branch man, both of whom were to become so well-known to Pendon visitors. *The Railway Modeller*, unaware of our predicament, made

A typical gathering of hostellers assembled outside Long Wittenham Youth Hostel. In a caption to this print written by Roye many years later, he incorrectly identifies the man on the left as himself, but it is most probably Roye who was the photographer.
PENDON MUSEUM
COLLECTION

the gratifying remark that Pendon was doing for the Great Western what Derby Museum had done for the Midland Railway.

One evening I was shaken to find that an intruder had been in Dartmoor. The outside lock had apparently been picked, and we concluded that money — of which there was none in the building — must have been the goal for, almost incredibly, none of the models appeared to have been touched. We dared not assess what the loss might have been.

A week after this, at 2 a.m., I was awakened by a sudden clatter in the hostel shop, followed a few moments later by the confused footsteps of what sounded like two men running away. I hurried down and, rather surprisingly, found the shop door still locked, but inside on the floor lay the metal cashbox, open and upside-down, with silver scattered in all directions. Apparently, the raiders had made straight for the box but it had a faulty fastening and when picked up by the lid, it swung open and emptied its contents with a crash onto the brick floor. The thieves grabbed £9 in notes and ran to the door. But this also had a faulty catch and they found themselves locked in. Then they panicked and bundled out of the window, leaving several pounds-worth of silver and £18 of cigarettes on the shelf.

The unlikely hitch that had sent them scampering was fortunate enough, but even more so was the fact that they had not chosen one of the hostel closing nights when I had been away measuring in Uffington, leaving the hostel empty. Apart from what there was in the shop, there was at least £50 hidden in my den, much of it belonging to Pendon. The next afternoon I opened several accounts in the Trustee Savings Bank and thankfully locked the stable door while the horse, or most of it, was still inside!

So odd excitements, unremitting toil, persistent worry, and several crises on the site made up the life of that harassed season. But despite everything, and with the invaluable assistance of Sandy and her helper, the ordeal of the summer was gradually overcome and left behind, yet not without the hostel suffering to some extent from the impossibility of my doing more than I was humanly able.

Towards the end of August, the YHA Chairman came out for a chat. There had been a couple of complaints and the Committee wondered whether certain alterations could be made. I said no-one knew the shortcomings better than I, but my tether was stretched already to breaking point and I was incapable, both for money and time, of doing more. That was why I had welcomed Jake as joint warden and why his letting me down had been almost a mortal blow.

The Committee met in September when they considered the whole difficult position. They admitted they were worried about it. It was not the odd complaint — all hostels had those — it was the general unsatisfactoriness of the situation, as much as anything else my overwhelming debts. Any improvements that they might have been able to make possible were out of the question if the very continuance of the hostel itself was as uncertain as my financial dilemma suggested.

From Pendon's point of view, I was content that the hostel had served its purpose well. It had got Pendon off the ground, helping to form a team, giving Pendon a home and a ready-made public that had taken word of it the length of the land. It had been a winner. But now it had become a drag, demanding more time than I could give it, more strength than I could go on expending, essential help for which I had no means to pay and space that Pendon increasingly needed. I realised that I should soon have to choose between the hostel or the models, but I could not continue both.

When I discussed the difficulties with Maeve Simpkins, she said that the Committee would never close a hostel — especially a popular one like Long Wittenham — if there was any way out of it at all. But even a small hostel, let alone a 40-bed one such as the Poplars, needed full-time attention and it was everyone's misfortune that I was powerless to give it all it needed.

When I saw Guy he said that though the passing of the hostel would be regretted by thousands, the alternative of letting three or four rooms in the house would be infinitely preferable to its insatiable demands and, even financially, it would probably be better. The advice of the Lomases was to close both hostel and shop — the sooner the better. All the Pendon team, with the exception of Jim Arnold, saw it the same way and Philip Rickard, who was as keen a hosteller as a Pendon supporter, summed it up by saying, "The hostel has given pleasure to a great many, but Pendon will give pleasure to far more. Pendon must come first."

Suddenly I realised that the YHA Handbook for 1961 was on the verge of going to press and if the hostel were not to continue, it must on no account be allowed to remain in the book. I rang both the Chairman and Maeve, begging them to press the Committee for a snap decision. It was a poignant thought that I had approached the Committee for the same favour six years before, when the birth of the hostel was in the balance. After some deliberation, they reluctantly agreed to let the hostel close on 1st November. They would put notices in all the neighbouring hostels and promised to mention that Pendon Models could still be seen at weekends.

So our last night was only a couple of weeks off. Before it came, however, I gave way to a special request to remain open on Bonfire Night, a Saturday, for a party of 21 who could not get in elsewhere. In its few remaining days, the hostel acted right up to form as regards difficulties — blocked toilets, gas run out just before supper when both spanners for changing the cylinders had been borrowed and not returned, the last normal Saturday — a pouring day when everyone arrived soaked (though cheerful) and the men's wash in the cellar was nine inches under water. In the hostel's first few days of life, the men had had to wash in the kitchen, and now, in its last, the circle was made complete. After this weekend, although two large parties were now booked for Guy Fawkes night, the hostel was officially closed and the YHA green triangle was removed from the hostel wall.

Then came the 5th of November and our last night went off with a bang in the truest sense. Roy and daughters contributed a large bonfire and a very fine guy, and when the flashes and crashes died down, Wynne produced quantities of hot soup and home-made sausage rolls in the dining room. Many then went to The Plough and, by the time they were coming back, some of the others had acquired an appetite for cocoa. It being the end, I made no attempt to hurry them and it was nearly midnight before the last turned in and the hostel fell quiet. I could hardly believe that none of this would happen again.

The next morning it was breakfast for 25, jobs done uproariously, a stamping of cards for the last time, followed by a showing of Pendon to the Swindon Wheelers Cycle Club. Then, the final departure, which I photographed, back view, as they went . . .

Nostalgia — yet unspeakable relief. But if it had worn me to a frazzle, it had also given shelter and comradeship to people from all over the country and all over the world. They had booked-in to make nearly 17,000 bednights and there was no doubt, however adverse the wind might now have become, that the hostel had given Pendon a flying start. On the wall of the house, near where the green triangle had been, there remained the Pendon sign, printed, for no discoverable reason, in maroon and cream, which said simply:

> PENDON MODELS
>
> SATS.
> OPEN   3PM
> SUNS.

In its isolation up there, it brought home how completely, for the first time, Pendon was on its own. The aim of the Three Poplars was now solely Pendon. The sign on the wall looked both lonely and challenging.

Meanwhile, after waiting nearly four months with no word from Mr. Clauson, the London counsel, we prodded him and it came to light that he had mislaid the papers and overlooked the case as a result. He then, however, got down to it and a fortnight later, at the end of August 1960, we received the draft of our Memorandum and Articles of Association. They made a formidable document in which lay all our hopes of recognition as a charity.

Mr. Clauson had arranged that an alterable maximum of 25 people might become Members of the Trust, with a required minimum of seven foundation members to sign the Memorandum and Articles. The Pendon team at that time consisted of six modellers — Guy Williams, Ken Budd, Paul King, Jim Arnold, Stewart Hine and myself — who would make up all but one of the necessary seven and by his creating for these (at our own request) the status of Permanent Council Members, our continuing control of the undertaking could be assured. We were the ones who had moulded Pendon into what it already was, who had set its standards of modelling and who knew what we wanted to make of it in the future. Other members could be appointed to Council as needed.

A 'Mogul' 2—6—0, No. 7329, passing the extensive sidings at Moreton with a down fast freight whilst in the distance 'Castle' class 4—6—0 No. 5037 Monmouth Castle *can be seen approaching with an express.*

For some time a big, quiet-mannered young fellow from Aylesbury, John Edmunds, a keen hosteller and a cyclist, had been helping Pendon in railway research and other ways. I decided to ask him if he would care to be counted as one of the regular team and become the seventh Member of the Trust and its Council, when it was formed. He cycled over from Aylesbury specially to accept and put his readiness to help into immediate effect by taking home my layout plan of the Vale scene to trace and have copies made.

The time had now come to decide the name by which the new Trust was to be known. 'Pendon Models' had served its purpose well enough at the start, but something better was now called for and I suggested to Guy that we name it simply 'The Pendon Trust'. He was in full agreement.

By coincidence, we received its draft basis and discussed the name on 31st August, St. Aidan's Day once more, and, this time, the coming-of-age anniversary of the founding of the Guild of St. Aidan. To think that the high ideals of the Guild had been born 21 years before came as something of a shock, yet since then a great deal had been done and whatever the present doubts about my financial state, there was no question that Pendon itself was a far more realistic affair than ever the Guild had been. But to make it legally secure was urgent and imperative.

However, the Registrar of Companies rejected the title 'The Pendon Trust Ltd' on the grounds that it was not explicit. He required a qualifying word to be added. There were trusts of a totally different nature — invest-

ment trusts, for instance — with which it could be confused, but the addition of the word 'Museum' would make its object perfectly clear. We therefore agreed to its becoming officially 'The Pendon Museum Trust Ltd'. For popular use, however, Guy and I arrived at a descriptive name that made a useful, and eventually a well-known, alternative — 'The Pendon Museum of Miniature Landscape and Transport'. Towards the end of the year a copy of the Memorandum and Articles arrived for signature by the seven subscribers, a work which appeared to say exactly what we needed. On 3rd February 1961, The Pendon Museum Trust Ltd, with its Registered Office at the Three Poplars, received its incorporation. Pendon, at last, was a body recognized by law, an entity in its own right.

Legal work, though, almost always proves to be more expensive than one has hoped and the forming of a trust had cost a hundred guineas and had taken a year and a quarter to bring to fruition. But, seen in a different way, from the far-off days of the Australian Central Railway, nearly forty years of striving had been needed to conceive it and achieve it in its final form.

Had it not been for my debts and the provisions of the Caravans Act, everything would now have been before us. As it was, the future was a very large question mark with a blank page beyond it. Anything could happen. A grant could conceivably save us or I could be bankrupted and everything could yet be lost, for though a Trust now owned the models, I found they could still for a period be confiscated and sold. Furthermore, the ground beneath them and the building in which they were housed, were still mine and had to remain so until the mortgage had been paid off.

On the brighter side, there came a very pleasant surprise. Without even a covering letter, the post brought me from the Rural District Council, subject to meeting their requirements, their Planning Permission and a permanent Site Licence for twenty caravans. I had won the first round and my spirits temporarily soared. Twelve months were allowed to bring the site up to standard but my hopes sank again when I was given a horrifying list of improvements that must be done. The Council said that they were not the least likely to lend any money towards the work. The choice therefore lay between building societies (which didn't usually finance caravans) and the bank, which was in the throes of a credit squeeze. Both, in turn, regretted they could give no help. So despite the cheering gift of the licence, the outlook appeared as bleak as before.

In 1961, steam on the railways was of course already on its way out, though it lingered for a few years more. Its shapeliness, its impatient strength, its liveness compared with the imperturbable diesels, were things that most people valued to a greater or lesser degree. Often at that time, I went to the mainline near Didcot, for no other reason

than the lure of steam. While it was there to be seen I must see it. A future without it seemed unreal and unthinkable.

A good vantage point was an overline bridge between the Moretons [2½ miles east of Didcot Station]. At that time of year — mid February — each evening in late twilight, seven passenger trains used to pass in quick succession behind Great Western steam. Looking down into the quadruple-track cutting from the high bridge, their thundering passing gave a terrific impression of power and purpose, with sparks rocketing and their lighted coaches half lost in swirling steam as they swept beneath — all the majesty, the beauty and the wonder of the railway that this generation was finding it necessary to destroy.

Side by side with the reconstituting of the railways, the ravaging of the countryside was gaining its appalling momentum. All Uffington's lanes had just been denuded of their towering elms, with nothing, of course, replanted to take their place. At Garford, Lyford, West Hanney, and Goosey, the dereliction amounted to literally thousands of elms swept away. The Vale, which had been a paradise of rich meadows clustered with soaring elms and nestled by old thatched villages and sleeping farms, was being changed into an uninspiring plain, mostly bereft of big

'Castle' class 4—6—0 No. 7013 Bristol Castle *passing the overline bridge near the Moretons with a down express.*   R. H. G. SIMPSON

Elms shading Northfield Lane near Long Wittenham in 1976. The loss of so many of these trees to Dutch elm disease and agricultural 'improvement' inflicted, in Roye's view, perhaps the greatest damage to his beloved Vale.

ROYE ENGLAND

Roye's own caption for this photograph is a simple one — 'elms on the north side of the Vale'. At one time the simple appeal of the scene was commonplace but today such incidental beauty has all but vanished from the Vale of White Horse. ROYE ENGLAND

trees but scarred by the deformed and mutilated survivors of once-shapely groups. Villages were under attack from a cancerous suburbia that was destroying their hearts and beginning to invade their surrounding fields, whilst the farms, now neither beautiful nor peaceful, were commonly sheeted in asbestos, paved in concrete, strung with wires and deafened by the relentless tractors. No doubt most of these things had to come, and, despite them, the Vale still had much that was peaceful and pleasant — occasional oases that had been missed. But with a little care, even the worst intrusions could have been less noxious than they were, and there was no case whatsoever for the wholesale slaughter of trees. No one, of course, could then guess that in time, the elm would be almost totally wiped out by Nature herself.

On 9th April 1961, Pendon held its first Council meeting, consisting of the seven foundation members. Guy was confirmed as Secretary and I was elected as Chairman and Treasurer. I should gladly have escaped the treasurership,

for I couldn't imagine anyone less likely to make an efficient job of it than I, but no one else lived on the spot or was really in touch with the ins and outs of what was being done each day, so I agreed to take it on.

It was at this meeting that we started the Friends of Pendon — a body of supporters who could join us (without voting rights) for a minimum subscription of £1 per year. Less than a week later our first Friend was enrolled — Flight Lieut. B.C. Chesher, a Pendon devotee of long standing. So started a source of support and income which, as it gradually built up, was to save the day. Without the Friends, when crisis came — as it surely did — Pendon would almost certainly have foundered.

It was June when we heard that both the Inland Revenue and the Ministry of Education had recognised the Pendon Museum Trust as a charity. That, at any rate, was a major success — no income tax to pay! The door was also open to apply for a grant from the Pilgrim Trust, although when we did so, we found there was a further

A quiet lane at Sevenhampton (near Shrivenham) in 1959.

ROYE ENGLAND

delay as their Secretary, Lord Kilmaine, had just returned from Africa and would not be free to visit us for a while. He would get in touch as soon as he could fit it in.

A much longer wait occurred for an estimate of the cost of improvements to the caravan site. The District Council had originally given us some idea of likely costs with an estimate of £1500, but, when the builder's quotation came through, the cost had swelled to the huge sum of £4,538. There could be no question of our raising the money, so Challenor advised trying to find someone who might possibly take over the site and its reconditioning on a long-term lease. At such a cost, this was a slender straw indeed, but if it failed, he said there would be nothing for it but to sell the site and its licence. When I objected that the field would one day be needed for a Pendon car park, he pointed out that unless I could keep afloat, there would probably be no Pendon to need one. Survival was what mattered and a licence for 20 vans was such a priceless possession that I must move heaven and earth to benefit from it — even if it meant transporting Pendon somewhere else in the future.

Time proved that our doubts over letting the site were well founded. When Challenor wrote offering a lease to four addresses provided by the Council, none replied. He sent to two more, one of whom ignored it, whilst the other was concerned only with buying, not renting. Challenor agreed that it would be folly to part with the site if there was any alternative at all. It would be a crippling way out, to be taken only at the last ditch. For Pendon, I believed it could even prove to be the end. So the dilemma continued. I dare not sell, yet had no way of raising the money needed to survive.

A majestic elm standing over an empty lane at the height of summer. The location is not recorded — a forgotten scene from a vanished land?
ROYE ENGLAND

CHAPTER TEN
1961–1963
LIGHT IN THE DARKNESS?

THE end of August came. Then, on its last day — St. Aidan's Day yet again — and quite unexpectedly, an enquirer who was interested in leasing the site drove up. His name was Kenneth Cope★ and he lived in Oxford. [★*This is not the gentleman's real name, for reasons that will become apparent.*] For an hour he looked round and discussed things and my first impression was that he was a reasonable man with whom to deal. In appearance, he had a mouth which I thought was inclined to be tight, but he had most genial and kind eyes that seemed to contradict this impression, and his manner was charming, with a good deal of humour thrown into his conversation.

We worked out a basis of an agreement by which he would do up the site to the required standard, leasing it for twelve years, paying £4 a week for the first four years and £5 a week for the remainder. This low rent would balance the high cost of the improvements. On expiry of the lease, he would have an option to renew, except on any part of the site which might be needed by Pendon for its car park. He was ready to close then and there, but I said I wanted to consult my solicitor first, so he agreed to wait.

When I rang Challenor he proved as enthusiastic as I was, and as surprised that the unlikely had happened. He drafted a copy of the proposed terms of the lease, which Cope confirmed. I was in Abingdon when Cope came with his wife to look around the site, but he told people he was taking over from 16th September. He obviously didn't intend to let the grass grow under his feet.

After ten-weeks' delay, Lord Kilmaine wrote saying he would like to come and see our work for himself, though unfortunately he could not spend more than an hour with us. He was elderly, courteous and kindly, and was appreciative of everything. There was only time to run three trains, but I showed him the Chapel group in detail. He said he had never seen flowers modelled so realistically. We discussed plans and needs and how we should apportion any aid we might receive. We suggested a total of £5,000 and he did not cavil at this, but he stressed that the decision lay not with him but with the Trustees as a whole, and Pendon would be difficult to describe to them. For himself, he said that though he went to many interesting places, his hour with us had added richly to his experience.

We were left with mixed feelings and complete uncertainty. Everything appeared to have gone off as well as it could have done while he was with us, but his reiteration that the decision rested with those who had not seen our work, and that their view was unpredictable, struck an ominous note that persisted in my mind.

It was November when the dream was shattered. Our application for a grant had been turned down, the reason given that our work was 'too different from other museum projects'. Presumably, had we been doing the same stereotyped work as so many other museums, we should have been helped, but having hit on something original, unique and of the utmost urgency, we must struggle on unaided. It was a bitter disappointment. It could have meant almost everything to us and, with help from the Pilgrim Trust, the threatening trough need never have engulfed us.

That summer, amid so much uncertainty, Pendon's own affairs had gone ahead slowly. With no weekday showings to hostellers, the number of visitors was cut down to less than half its former figure, but attendances by the public on weekends were very heartening. At busy times I was sometimes showing for as much as seven hours on end. With the extra mid-week freedom, I was able to do a good deal of vital fieldwork in the Vale, but modelling suffered, as usual, from too many interruptions.

Cope decided that before starting work on the site, he wanted it cleared of all its vans. He would not be interested in it unless he had a free hand while doing the improvements, and, as the site was not yet his in name, he asked me to give everyone a week's notice. They could come back when the site was in order. As I had virtually no option, I did as he demanded, to a panic reaction, for endless difficulties would arise in forcing so many families at once to find alternative sites. But he remained adamant, and, as my position was too precarious to cross him, the exodus duly followed about ten days, later. As it proved quite impossible to place my four vans elsewhere, he agreed to allow these to remain, but, even so, I was worried about them. With site rent inevitably rising after the improvements, they might well be running at a loss and I still owed (jointly with an elusive Jake) nearly £1,000 on them.

In the early part of the year, a new face drifted into Pendon's world. The first time I remember him was when a not-very-large schoolboy, somewhere in his teens, said at a showing that he would like to help in any way he could. At the time there was nothing on hand that I felt he could manage, but I said I should be glad of his help when something turned up. His name was Paddy Burridge and he lived in Sutton Courtney, only a few miles away.

He matured fast and, at the beginning of the autumn, he said he would like to have a shot at village modelling. Whether he could reach the artistic standard we were setting seemed very doubtful, but he was keen to try and we badly needed another village modeller. He took home all our photographs of the Berrycroft group from Ashbury. This was a row of cottages set near the Manor on the wooded brow of the slope into the Vale, and the model could be placed as close to (or removed from) the public as its workmanship allowed. Paddy proposed leaving the thatching to me and also suggested my putting on the finishing touches of colouring to integrate it with what had already been done. In this way, the door was opened to the team work that was to become such a happy feature of Pendon's modelling.

I still needed some details of Berrycroft, so I revisited the site. It was heartbreaking how that row of cottages had been ruined — by building dreadful extensions front and back, by television masts with wires and guylines in every garden, by the massacre of a most beautiful group of trees shading one end and by filling in a gem of a dingle that had run between the cottages and the grounds of Ashbury Manor. Originally said to have formed part of a surrounding moat, it had become a rugged little ravine, luxuriantly treed. But thousands of tons of soil from the site of the new Pressed Steel factory at Swindon had recently been dumped on farms all over the Vale and whatever the justification may have been elsewhere, here there was absolutely none. All that was left was a dead-level stretch of grass from cottages to manor house, serving no purpose and taking every scrap of inspiration out of one of the loveliest spots beside the Vale. But when I said to an inmate of the cottages what vandalism it was, she replied, "It's better like this. The dingle was no use, except as a rubbish tip." That seemed to me to typify the apathy which had descended like a blight on the villages of modern times.

Paddy's arrival had a number of benefits, but one of the most important of his initial contributions was to prompt me into producing a definitive design for Pendon Parva village. I knew fairly well what I wanted to include and had often thought about it, but a clear picture as to how they should fit in had remained elusive. It would be far from easy to arrange buildings of all types from a score of villages to make a completely natural composite one, placing each building or group in a suitable setting, necessarily using its actual slopes and at the same time arranging each so it could be seen to advantage by the public. But as I discussed my ideas with Paddy one morning, the picture began suddenly to take shape. I spent nine hours on it that day and a good deal more than that during the week, and everything fell into place as though pre-cut, like a jig-saw. What had persistently eluded me for years was suddenly arranging itself, almost involuntarily. It made what I thought to be a most convincing whole, thoroughly typical of the hill villages beside the Vale.

The only trouble was that so many buildings clamoured to be included, and were necessary to make a balanced village, that it was unlikely, at the rate things were going, that some of them — perhaps many — would ever get modelled. However, we could only design the village as it needed to be and trust that somehow, some day, it might be completed. The whole of Pendon had been built on that premise. [Although subsequently subjected to innumerable detailed revisions, the basic plan which Roye and Paddy sketched out in 1961, has remained within the final version of Pendon Parva village, as it nears completion nearly forty years later.]

For a few months now I had been gaining the impression that Cope was not going to be very co-operative. Winter had clamped down just before Christmas, turning the site into an icefield, which threw out his programme and made things difficult. By the time the early spring of 1962 had arrived, he had still, for one reason and another, not signed the lease. This, of course, was to his advantage for it meant that despite the loss of my £8 a week site rent when the site was cleared, he had not yet had to pay anything in its place. He did promise the arrears in due course but meanwhile, it was putting me in a serious jam. This, I felt, was not worrying him unduly.

At the tail end of March, however, he handed over the signed lease, though it was still not stamped and therefore not binding. But to my relief, very soon after this he began to be unexpectedly helpful.

It started with a suggestion that I should allow him to make a shared car park at the end of my land, where we hoped the building for the Vale scene would eventually stand. Though it would be for the use of Pendon's visitors equally with the caravan people, there would be no cost either to Pendon or myself, and when the land was needed for building, we should take it. He wanted this as a gentleman's agreement — he said he was averse to paying legal fees if they could be avoided. Challenor consented as he said it would imply no claim whatsoever on my land.

Cope later enlarged upon his preference for doing things in an informal, friendly way. If everything were kept strictly legal, he would give me only what was due, but if we built our co-operation on a broader basis, he would often give more. He illustrated his point by saying that although he didn't want them, he would consider taking over my four headache vans. He would presumably keep them on the site, and I estimated that when refurbished, their rent should give him a satisfactory margin of profit over their instalments. He was in a position to cope with repairs and letting — I was not — so good luck to him!

Although life was still full of worries, Cope's increasing helpfulness began to give me hope. As I came to know him better I thought I sensed a human side beneath the business exterior and a lot of small things seemed to point

An intimate corner on John Ahern's legendary Madder Valley layout. A small Manning Wardle locomotive is seen shunting an open wagon into the premises of the Lower Gammon Sawmill and Timber Company.
CTY. DAVID KITCHINER

to his being what he claimed — a good friend to those who merited his friendship. I was especially reassured when he accepted my invitation to become a Member of Pendon.

I was reassured too, by his insistence that in anything he did for me, there would be no strings attached. Then he surprised me by asking how far I would be willing to accept help in ways quite apart from the site — in my own affairs, or in the development of the Museum? I replied that any help which brought the completion of Pendon nearer would be more than welcome, always providing I lost no sovereignty in being able to give the land and the house to the Trust when the time came. That, he assured me, was the last thing he would try to prevent, but what I needed, he said, was unbroken time for modelling, enough money to live on without worrying, and somewhere to work without interruption. I said that I couldn't agree more but it was an impossible ideal. "If you will let me", he replied, "I can give it to you. I will renovate the house and put in a warden to run it and the site. You will lease it to me, and the rent, together with the site rent, will give you enough to live on with no ties at all. I'll build a workroom for you in the garden, where you can work in peace all day. Go and think it over, the decision rests with you."

In that time of debt, doubt and frustration, with the foundering of Pendon a distinct possibility, it looked like salvation. But having trusted Jake and been let down, I was more wary now and I wanted time to see how things were going to shape when the first flourish of trumpets died down. I spoke one lurking thought — however far-fetched it might be — that if I accepted help at the rate at which he was offering it, I could conceivably end up entirely dependent upon him. With my debts such as they

were, if he wanted he could lead me on, then drop me and take over the whole place when I failed. He replied that our relationship had to be based upon mutual trust and as an indication of his good intentions towards Pendon, he made a further offer to pay off the building society at a later date, which would then leave me free to transfer the whole of the land under the present and future Pendon to the ownership of the Trust, together with right of access. We shook hands on that and he said, "Do you still want proof that my desire to help is genuine?"

On a hectic Easter Monday, with two parties arriving for a special morning showing, a modeller from Harwell asked to see me — Malcolm Deere, whom I already knew from a visit to Pendon some time before. He came, he said, on a very special mission concerning his great friend John Ahern, who had died comparatively suddenly a short while before. This was the modeller who, even in his lifetime, had become almost legendary through creating the Madder Valley layout, doing so at a time when no one, except perhaps myself in the then-unknown beginnings of Pendon, had attempted anything approaching such ambitious scenic modelling. Malcolm had come at the request of Mrs. Ahern to ask whether Pendon would be interested in the permanent loan of the Madder Valley.

There was no time for discussion then, but here was an outstanding opportunity, and I said we would definitely be interested, provided we could cope financially. Its advent was bound to create expense, but, apart from that, it would fit perfectly into our scheme of things, for its scale and period were the same as Pendon's and when the Relic Room was finished, there would be ample space to show it.

At the Model Railway Club Exhibition in London a few days later, Guy mentioned to Cyril Freezer *[Editor of*

Jessamine Cottage, Badbury.

ROYE ENGLAND

the 'Railway Modeller'] that we might be offered the loan of the Madder Valley. "If you get it", exclaimed Cyril, "they'll have to build a trunk road to Long Wittenham! It may not be up to Pendon's standard of accuracy or finish, but it's full of atmosphere — a beautiful thing and one of the most famous layouts in the world. With that as well as Pendon, you'll become a place of pilgrimage."

Meanwhile, Paddy had been continuing his experimental work on the Berrycroft row, but the model had some deficiencies and, rather than start again, we set it aside and began work instead on Jessamine Cottage from Badbury, a small one which would be seen quite closely, set just below the Chapel group. When we went to measure it, we found it empty and about to be pulled down. Then, little by little, it dawned on us that there had been more than one lone cottage. A patched wall at one end of it, a distorted plum tree behind it, and traces of foundations. With a small iron shovel that we picked up in the garden, we dug and revealed steps, then more foundations. In the next village we found Miss Gullis, the old lady who had lived in Jessamine all her life, who not only told us a lot about the cottages but also looked out three old photographs showing it in its original state. There had, in fact, been three cottages and a vertical-planked shed, and, by putting all our gleanings together, we were able to evolve quite a reasonable reconstruction. So at Paddy's hands, the Jessamine group began to grow again out of the past.

In Chiseldon, on the hills at the further end of the Vale, was a delightful little community which went under the name of Canney — three rows of old thatched cottages set in an isolated spot dominated by big trees. One of the rows was threatened with demolition and all attempts to save it had failed. A builder had bought the site with permission to erect several bungalows. June had come when I was told by a signalman from Chiseldon, who was giving me cups of tea in Marston East signal box, that zero hour for the doomed row was almost upon it.

A day or so later, in steeping sunshine, I measured part of the front. It was still such a peaceful spot, a tiny corner of an Old England that lingered almost untouched in its seclusion, away from all roads, approached only by a narrow footpath under mighty trees. Tennyson could have been describing it, its little gardens and its stillness as I found it that drowsy morning, when he wrote 'the moans of doves in immemorial elms, and the murmuring of innumerable bees.' I went to see the builder who was preparing to destroy this paradise and asked how much time I had left to measure it. He assured me that nothing would be done just yet. I found him unexpectedly ready to be helpful and he promised he would let me know before a start was made.

His telephone call came very soon at 7.15pm the following Friday. Plans had changed and demolition would start tomorrow. It caused me something of a panic for, as yet, only about an eighth of the row had been measured.

I packed the rucksack to sling on my bike, caught the 8.47 from Didcot (which came in twenty minutes late owing to trouble with its diesel) and eventually, cycling from Swindon, arrived at Canney at a quarter to eleven. The work of destruction had already begun and all the various lean-tos at the back were removed and reduced to piles of debris. But these were recent additions and only at the east end had the original cottages been invaded by the removal of some thatch. I spent the night in the upstairs room of the cottage at the west end of the row. It was perfectly sound and, of course, empty. The night was moonlit and deadly quiet.

In the morning, a day of sun and cloud, I took further photographs and had begun measuring when two men brought a lorry through a field to attack the thatch from the rear, there being no access at all from the front. They showed quite an interest in what I was doing, and when on the roof preparing to start, they most obligingly measured chimneys and height of thatch for me. Then they began their mission of destruction, looping a steel cable around roof beams, windows, or anything above the walls and hauling with the lorry to drag great masses of thatch and old wood into the garden below. A horrible but morbidly fascinating sight.

For several hours I measured while this was going on, then cycled to Swindon to catch the train home for the Saturday afternoon showing of Pendon. When the showing was over, I again caught the 8.47 back to Swindon, arriving at Canney with enough light left to do a further half-hour of measuring. The east cottage was now largely roofless, but, to my relief, the rest of the row was still intact and I spent another (and last) night in the cottage at the west end. Tomorrow six men would be working on the demolition and it was an eerie thought that after giving solid shelter to forgotten generations for hundreds of years, this cosy little upper room would tomorrow be no more than a heap of rubble.

'The moans of doves in immemorial elms, and the murmuring of innumerable bees'. Canney Row awaits destruction.   ROYE ENGLAND

THE DESTRUCTION OF CANNEY ROW, 1962.

The western end of Canney Row. To speed the task of recording the buildings, Roye camped out in the upper room of this cottage on the night before it was demolished.

ROYE ENGLAND

After giving solid shelter to untold generations, Canney Row meets its end.
ROYE ENGLAND

Next morning was a race against time. Destruction started apace and my survey went on, often with no more than minutes to spare before the spoilers caught up with what I was measuring. For three and a half hours I kept just ahead of them and completed my work as the west cottage began to fall. Then I went into Swindon to buy a replacement film, entirely forgetting, with so many men at work at Canney, that it was a Sunday.

There was still time to cycle home to three showings and I did so with the satisfaction of having saved Canney Row from oblivion — whether on paper, as at the moment, or as I pictured it, one day set again under its great elms in Pendon Parva village.

On 2nd August 1962, Pendon held its first AGM, followed by a Council meeting. We discussed at length all of Cope's offers, and while acknowledging the need for caution and with one or two tentative reservations, we unanimously agreed to accept Cope's help.

Optimism was the keynote of mid-1962. Thanks to an article in the *Railway Modeller*, we had never had such attendances. The Madder Valley had been accepted, the Relic Room in what had been the dormitory end of Marilyn was under way and track and scenery for the extension to Dartmoor was to come next. The repayment of the mortgage by Cope was imminent and then Pendon would be given its own land under its buildings, with a car park to follow. The growth in visitors and Friends of Pendon, in helpers and potential helpers, all told of advance.

Bearing out this impression of well-being, Cope now proposed trying to take out a further and much bigger

mortgage on the property, the value of which had, of course, increased out of recognition since the start of the first one. After reimbursing himself for the cost of clearing the first mortgage, Cope proposed to use the money to improve the house and to hasten Pendon's programme of building and re-building. Almost every time I discussed things with Cope at this stage, my hopes rose. "I have no longer any qualms", records 'Outline', "that Mr. Cope is putting Pendon first in everything and there is no knowing how far this help may lead us. It could even prove, in the end, as potent as the Pilgrim thousands could have been."

There is a saying that the darkest hour is just before the dawn, but Pendon was to find that it could be brightest before the dusk . . .

Cope now made a new proposal. To do everything that he had offered would take a great deal of capital — all that he could put into the place and as much as he could borrow on it. But he also pointed out that no one was going to lend him money to improve a property that was not even his own. So he suggested — and shook me in doing so — that as soon as he had freed me of the mortgage and the first piece of land (under the Museum building) had been transfered to the Trust, I should make over completely, though with safeguards, the remainder of the property into his name. He would then take out whatever mortgage was possible and effect all the improvements. The safeguards would include an agreement providing for the whole to be taken back fully by Pendon, as soon as the money could be raised to repay him its value. This would be based upon an independent valuation. Until then he would provide me with enough income to live simply and to give Pendon the whole of my time.

Yes, I saw the dangers. The money to reclaim might not be available when needed and the value of the property could soar permanently beyond Pendon's reach. On the other hand, if Pendon and myself were put on our feet in the present, there might be no financial problems to consider in the future. It meant placing myself in his power, but, since the lease was still not stamped, he was already leaving himself equally in mine, spending thousands on land which I could take back, together with everything he had done on it, any day I chose. I reflected on Cope's suggestion for a period of days before I said that I was willing to go ahead, provided no unforeseen snags cropped up. Cope then announced that he would order the concrete blocks for the new workroom that morning.

Meanwhile, Mrs. Ahern had asked me to go to London and discuss arrangements for the Madder Valley. She lived

Guy (left) with two helpers, working on the new extension to the Dartmoor layout. The block walls mark the point at which 'Marilyn' had recently been extended.   ROYE ENGLAND

A second view of the extended layout. The nameplate leaning somewhat casually against the control panel is from 'Saint' class engine No. 2935 Caynham Court.
ROYE ENGLAND

in a quiet, old-world house, lying behind a creeper-grown garden wall — an oasis of country peace in the midst of busy St. John's Wood, and she could not have made me more welcome or have been more charming.

The Madder Valley was stored in the attic, its baseboards stacked on edge with only their undersides visible, and its buildings, vehicles and accessories tied in haphazard bundles in boxes and a cupboard. It looked, in that state, like so much junk and it was fortunate indeed that Mrs. Ahern realised what could be made of it. She was ready for it to go to Pendon on permanent loan at any time and made the very helpful offer to pay for glass to enclose it. In addition to the Madder Valley itself, Mrs. Ahern also loaned us several treasures for the Relic Room and she rounded off a delightful visit, just as I was leaving, by becoming a Friend.

Back at Pendon, we were also making progress with the Dartmoor layout. Through no little effort, Paul, Guy and some helpers had extended Dartmoor so that it now consisted of an oblong of about 100 feet of single-line track in place of the previous 60 feet, giving a great sense of space. But, best of all, it made room for so many more people, all of whom could see the trains at close quarters. We optimistically looked on this as the first step towards the taking of motor coaches and, through them, to paying our way.

There was still no-one but myself who could give Pendon's showings, which I now sometimes had to do for as much as eight hours on end without food or any break. I tried to prepare, as reliefs, two or three of our helpers, but whilst they ran the trains happily enough, none of them rose to the commentary. Paddy, on the other hand,

Looking in the opposite direction, the control panel largely obscures the model of Walkham Viaduct. The bare baseboards in the foreground would eventually become the site of the model of a typical junction station, for which Roye had chosen the name 'Pen Tor Road'. ROYE ENGLAND

Several of Pendon's earliest supporters, photographed alongside Dartmoor in about 1963 — Paul Counsell (left), Guy, Paul King (seated) and at the rear, Jim Arnold. ROYE ENGLAND

often working in the hut, drifted as a matter of course into both train operation and my much-repeated spiel. One day, several long-distance visitors begged for a showing just as I was going out, and Paddy, for the first time, took over. Since the initial showing of Pendon on a table in the former bar of the Three Poplars, eight years before, in which time 16,500 people had seen the models, this was the first showing that I had not taken myself. It was a strange feeling to be cycling away to Abingdon while the trains ran for visitors at home.

Less positively, things with Cope were not shaping as well as I had hoped, The promised workroom was to have been completed during the summer, yet by early October, only the footings were started, mostly with our own labour. There were other delays, too, which were more worrying. In July, Cope had asked me to get a settlement figure for the mortgage. By August he had not paid it off, so he asked me to get it again. When, in September, I had to apply for it a third time, it came with his undertaking that he would see to it that month. But October came, then November, and in each of them, with no move made, a revised figure was needed. It made me appear to be playing a game with the building society. Cope put it down to his being too busy to deal with everything on time, but he also admitted that sometimes shortage of ready cash caused him to put things off.

I was becoming increasingly worried. For one thing, Cope favoured having no legal agreement between us because it would be so complicated and cost the earth. But purely verbal promises could obviously fade and intentions change. The more I thought about signing the property over to Cope, the more afraid I felt of it. So I went to Bristol to talk it out more thoroughly with Guy and Ken. Unfortunately, Ken was away, but Guy and I had a four-hour discussion, then I telephoned Paul and gave him the main facts as we saw them. We came to two unanimous conclusions — we must not part with the freehold without a legal document to protect its return and in any case, it would be better to struggle on and hope to keep the property than to get help now and then find it so overburdened with loans, or with appreciation in value, that we might not be able to redeem it.

When I arrived home after dark, Cope was still there, so I took him up to my den and broke the news. He was visibly taken aback, but showed no irritation. He said that it had put him in a difficult position as he had now ordered the timber, as well as the blocks, for the workroom. When I pointed out that we dared not have any improvements done, however desirable, if they might endanger the redemption of the freehold, he insisted there was no question of a such a thing. If that was all that was disturbing us, he would meet us by asking no more than the present amount of the mortgage by way of eventual settlement. That was quite a different matter from the

'independent valuation' that till now had been his condition of redemption. I then said we felt unable to do anything that was not legally provided for and he replied that he was perfectly willing for this if we wanted it. I rang Guy and he agreed these changes threw a very different light on it and thought we ought to reconsider it accordingly.

Next day Cope and I worked out a basis of the agreement, making it as simple as possible but covering all the major points, especially with regard to the return of the property. But when I took the proposal to Challenor, he said it was completely unpractical, and that no solicitor would ever draw up such a document, for it would not be capable of safeguarding the property as we intended it to do. He said an option for us to repurchase could be placed on the property for a nominal sum at a given date and this would be inviolable, but, before anything could be done, Cope must be represented by a solicitor, who would make a concrete proposal. When I told Cope this, he said it would double the expense and he was not doing it. Challenor insisted, saying his job was to protect Pendon's interests and mine and nothing would change his attitude. Had I been more perceptive, I should have seen it as the very red light of danger.

Cope, still refusing to budge, said this had dragged on for so many months, it must be settled simply and quickly or else dropped altogether. Either we circumnavigate Challenor or this was the end of his help.

We all get blind spots at times, but this was a most unfortunate moment for me to have done so. As I saw it, just then there was little material inducement to Cope to continue. He could still have the lease for the caravan site on the same terms as originally agreed, without any of the trouble or expense of the massive additional assistance that he was now offering. The only real compensation for it all appeared to be the satisfaction of furthering a cause. Since I had given so much for Pendon, it seemed natural to me that another of its Members, with the power to aid it, should be willing to do the same, especially as Cope had said how proud he would be when Pendon was a flourishing concern.

I discussed it all again with Guy. We compared the hope of prosperity and advance (albeit coupled with the conceivable loss of the land should things go wrong), with the unending state of financial frustration and my own equally conceivable failure, together with Pendon's, if we turned the offer down. There could be risks either way, but the greater one might well be my own instability. Cope might get slack in his help as time went on, but even if he produced only half of what he promised, it would be a godsend. Nothing ventured, nothing gained . . .

It was the first week of December when I told Cope we had come to a decision. Since a legal agreement, through no-one's fault, had become impossible, if he were willing to keep to his agreement to return the land to Pendon and trust us, we were ready to go ahead and trust him to do all he promised, which we accepted with gratitude. He grasped my hand and pressed it most warmly.

I rang Challenor to tell him, but he was out, so I left a message. As a binding agreement was unattainable, and as he was unwilling to act for us without one, we were most reluctantly turning elsewhere. I then went to Geoffrey Craik, another solicitor in Abingdon, who had been very helpful when Jake and I were trying to arrange our ill-starred partnership. As I expected, he said he hesitated to undertake any conveyance which left Pendon and myself so completely unprotected. He would have to think it over before acting. But I told him it was the only way of getting Cope's backing, the alternative seemed a greater danger, and we had decided to take the risk. I asked Craik, despite his doubts, to put it through.

The new year of 1963 came and in due course he told me the conveyance would be ready for signing in a couple of days. However, as I was asking him to do this against his own advice and it could conceivably go wrong, it was only fair to him that I should sign a statement for his files absolving him of any responsibility. It was a chilling document, making it perfectly clear that once the conveyance was completed I should have no further legal interest in the property and that if Cope so wished, he could turn me off as a trespasser. In spite of an indefinable qualm lurking inside me, I put my name to it.

But the signing that was to follow was the one that mattered, and by now, whether I rejoiced in it or dreaded it, I felt myself forced to admit there was very little option. There was no prospect of paying off the old debts (whose accumulated hundreds must be a long-continuing peril) and, beyond all this, there was a new threat hanging over me. When Cope first asked for a settlement figure for the

mortgage, he said there was no point in my paying the current monthly instalments. But the same happened month after month, from midsummer into the snows of winter and the arrears had now escalated to such a figure that there was no longer any hope of my catching up on them. That alone, as I saw it, left me powerless to turn back.

Like it or not, here was a parting of the ways. I told myself I could delay until the property was taken out of my hands by force, leaving Pendon with virtually nothing, or I could give it now to Cope, a Member of Pendon, with the prospect of major help if he kept his word. Then Craik 'phoned — the conveyance was ready to sign the next day.

"So it looks", soliloquised 'Outline', "as though this will be the last night I shall ever spend in my own house. It is a rather momentous feeling. But as long as Pendon goes ahead and can own it in the end, I shall be more than content.

"I went out last thing — after 1a.m. — as I have often done before, to look at my little bit of England. Tonight it is sublimely peaceful — a brilliant moon in a clear cold sky lighting, almost as day, the fields of snow that cover everything. I thought back to the first nights I had stood there, where apple trees grew where Pendon now stands; to the heyday of the hostel, when I had stood looking across moonlit summer grasses to the hut where thirty boys and men were sleeping; of all the hopes and struggles of the last eight years that made the hostel what it was and Pendon what it is; and to the new regime, so nearly on me, with all its uncertainties which could spell ruin, yet with such possibilities as may prove the turning point of all my aims, the starting point of Pendon's firm advance."

For better or worse, I signed the conveyance documents the following afternoon.

'Barnum' class 2–4–0 No. 3222 — the prototype for Pendon's model. The date and location are not recorded but the destination board on the LNER coach in the background indicates a service on the Banbury, Oxford, Swindon route.
ROYE ENGLAND

ROYE ENGLAND

Winter at 'The Three Poplars'.

CHAPTER ELEVEN

1963
THE DEPTH OF THE TROUGH

FREEZING weather before Christmas 1962 had turned to snow falling continuously for two days after it — the precursor of the stiffest winter of the century. Plans for the Relic Room had been shaping well and they had a boost when Tony Chapman *[a lodger in one of Roye's rooms in the Poplars]* offered to take charge of the relics as his special province. When the snow came, neither he nor his brother Alan, who also had a room in the house, could go to their outdoor jobs, and with unlimited time on their hands, construction in the Relic Room went ahead beyond all expectations. In two loads I ordered 2,000 feet of timber and 31 sheets of hardboard for relic display and we kept our fingers crossed that they would arrive, despite the several inches of lying snow. Most fortunately, both loads did.

Before long there were drifts that made the yard impassable and we cut deep paths through them, with another long channel to the far end of the models. The cats were thrilled with it, tearing along great white cuttings and bouncing out at each other round the corners. Tony then ushered in the new year by working on the timbers of the

first display recess from midnight until quarter to three. He could get on best when the mood took him, and it came at strange times.

Just before Christmas I had gone for a couple of days to Manchester, bound for the model railway exhibition there and staying with Jim Whittaker *[an outstanding modeller of Great Western rolling stock in 4mm, and later 7mm scale]*. As far as Wolverhampton, the 13 coaches of 'The Pines Express' were hauled by No.7030 *Cranbrook Castle* and the rapid withdrawal of steam made me realise that this might well prove — as in fact it did — to be my last time ever behind a steam locomotive in a regular express. Masses of lingering steam mingled with the misty air and often blended into snowstorms as well, to make a softly beautiful countryside seen in comfort through windows which, unusually, made no attempt to mist over.

In Birmingham it was very appropriately snowing lustily while we waited at Snow Hill station. A little woman who sat in my compartment for a short time gave a sigh and remarked wearily "Isn't railway travel boring!" She had said it to quite the wrong person and I replied that "I

A wintry scene at Banbury in January 1962. 'Modified Hall' class No. 7902 Eaton Mascot Hall *is seen waiting with a northbound train to Leamington and Birmingham Snow Hill.*
R. K. BLENCOWE

love every minute of it". She looked so surprised that I added, "There's so much to see". "I suppose there is", she replied weakly, without any conviction and without the least attempt to glance at the scenes outside. I felt sorry for her.

During January it was announced that every main road in Oxfordshire was blocked by snow. At Clifton Lock the Thames had frozen over, though water still rushed over the weir beneath the ice. Yet whatever the trials of the freeze, all was progress in the Relic Room. Both Tony and Alan still chose to work through each bitter night, doing spells of carpentry, then huddling to thaw out over a calor-gas fire behind a blanket hung across one of the recesses. They seldom finished before three in the morning, but, despite this unlikely choice, work went ahead so well that by mid-January, all three recesses were built, in position and lighted.

The next item was staging to support the Madder Valley — and the problem of its cost. On 23rd January, through a fantastic and slippery morning of ice, rime and fog on snow, I cycled at snail's pace to Didcot, bound for London to see Mrs. Ahern again. Only one of the four morning trains was running, but I was lucky, for it came behind two diesels after I had waited only half an hour — the 7.12am from Bristol which eventually drew into Paddington at 12 noon!

I reached Mrs. Ahern's house an hour and a half late, but she was as charming as ever. After explaining the difficulties, I asked would she be willing to lend us £25 for staging, which we would repay out of our earnings in the

The hard-packed snow and enormous icicles suspended from the roof of 'Marilyn' bear witness to the hardest winter of the 20th century — 1963. Across the field beyond the washing lines, even the River Thames had frozen over.   ROYE ENGLAND

Reassembling the Madderport section of John Ahern's 'Madder Valley' layout in the new Relics Room at Pendon.   ROYE ENGLAND

summer. To my surprise and joy, she said that £25 might not be sufficient. We must not be crippled for lack of cash and before I left she gave me a cheque for £50, which she did not want repaid!

Through February and into March, the work on the Relic Room went on and, little by little, we started to get the relics into their cases and recesses. Then Malcolm Deere brought the Madder Valley buildings, and the bases with their scenery arrived in a removal van a couple of days later. Everything was dull with dust but I cleaned the majority of the buildings by rubbing them over with breadcrumbs, which brought them up wonderfully. The diversity of their character and their individual charm amazed me when I came to them like this, inch by inch, at close quarters, and I was especially struck by the naturalness of effect that John Ahern had gained in them with the minimum of trouble. Judicious detail here and there, touches of paint exactly where needed, and the buildings lived. It was not the meticulous type of modelling that we were doing at Pendon Parva, but the impression they gave was convincing and delightful.

A lot of work remained to be done on the scenery. Apart from damage in one or two places, the landscape was at present in very obviously divided sections and one long stretch had literally been sawn in half near the tunnel. Worse than this, at the further corner near Much

Madder, there was a large gap where John Ahern had started alterations but left them so unfinished at his death, as to make his intentions indecipherable. All we could do was to restore the corner as nearly as possible to the original plan — a difficult job demanding both character and colouring to blend imperceptibly with the adjoining scenery.

Alan so far had done carpentry and general painting for us, but he now said that although he had never tried any modelling, he wanted me to entrust him with the restoration of the Madder Valley. I hesitated. It was not mine with which to take liberties. But Alan had an artistic bent and, in any case, if he failed to make the grade in filling the gap in the layout, it could be taken out again and no harm done. Almost all that day he worked at it and he astonished me by what he achieved, blending everything in with the greatest success. He certainly had the gift. From this he later went on to the fusing of section joins, then the fitting of backs to certain buildings which now, for the first time, would be seen from the rear.

It was with some difficulty that Malcolm and Alan placed all the buildings in their settings. John Ahern's photos often showed the same structure in two or three different positions — even in different parts of the layout. But in the end it all worked out. So, apart from operation, which we had not yet attempted, the only lack now was a

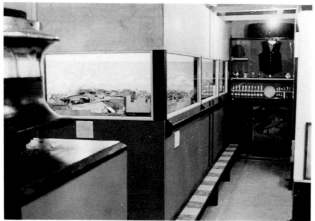

Pendon Museum's first Relic Room. The view shows the 'King' chimney (left) with the 'Madder Valley' layout within its show-case beyond. At the end of the aisle the showcase contains a display of GWR cutlery and several items of uniform.
ROYE ENGLAND

sky. The model's original pale blue background had disappeared, and, to replace it, I discovered at Kettle's in London, a most natural 'sky' paper. It brought to the Madder Valley soft clouds and sunny skies that proved its ideal completion,

Easter was now perilously close and with a lot still to be done, as we had promised the opening of the Relic Room and the Madder Valley for Good Friday. Three hectic days (and nights) of effort brought us within sight of the goal, but in the final rush we finished literally minutes before the 3 o'clock influx. It all looked very attractive and it gave Pendon, for the first time, the appearance of a museum. One recess displayed a variety of paper relics, the second contained pictures and photographs, the third signalling equipment, and at the foot of each stood a polished brass engine nameplate. Opposite these stretched the Madder Valley, seen through glass on two sides of its 'U' formation. There were four locomotive chimneys on

The Gammon Magna end of the 'Madder Valley' layout. These views illustrate the considerable problems of piecing together the layout.
ROYE ENGLAND

A later view of the area seen opposite shows additional displays of engine nameplates and small cast-iron notices and wagon plates.

ROYE ENGLAND

In another alcove, paper relics including timetables, luggage labels and tickets were displayed, whilst in the next area . . .

. . . illustrations of early railways, crests and the nameplate from former 'Star' class engine Westminster Abbey *(the first engine Roye saw on his arrival in England) were set out.*

ROYE ENGLAND

individual stands, a case of railway lamps, another case adjoining it with more signalling instruments and yet another containing one or two items of railway uniform and some small relics. Even though it was not complete, there was no doubt that the visitors liked it.

That weekend we had a record Easter attendance of 129 people and the total of our takings to date crossed the £1,000 line. Were these advances, in amenity and in the public response, going to be the start of a new era?

Unfortunately, my own finances were getting ever more precarious for, although I had signed the conveyance, Cope had still not completed the transaction by settling the mortgage. The longer Cope put off the settlement (and the other help he had promised) the deeper I became submerged in debt and, of course, more dependent upon him to pull me out. My total owings had now reached £600 — no small amount in those days. *[Much to Roye's concern, Cope prevaricated over a range of details and did not sign the conveyance until 16th May. Thereafter, Pendon was in Cope's hands.]*

It was now early June and the first disappointment came. Cope looked in, hurriedly as so often, but I persuaded him to spare half an hour. I told him that the crisis which had been building up for months had now reached desperate proportions. How soon could the loan be obtained to meet my accumulated debts? I also asked to have the £10 a week he had undertaken to give me. To my dismay, he said quite bluntly that he could do nothing at all at present. A number of factors had made ready money very short and the bank had declined to lend more than a couple of hundred pounds above what he had just paid out on the mortgage. What, I asked, about the transfer of the land under the Museum into the Trust's possession, which was to be done immediately he took over? He assured me that it was quite safe, but he now claimed that it could not officially be made over until its boundary was fenced off, and he couldn't divide it yet as there was no money to buy the fence. He left me in a maze of dread and uncertainty.

With progress which was anything but smooth or inspiring, the workroom had for some time been creeping ahead, but before long Cope was letting it be known that he was far from pleased with the way that it was hanging fire. I pointed out that his offer had been to build a workroom, not to expect us to build it, but he brushed this aside. Surely, we were willing to help ourselves when he was going to do so much? Its completion was now urgent since before he could give me the help he had promised, the house must be let to bring in the money for it. Before it could be let, it must be renovated, but that couldn't be done until I moved out. This depended upon there being a workroom into which to move. It was up to me to get it built!

In the final part of the Relic Room, the displays featured signalling equipment and a large map of England and Wales on which were arranged a collection of railway buttons from uniforms of many of the pre-1923 railway companies.   ROYE ENGLAND

By mid-July our relations were worsening. When I tackled Cope about lack of progress, he submerged me in a tirade of disapproval in all directions. He was fed up with everything and everyone, on the site and off it. He was getting co-operation, he declared, from no-one. Look at the workroom — not another stroke done! Look at the wilderness surrounding it (which I thought was indescribably beautiful) which he had asked us to cut down! While that 'mess' remained he was doing no more. In fact he had done all he was going to do and now it was up to me.

If this were all he was going to do, I asked myself, what had he done — apart from acquiring a valuable property for a song. The promised workroom had so far been worked on and financed — to the extent of £60 — entirely by Pendon. The transfer of Pendon's part of the land to Trust ownership was now, as Cope put it, "a thing we must do when we can". There was no longer any mention of help with my debts, and though for the time being I was allowed to collect the fluctuating rent from the rooms in the house, its average was so much below the £10 a week I had been promised, that it left me deeper in debt with every week that passed.

Despite the anxieties, we were still making progress on the Museum. A comparatively new recruit — Ed Wheal — not quite out of his teens, but six foot five tall, undertook the engineering side of the Madder Valley, while Alan continued at intervals to work on the scenery. Before long, Ed had the first train running from Gammon End to Much Madder. After the passing of years, life came back to a layout which had become a legend but which might never have run again. The *Railway Modeller*, in its August issue, gave Pendon a centre-page spread featuring the Madder Valley, where they claimed 'Pendon is today the greatest single source of inspiration for the serious modeller.' We might be on the rocks, but we were also getting a name.

Towards the end of August, Cope said he wanted to take the house in hand for renovation in the coming winter, so would I please ask my lodgers to begin looking for somewhere else. I reminded him that he had promised to give me enough to live on from the time he took over and asked what he proposed to do for me when the house was emptied and no rent was coming in? After initially disclosing that he hadn't really thought about that, he promised me a caravan to live in for the time being. What, I asked, would I do with all my things, pointing out that the workroom had been promised for their temporary storage? His reply was simply to ask what I was doing about getting it built. For his part, he said he would do nothing more about the workroom, so that looked like the end of it unless we did it ourselves.

The next day Cope told me openly that he had completely changed his mind since taking over. He was no longer helping Pendon — he was going his own way and we must manage as best we could. To excuse this flagrant about-face, he merely dragged out the old irrelevant let-out that the site was in what he called "such a mess". Things had not worked out as he expected and he was very disappointed. I said that I was disappointed too and then asked him that, since he now said that he regretted having taken it over, how would he feel if we found a means to repay him and take it back? He said that he would be very thankful.

I rang Guy to discuss our crumbling position and we were agreed that the only hope now was to move heaven and earth to get the property back. At his suggestion I went for a chat with Mr. Sherlock at the bank. He said that there was nothing the bank could do over such a long term as we should need, but it was possible that a building society might give Pendon a mortgage. The first thing was to approach Cope and ask would he let us reclaim it for what he gave, plus his expenses — which in all fairness would be the least he could do. In trepidation I put the crucial question to Cope the next day. "Yes", he said, "that was quite fair". It was a relief to have some co-operation again, but the huge question now was could we raise the money?

Whether we reclaimed the place or not, there would, of course, remain the deadweight of debt that was ever more dangerously dragging me down. It was a threat that I had to face up to and I knew now that though I had been fighting against it, there was only one possible course left. Irrespective of what it might cost in my work for Pendon and notwithstanding my lack of formal training and my age, I must get a job.

But before I could do much about finding a job, Cope gave me the ultimatum that the house and its outbuildings must be emptied, both of tenants and contents, within a month, as he had decided to renovate the lot together. He would try to give me a caravan in which to live. In the continuing absence of the workroom, I again asked about my things. "Find someone in the village to keep them for you", came his answer. That, I knew, was impossible, so said so. But instead of softening, he stepped up the blitz. "If that is how it is", he returned, "I'll have the house emptied by Saturday!" When I looked aghast he added, "and if you can't do it, I'll do it for you."

The whip was in his hand. He could do exactly as he said. He could, if he wanted, dump all Pendon's possessions, along with all of mine, in the road and then have me moved on by the police. The law was on his side — all security had been signed away. Almost everything that had held promise had failed. All that Pendon had striven for, all that it had achieved, no longer counted. The closing of the Museum could be the next blow and its fate rested with Cope.

We had reached the depth of the trough.

CHAPTER TWELVE
1963–1967
THE STRUGGLE TO REPOSSESS

OF one thing I was determined. If Pendon had to go, we should not give up. The modelling must go on, nonetheless, and we must hope that somehow, somewhere, someday, a new start might be possible. Kipling could have been looking ahead to the troubles at Pendon when he wrote 'Or see the things you gave your life to broken, and stoop and build them up again with worn-out tools.'

But it was not only Cope's offensive that was driving me to distraction. The grocer had just sprung on me the news that the firm was liquidating at the end of the year. They were letting me know now to give me time (10 weeks) to pay off the £105 that was owing. If a job of some sort had seemed inevitable before, this new ultimatum made it doubly imperative. But could I get one? With no training and uncertain eyesight, it seemed unlikely. Yet it seemed the only chance.

Alan was also looking for work, though not of the kind that I could do, and to try to get him fixed up, I telephoned in vain to every firm we could bring to mind. The list included the MG car factory at Abingdon. "Sorry", I was told, "we have no vacancies for men in their twenties — nothing but a clerical job for a man of about fifty." I caught my breath and asked could I be considered for it? I wrote, formally, the same day, went for an interview four days later — and started in the Production Control department at MG the following Monday. It was a 5-day, 38-hour week, with a starting pay of £14 10s — good at that time — and which would be increased after three months.

The solution to the dilemma was so sudden, it seemed almost to have dropped from heaven — as I indeed believed it had. I found myself completely happy there, and however badly things might be at home, there was now the real hope of gradually clearing the debts — a first and essential step towards securing a future for Pendon.

Financially, this was the start of better days, even if, on the £11 or so that I brought home after deductions, it would take several years to get clear. But, apart from this one bright spot, there appeared to be nothing but frustration still ahead. Pendon was now badly hit by the loss of so many hours of my time each day. Weekends were almost always taken up with showing, so our essential measuring and data collecting in the Vale was out from now on, unless someone else could be found to do it. Above all, we were not to know how far Cope meant to act on the threats he made and the collapse of our independence was still having a devastating effect on the morale of our helpers. We found ourselves in a Sargasso Sea where we could hoist our sails, but there was neither breeze nor current to take us further.

If only we could reclaim the property, what a different vigour would now come into everything! Then it occurred to me that with my new found status as an employee at MG, it was just possible the bank might co-operate. Mr. Sherlock was on holiday, but his deputy listened to the whole depressing story. He said that he knew Mr. Sherlock would want to help if he could, but the security was so frail that it was very doubtful indeed whether they could take it on. However, he would get in touch with him and telephone me in the evening.

When the call came I almost dreaded taking up the phone, but when I did, he asked that if they advanced me £1,500, Could I reduce the debt to £1,000 at the end of the first year and repay completely in three? It would mean giving up the whole of my earnings from MG for that period, but there would be house and site rent that would help see me through. I gave my word and he promised that the bank was therefore prepared to make the loan. I put the phone down, jubilant yet fearful. Things could still easily go wrong. Then, with my heart in my mouth, I rang Cope.

When I explained that I had found the money to buy back the property he said, "That's a great surprise. But", he continued, "don't let us do anything in a hurry. I'll come one evening and we can discuss what to do." The conversation was quite brief, but he made no suggestion of refusing. The biggest hurdles of all appeared to have fallen in a single day and in my relief after being so overwrought for so long, I crumpled up on the bed and cried. I had never wept for joy before, but my life's work seemed suddenly to have become real again and it was like releasing the trigger on a pent-up spring.

Through eleven long days I waited impatiently for our promised talk. Then Cope came to see me — and declined to sell back the property. He had been to London and had seen his solicitor who was strongly opposed to his parting with the place. He had taken on commitments to Pendon and me and would fulfil them. He continued by saying that he would not do up the house until the new year and then, rather than turn me out, I could move from room to room as each was done. When the rent from the rooms ceased, he would try to help me with some cash in place of it. He then suggested that I should look for someone to finish the workroom and he would pay for the walls and roof if we could manage the rest. The land under the Museum was already earmarked and registered for Pendon, though he would not complete the legal

This view was taken inside Roye's room in the youth hostel in 1954 and shows the early stages in the construction of the Chapel Group.
ROYE ENGLAND

transfer until the house was renovated. But we need have no fear for our security.

In the Museum itself, things did of course appear to go on much as before, but they were forced now by a dogged determination to get through, rather than by the old, spontaneous enthusiasm. My modelling continued, though it was cut down to an hour or two in the evenings and on weekends, but Paddy was going ahead well with the Jessamine group.

Meanwhile, Alan had been chafing to start modelling for Pendon Parva village, and though a certain amount still needed doing to the Madder Valley and in the Relic Room, I agreed to his taking the Gosditch group from Uffington. He chose Upper Cottage for his first attempt — the smallest and one of the prettiest of the cottages, though not the easiest. For about a month he stuck at it and everything went well. Then, as expected, distractions came, together with uncertainties and, to my disappointment, no more looked like being done.

Christmas came with five clear days at home — and I never felt less elated at the prospect, or less in the mood for modelling. I did feel intensely relieved to be spared for a short time the nightmare journey to work in Abingdon, over frosty roads seething with traffic, but once I arrived I was as happy there as at home, and often happier. "There", records 'Outline', "it is warm, friendly and peaceful; here it is cold, lonely, and one long succession of strivings, anxieties, frustrations and disappointments. I think the shattered hopes of this year have worn me down more than I realised." I did, however, get back to modelling that holiday, even if it was with an effort and anything but a light heart. A few days later the diary notes "The last day of 1963 — and Alan has suddenly started modelling Upper Cottage again; a ray of sunshine in the evening of Pendon's darkest year."

Early in 1964, the workroom was stirring again. Cope had recently commissioned two brothers named Phillips to put up concrete walls, but by the end of January they had made no start and he asked me to get an estimate for the whole job from a regular builder. When it came, it amounted to £550. Cope said that was impossible and he wondered whether Mrs. Ahern would think of financing it? She had tentatively offered us help in a building extension of one kind or another, as a memorial to her husband.

I had, of course, already told Mrs. Ahern of the turn things had taken and she had been aghast at our predicament. When I now saw her again, she was even more pessimistic, but she maintained that we must not give up until all was finally lost. The immediate need was for a finished workroom, which would at least help to lessen our troubles. But it must be on land owned by Pendon. So her offer was that as soon as the ground under Pendon was made over to the Trust, she would contribute £500 towards the cost of the workroom, but until that condition was met she would do nothing.

When I rang Cope he said he was not going to be told what to do. We wanted the workroom done as soon as possible and to wait while land was legally transferred would be bound to make for a long delay. He was a man of his word — the land would be ours when the workroom was built. So he would pay for the building work for the time being and go ahead without letting Mrs. Ahern hold us up.

It was another month, however — the beginning of April — before anything practical happened. Then the Phillips brothers turned up to make a start, and within a

A closer view of part of the Chapel Group under construction. Roye took very few photographs of work in progress and this is, therefore, a comparatively rare opportunity to look within one of his models.
PENDON MUSEUM COLLECTION

Part of the finished Chapel Group, including the truly remarkable miniature garden in front of 'Middlecot'. The cat asleep on the wall by the open gate was modelled to dimensions that Roye took from one of his own pets.
PENDON MUSEUM COLLECTION

couple of hours, the walls were standing to window level. I rang Mrs. Ahern to tell her the good news and that Cope had agreed to pay for the work until the land was made over to the Trust. But she shattered me by replying that she was paying for no work retrospectively. Whatever was built before the transfer of land was of no interest to her and would be paid for by Cope alone. I was flabbergasted. What we both aimed for was a workroom on Trust property and I thought that when we could produce that,

it would fulfil her requirements. She said certainly not. We had better stop the work at once. She was very angry at the way we had misrepresented her offer, at which point she hung up.

That was the death blow to the workroom. Building work stopped and it remained half-finished — a lost cause. After a time, moss and weeds began to grow on its concrete floor. It looked more like a ruin than anything else and we christened it 'Pompeii'.

By the end of the 1950s, the Chapel Group was substantially finished but final detailing and installation in the landscape took another five years.
PENDON MUSEUM COLLECTION

The finished Chapel Group set within Pendon Parva village.   A. E. SMITH

Things hastened slowly that year, the only encouragement being that attendances, unaffected by the prevailing uncertainty, continued to be good. But the urge to model had by now completely left me — perhaps after twelve constantly interrupted years on the Chapel group it was not surprising — and while I felt as stale as this, it was pointless to force it. So I gave way to, of all things, a lifelong craving to write music. The evolving of a piano sonata offered a blissful relief from the miseries that were Pendon. *[The views of a professional musician to whom the work was sent, were less than favourable. Although the critic was able to commend Roye's 'fertile mind and musical ear' and felt the melodies justified his developing the art of composition, most of the remaining comments were distinctly discouraging. 'Cold, bleak and apparently purposeless . . . non-existent counterpoint . . . phrasing, harmonies and development of themes are all very bad' were some of the comments. Given the circumstances under which the work was composed, the bleakness is perhaps not surprising and despite the weight of criticism, Roye kept both the work and the letter until his death.]*

Towards the end of September, Cope let the house, outbuildings and grounds — everything except my one small room and the land actually under the Museum — to a family named Hall. This meant that the renovation of the house and its buildings had been tacitly dropped.

Jim Hall had been a farmer and he brought with him ponies, calves, dogs, cats and rabbits. So the old stable reverted as a matter of course to its original use. The dogs mixed unexpectedly well with my cats, and the cats among themselves decided, after a rather chilly start, that they could get on with each other. I also found that I could get on with the Halls, the only difference being over the land for the proposed car park. I said this was under promise to Pendon, and Cope, by our agreement, was not free to let it. Jim could be peppery and he answered hotly that he knew or cared nothing about that. He was renting the lot. When I tackled Cope he replied, in a slightly off-hand way, "Oh, I didn't think of the car park. I've let Jim have the whole place. We must try to get it straightened out." But he never did.

On the other hand, to our relief, Cope now began talking again of transferring the land under the Museum. At Pendon's expense, the concrete posts of the required dividing fence had been erected, but now Cope's solicitors took exception to a reference to the proposed adjoining car park. Cope then came into the open by stating that though he was making us what he called a 'gift' of the land under Pendon, he was not extending it to include any access, except by foot. Entry for vehicles he would not sanction. Later on, if the Halls left, cars would probably be able to use it, but he was not making a legal issue of it.

After a lull, the document came through for signature and the seal of the Trust. But it was nearly six weeks later, at the end of January 1965, before it was finally put through. Then, at last, Pendon possessed a small foothold

The Chapel Group is arguably Roye's greatest individual achievement as a modeller. The complex shapes, the differing textures and colours, and the subtle effects of weathering are all beautifully captured in what are virtually perfect miniatures.

A. E. SMITH

of its own from which it could not be ejected — a major gain. Yet our holding was painfully small by comparison with all that we needed, and it was enclosed within a few feet on every side by land that belonged to other people — an unhappy and crippling fact to temper our pleasure.

Home from work one evening, I found a GWR crescent nameplate awaiting me — *Westminster Abbey*. I had put my name down for it a dozen years before and it was all of forty years since the 'Star' class engine bearing that plate had taken me from Plymouth to Paddington on my first, never-to-be-forgotten day in England. Since then the engine had been rebuilt and the words 'Castle Class' added to the plate, but careful enquiry established that the plate was the original one. Pendon paid what we thought then as the high price of £15, little realising that before long, its value would have soared by over 500%!

Unexpectedly, Mrs. Ahern wrote saying that now the land was ours she would like to make us the gift of a workroom, hoping that I would get back to modelling when I had the additional space. A fortnight later, Malcolm Deere came on her behalf, saying that she pro-posed giving us a pre-fabricated cedarwood shed instead of the workroom that lay half finished. When I raised the question of finishing Pompeii, Malcolm said that it was the shed or nothing, so we gratefully accepted what she was prepared to give us. Years later, when Marilyn was being replaced, we realised that the decision had been fortuitous as a completed Pompeii would have been a hindrance.

We chose a building measuring 24ft by 9ft — the largest which would fit into the only land we had available for it behind the Dartmoor extension. Though the cost was all but £300, Mrs. Ahern confirmed her willingness to give it to us in memory of her husband. We proposed calling it 'The John Ahern Memorial Workshop', but amongst ourselves it became simply 'The J.H.A.' Our spirits were further raised by the efforts of Paul, Guy and Dave Badminton to bring the newly extended Dartmoor layout into operation and by the arrival from Guy, quite unan-nounced, of a little Southern Railway 0-4-4 tank — an M7 class engine — our first non-GWR locomotive which provided a lovely contrast to the rest of our stock.

Little Chapel Cottage. Comparison with the photograph of the original cottage on page 85 shows just how well Roye's model preserves a record of another lost corner of rural England.
                                                                                        A. E. SMITH

The Museum site with the 'John Ahern Memorial Workshop' squeezed into the area between the Dartmoor extension and the boundary fence that divided the Museum's land from the rest of the caravan site.

A. E. SMITH

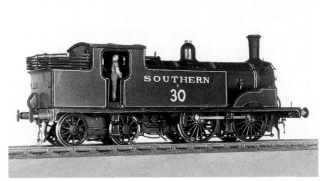

Guy's model of the Southern Railway 'M7' class 0—4—4T, the first non-GWR engine that Pendon received. A. E. SMITH

Only a week or so later we received another boost. At the end of a showing, one of our Friends — Howard Fuller and his teenage son Peter, offered to come on Friday evenings to do whatever needed doing. Howard was of stocky build, with a broad smile and eyes that lighted at times to a delicious sense of humour. Like Paddy, he could be somewhat peremptory in manner, but in both cases we realised that it was the result of a forceful and go-ahead personality. Howard was to become one of the most practical, energetic and resourceful of all our helpers.

The Fullers lived in Steventon, on what had been the GWR mainline through the Vale. We had just obtained official permission to remove any relics we could find at the recently-closed stations at Steventon and nearby Wantage Road. A word about it to Howard was all it required, and next evening, he and Peter arrived with a Dormobile and trailer crammed with loot. It ranged in size from a tiny glass phial from Wantage Road, marked 'GWR Sal Volataire — One Teaspoonful' (for fainting ladies in the Victorian era?) to two platform nameboards from Steventon, each 14 ft long. But the most useful relic was a stool from Wantage Road which proved an ideal seat for the operator of the Dartmoor control panel. *[This stool remains in service to this day.]*

By now I was modelling again, making good progress on Badbury Farm. In all ways Pendon was looking up. Before the end of the year, Ken Budd brought a friend named Ruth Bwye to a showing. She had offered to take over the correspondence to the Friends of Pendon, a nightmare task which had so far defeated six people in turn. We had already lost many Friends through our failure to keep them in touch, but Ruth was bright, efficient and soon had things going as never before. When the pinch came later on, Pendon would not have survived without the regular income from the Friends that Ruth's work made possible.

The new year of 1966 opened with tragedy when John Edmunds, only 23 years old, was killed in an unexplained road accident near his home. He was a Founder-member of Pendon and our youngest Council member, an excep-

tionally nice fellow. His people took the loss of their only son with the greatest fortitude and later gave Pendon all his railway books as well as a collection of Great Central Railway engine works plates.

At one of the showings soon after, I found myself chatting to a visitor who had been a number of times previously and had become a Friend. He had a soft voice and a quiet, rather self-effacing manner. He casually remarked that he did woodwork and if there was anything we wanted in that line, he could help. So Tony Smith from Henley slipped into the fold. Even when we realised what a skilled worker he was, we little foresaw the amount and quality of the help he would give us — in modelling and so much more besides.

Meanwhile, Marilyn's chronically leaking roof was giving us ever more anxiety. It was no use having magnificent models if the building was going to crumble around them or allow them to be ruined by damp. So we decided to make an immediate fund-raising effort towards rebuilding. Guy wrote to Paul Counsell (whom I had met in Bristol in 1951) and with whom Guy was still in touch, asking if he could suggest anywhere that we might apply for help. He answered by tentatively offering us a personal loan of £500 at building society rates, without a fixed date for repayment. It was a wonderful offer and it gave our plans a big boost.

Then, before we could go into it any further, came a thunderbolt. I returned from work on 2nd May to find a message awaiting me — would I please ring Mr. Cope? When I did so, he made my head spin. He had decided to sell the property. Would we be interested in buying it back?

Hopes and fears chased each other madly. Heaven and earth must be moved to meet this challenge. Cope pressed me to give a rough idea of what we might be able to offer and after a long phone call to Guy, I suggested £3,000, which we felt probably covered what he had paid out on the mortgage and on site improvements. This he said he could not possibly accept. His accountant had recommended £7,500, but he thought £6,500 might be right. I said that we should never be able to raise such a sum but he replied, "Well, see what you can do." He was not in a hurry and he assured me that he would like us to have it if we could. It seemed quite to have slipped his mind that he promised it to us in any case, free of expense at the end of a number of years. But recrimination would only have wrecked our chances and at least it was a help that he was not going to press us for time.

We soon realised that it was out of the question to think of buying back the caravan site. Cope fortunately agreed, however, to sell the house and some of the surrounding land, including the site drying ground and the playground separately. For these alone he asked £4,000, or perhaps

The model of Badbury Farmhouse, largely complete except for a small area of thatch on one of the outbuildings. Rather unusually, the other slope of the roof on this shed was tiled!
PENDON MUSEUM COLLECTION

A comparative view of the real Badbury Farmhouse reveals, once again, the skill and the sensitivity with which Roye modelled his subjects.
ROYE ENGLAND

The front of Badbury Farmhouse is not seen by the public at Pendon, but it is modelled with exactly the same care and attention to detail as the visible parts, to act as an historic record of another lost building.   PENDON MUSEUM COLLECTION

£3,500. We had let him have the whole property, valuable caravan site included, for less than a third of this sum, but he refused to come down.

It was fortunate that that year, when we needed every penny we could raise towards a deposit, attendances were unexpectedly high. Yet despite this encouragement, we were no nearer finding the money to repossess and without the land back, there would be no solution to the parking problem and nowhere to erect a building to house the planned Vale scene. To meet this latter contingency, Paddy began working on a design for an Upper Hall above Dartmoor and the Relic Room. He thought that this might be preferable from the point of view of both space and cost and his arguments I found convincing. *[As many readers will know, this in fact became the final arrangement of the exhibits at Pendon.]*

Amidst all the anxiety, modelling of the village continued to move forward. Perhaps the most surprising recruit at this time was Peter Buddle, a boy of under 12 years from Oxford, who had been brought to Pendon by a school friend and said he wanted to model for us. He served an apprenticeship with some small building intended for Dartmoor station surroundings, after which he started on the less-than-easy Shotover Cottage from Uffington. Working at home and without any help, he brought it to Pendon, finished, on his thirteenth birthday. He had made an excellent job both of the cottage and its garden. He

then went on to other cottages and was to become one of our most regular modellers over the next ten years or so.

Christmas that year (1966) brought me ten days' holiday in which I reached my target of completing the main roof of Badbury Farm house, with its 4,375 tiles. The opening of the new year brought a bitter-sweet gift of £50 from Mr. and Mrs. Edmunds in John's memory, on the first anniversary of his death. It could not have come at a more opportune time and it was good to know that although John was no longer with us, his help to Pendon, even if indirectly, was still going on.

As a break from all the worries over the site, I went one morning to Didcot to see *Pendennis Castle* on an enthusiasts' special to Birkenhead, which we were told might be the last public run of steam on the Western Region. When I came in sight of her, she was backing onto the 11-coach train in the station — the platform a solid mass of humanity, overflowing in a big way onto the track to take photos, under the watchful eye of the police. Everyone seemed to be carrying either a camera or a tape recorder and the atmosphere was tense with excitement and emotion. Only an occasion such as this could express the extraordinary depth of affection in which the steam locomotive was held.

Pendennis Castle looked magnificent — a gleaming titan of polished green and brass and copper and steel — bursting with life and power. I pushed my way to a platform

One of Pendon's earliest engines at work on the Dartmoor layout. The pannier tank emerging from the tunnel, with a short train comprised mainly of loco coal wagons.
PENDON MUSEUM COLLECTION

The Collett 48XX class 0—4—2T, sandwiched between two superb scratchbuilt models by Ken Budd of GWR autotrailers, crossing the Walkham Viaduct.   **PENDON MUSEUM COLLECTION**

edge well ahead of the train as loudspeakers invited passengers to take their seats. The engine gave a long, triumphant whistle, a diesel somewhere out of sight bellowed a salute, *Pendennis* replied, and then, amid a cloud of steam, she moved slowly forward with an echoing blast. As the line diverged from the platform, she gathered speed and passed at a little distance, looking absolutely superb, wreathed and crowned in steam, seemingly as young and as vital as when she left the shops at Swindon more than forty years before. She bore away, curving her train towards Oxford, her flickering plume at its head growing smaller and its rhythm faster until it was lost to sight, perhaps, as we then believed, for the last time ever in these parts where once she had been so much at home.

On the platform, as the throng began slowly to disperse, four men greeted me and drew me aside, all smiles. "Do you remember us, in the Transfer at Swindon? You used to take photos there, and you brought a couple of your engines down to show us." That was fourteen years before, yet they had picked me out in that crowd! I brought them home and showed them the same engines running now through our Dartmoor scenery. They were

delighted with everything and some of the information they volunteered proved most valuable and interesting.

It was now more than nine months since Cope had first offered the property and he was now pushing us to find the money. Pendon's life was again at stake. Any port in a storm and, on the spur of the moment, I made for a very unlikely one. A local doctor had once casually mentioned an interest in railways and, though he was no more than an acquaintance, I called on him to ask whether he could help us in our predicament. He said had I come six weeks earlier he would have given us a loan, but he had unexpectedly bought a house for a large sum and was powerless to do more. All he could advise was to try the bank again. If my own bank would do nothing, I should try another. He thought his own, the National Provincial, might be more helpful than some.

Paul Counsell, however, was proving a great champion of our cause and he now suggested, as a last resort, providing us with a guarantee if it would bring a loan within reach. When I rang Guy to tell him, he capped this news by telling me that Donald Mackay, an insurance director and a friend to both Guy and Paul Counsell, had just pro-

Pendon's first engine, Collett 56XX class 0–6–2T No. 5624, working an impressive milk and parcels train across the viaduct.

posed helping us in precisely the same way. So, armed with these new offers of support, I went to the National Provincial Bank.

The manager was away but his deputy entered thoroughly into the dilemma. After weighing everything, he said it was a borderline case. When the manager, a Mr. Morris, came back he would put it to him and I could come and see him again if there was any point in doing so. An appointment was duly arranged.

Mr. Morris proved to be a most likeable man, downright but approachable and he seemed genuinely interested in helping us. On the strength of the two guarantees, if they worked out as we hoped, he would consider making us a loan. A couple of days later he offered to lend us £2,500 to be repaid at the rate of £600 a year. That would be tight, but we believed we could manage it. As soon as we had the go-ahead from Donald and Paul to cover us 'jointly and severally' for the total sum, the formalities

could be put through. With Paul's loan of £500 and £100 from Pendon funds, we had £3,100.

There remained, however, the problem of raising the £400 difference between Cope's price of £3,500 and the amount we had secured. In desperation, I approached the owner of the house next door, Mr. Heard, in the unlikely hope that he might give us a loan. This he declined to do, but instead, he offered to buy the garden between the two houses for the £400 that we needed. Though we could not really afford to do without any land that we might subsequently need, this would at least resolve the immediate crisis. So I called in a surveyor, and together with Mr. Heard we measured the plot up. Our troubles seemed to be clearing.

But the following evening Cope telephoned. We had been seen measuring the plot with a surveyor, a builder had got wind of it and had immediately made an offer of £1,200 for the piece of land and part to the rear that was to be within our car park, provided Cope honoured his promise to return this ground in the future.

Cope was obviously tempted to sell to the builder but he now said that instead of selling to the builder, he would let us have the property, plus the plot to the rear, for £4,000. We could pay in cash the £3,100 that we had raised and the remainder as and when we were able. So the intervention of the builder had meant that an extra piece of land was now to be included in the sale, and, although the cost had risen, when coupled with Cope's new terms this was quite acceptable. Guy closed with him then and there.

Again it looked like success but yet again there was disappointment. This time it came from Cope's solicitor, who turned down our draft contract and substituted one which we saw as quite impossible to fulfil — £3,500 down and £500 to be repaid in two years, the completion date being four days ahead! Guy was furious, saying that no-one could do business if deals meant nothing when they were accepted. I telephoned Cope and told him these demands were out of the question. He pointed out, however, that if we sold the garden part of the side plot to Mr. Heard for £400, we should have the required deposit. This appeared to be true and we should still have the extra piece left to form the basis for the car park. But our total repayments would soar to £80 a month over five years. Could we afford it?

Howard, who by now had become our Treasurer, was in America, so I spent an evening working out our income and expenditure, then rang Guy to discuss it. Though it would be touch and go, we believed we could just survive. Council had given Guy and myself a mandate to act as we thought best, and, with Cope now pressing insistently, there was no time to spend on deliberating. So we took the decision to accept the contract as it stood. But both our guarantors were on holiday and nothing could be done without their signatures.

A week later, Cope rang me at work, very annoyed at the delay. His solicitors were advising him not to wait for us, but to put the property on the open market. To make matters worse, even though both guarantors had returned home, nothing came through. More than three weeks later, despite urgent phone calls, we still had no definite answer and Cope was now getting dangerously restive.

We then learnt that Paul Counsell was ill, but that he hoped to sign shortly. Yet another three weeks passed, bringing us to the beginning of November and when I rang Guy in desperation, he said that as far as Donald was concerned, the reason for his delay had just come to light. His bank had objected to the lack of security, but when we offered the property itself as security (which we could have done weeks before had we know of the need), the way seemed clear.

Two days later I rang our own bank. Donald had still not signed. Cope telephoned me soon after, now in a state of exasperation. He would set a short time limit and then wash his hands of us. Six more days passed and still not a word. The suspense was unbearable. After all our battling, was this going to be the end?

On the last night of the six I came back from work frustrated and miserable. Suddenly the telephone rang. It was the National Provincial Bank. Both guarantors had signed and the document for the loan was ready for stamping! I banged the phone down and grabbed the nearest object — Black Pudding, a very surprised cat — and upped her nearly to the ceiling. She loved it. I put Schubert's 'Great C Major' symphony on the gramophone and had tea to its triumph. Then I rang Guy. "I've great news for you." "Yes", said Guy, "so have I for you. I've just signed the contract!"

So he beat me to it and, after spending an hour with our Bristol solicitor, he paid over to him the £400 deposit. Completion date would be named in due course. This time the deal was fact, not fiction.

Roye, posed with Fluff (one of his many cats) amidst part of Pendon Museum's collection of railway relics, c.1966.
PENDON MUSEUM COLLECTION

Alan Chapman's models of 'Upper Middle Cottages', after installation in Pendon Parva village.

CHAPTER THIRTEEN

1967–1971
BREAKTHROUGH: PENDON, HENDON, CRENDON

Saint Dunstan *with the Dartmoor express crossing Walkham Viaduct.*

A. E. SMITH

AT the beginning of December we held an enthusiastic gathering of 22 Members of Pendon. A two-hour Council meeting followed, with everyone present, at which we signed and sealed the documents for the Conveyance. Completion date had been fixed for 14th December. For repayment we had committed ourselves up to the absolute limit. There would be five very lean years ahead, but we now had everything to work for and we felt confident that unless anything very unforeseen happened, we should win through.

Completion day came. After so many disappointments, what had seemed something between a nightmare and a fairy-tale suddenly became a proud reality. The Poplars, including most of the land for a car park, was the legal property of Pendon, and if we paid our way, we could not be turned off. The first thing I did was to put the signal to clear, where we intended that it would remain, a witness to all the fresh hopes ahead.

Modelling, about this time, was going on in several directions. There were now three lighted coaches built by Stewart and, for some time now, these had been running in the express, giving *St. Dunstan* an impressive train of thirteen coaches. However, Guy fitted the Bulldog class engine *Sedgemoor* with lighting and, with Stewart's coaches transferred, we were able to show for the first time a complete, lighted train. It looked most convincing in

semi-darkness on the viaduct, with the moonlit sky beyond.

At the same time, Alan, temporarily out of work, suddenly began modelling again, starting the long row of Upper Middle Cottages. About nine days later they were built and being thatched. He had been working on them for something like ten hours a day. With Alan it was all or nothing. He then started on the adjoining row and had built it to roof level when the inevitable interruptions came. He completed the thatching of the second row, but the spell had been broken and he did no more to either of the pair. How much, how very much, could he have given to Pendon at that time, if only his application had matched his artistic skill?

The village models were still being shown with the Dartmoor scene, which was far from ideal. So we now decided to convert the cedarwood building which Mrs. Ahern had given us — 'The J.H.A.' — from temporary storage into a home for the growing Pendon Parva. This would also allow us to start a small shop for the sale of postcards and souvenirs. The only disadvantage was that an extra helper would always be needed. John Shingleton circularised more than twenty possibles in the hope of forming a rota and, although the response at that time was not what we had hoped, when the time came the helpers came too. [*This was the start of the rota of volunteer helpers that*

Pendon's famous model of a long coal train, quite out of place on a Dartmoor branch, but a spectacular sight nonetheless. With the exception of the guard's van and the engine, the train was entirely handbuilt and painted by Tony Smith.   A. E. SMITH

has continued to provide all the staff for public showings at the Museum.]

For several months our tenant, Mrs. Hall, had been seriously ill and in mid-August (1968), she passed away. Jim Hall gave notice to quit four days later and decided to leave at once. We found ourselves faced with the frightening prospect that with the Halls gone, we had to find the £80 a month rent that they had been paying from other sources. Moreover, costly repairs and improvements to the house would almost certainly have to be done before we could let it again. At present there was no indoor sanitation, no proper bathroom, not even a convenient kitchen, and one room, at least, was seriously damp.

In the face of threatening disaster and Pendon's complete inability to meet it, Howard and Paddy came forward with designs for a bathroom-cum-toilet, new kitchen, stairs and porch, besides damp-proofing and a lot of redecorating both outside and in, the cost to be met by themselves until Pendon could repay. The work would be done by all who were willing to help. Such was the sense of urgency that the huge work began the following day.

Floors were ripped up, electric wiring almost entirely renewed, rotting window frames replaced, damp walls lined, a concrete floor laid, a hot-water system installed, walls built in the cellar to support the bathroom which took shape above, drains dug, stairs demolished and built afresh elsewhere as a new landing appeared. Howard and Paddy worked almost every evening and every weekend whilst Tony Smith did our woodwork at home and came on weekends to fit it. Others helped but these three bore the brunt of it, often tired out, sometimes discouraged,

but always pressing on because they believed Pendon's life hung on what they were doing.

Weeks passed by, then months, but still the work went on. By now the pressure was slackening somewhat — no one could keep it up continuously for so long — but an unexpected turn came when a father and two sons who were desperate for accommodation moved into one of the completed rooms, cheerfully taking the rest as they found it. Unfortunately, they did not treat the place very kindly, but at least their rent was coming in while renovation went on.

Besides Tony's help in house renovation, he had lined the J.H.A. with softboard and made for it a large new showcase to take the village groups. We decided also to move in the existing showcase from Dartmoor to show unfinished models. To do this entailed a long detour round the garden to reach a door in the J.H.A. that was wide enough for the case. Paddy and Dave Badminton lifted the case unseen from inside it, shoulders against the underside of the floor and Chris Kirby followed, shouting directions as they went. One of the funniest sights I remember was that 7ft case trotting down the lane like a huge beetle on four human legs!

Guy had recently taken our railway modelling a step further by producing for our Southern Railway M7 0-4-4 tank, an attractive 3-coach set from the 'Atlantic Coast Express', but the greatest boost in rolling stock came from Tony, who started building private owner coal wagons to a very high standard early in 1969, averaging more than one a week for the rest of the year. Eventually his private owners formed a complete coal train which replaced the 70 mixed wagons that we had previously run behind the '28'. An entire train of colliery and coal merchants' wagons was, of course, a very usual sight in the 1930s. One day, as an experiment, we combined the coal train with other wagons, making a vast train of 105 vehicles. This was the most that the GWR allowed, but our '28' took them steadily and in fine style. We had certainly proved that when the time came, 100-wagon trains would be feasible on the Vale of White Horse layout.

The caravan site, now taken over by a Mr. Sylvester, was still sentried by our signal, once such a hot topic of controversy. But Sylvester was now on the point of bringing several new vans onto the site which would engulf the signal, so he asked would we please move it to our own land. This would be a major operation and we went into it at length without finding a clear solution. Even the Post Office engineers said they would prefer not to touch it with caravans so near, but Sylvester said these could not be moved. He then sent word that he could wait no longer if we had not removed it by the weekend, he would have to take it down for us.

This produced a panic, for his doing so would probably wreck it. In a further effort to get something done, I approached the Rover Scouts, the Army and the RAF without results, and, on the deadline weekend, the only Pendon helpers we could muster were Howard, his son Peter and David Kearsey, who gave up another engagement to help us out. Between them they stripped the post of its fittings and made a start at taking it down, leaving it standing at a slight angle with a rope retaining it. Until we could collect about a dozen helpers to lower it gently, they dared not take it further.

A few evenings later I came out of the house and glanced at the dismantled post. In that moment its lean increased and it slowly, almost gracefully, fell to the ground amid exclamations from a group gathered about it. It could easily have been snapped by the impact and I strode livid to the scene of the crime. But it had been done most skilfully, singlehanded, by a trained man who had been specially hired without my knowing — a great burly, bearded fellow, who had raised a mound of earth to cushion the fall. My wrath subsided.

The signal remained where it had fallen until the following weekend when twelve came to an emergency working party. They included John Wiltshire, a new convert, who was later to become a prominent member of the team, and a Western Region signal official, Mr. Mundy, who generously stayed the whole day to advise us. The 38 ft post was heavier and more awkward than we expected, but with crowbars, rollers and ropes, we inched it over the uneven ground towards our own land until eventually it lay beside the 6 ft hole that had been dug for it.

What happened after that I was unable to see, as I was showing all afternoon. Getting the butt into the hole and standing all thirty-odd feet of it on end must have been an arduous and nerve-racking business. During the showings, recurring shouts of "Heave!" came floating in to me. But they won, and when I came out at quarter to seven, the great post was vertical and they were fixing three guy lines. In its new position close to the Museum it looked higher and more imposing than before, even though none of the fittings had yet been put back. Mr. Mundy estimated the date of the signal to be somewhere near 1905.

By the loss of the site drying ground in the final settlement with Cope, we were forced back to Paddy's earlier proposal to build an Upper Hall for the Vale scene and, with this concept in mind, the proportions of the village and the Vale scene as a whole had to be reconsidered. I put a lot of work into a revision of the main plan. It turned out very well and I found that the tentative layout that I had designed some eight years before, fitted quite happily into this new configuration.

Several buildings for the Brook section of Pendon Parva had by now been built by Peter Buddle, and the time had come to go in full detail into their setting and contours. Howard and I worked out the most probable geology of this lower part of the village, and hence, the formation and development of the streams, pond and, to a lesser extent, the roads. With this as a basis, I designed a compatible scene to incorporate the buildings and other features in an attractive arrangement for viewing.

Howard then took over, and, by making a box-work of card, translated this plan into three dimensions, remarking that it was like exploring an unknown country — you kept coming on hills and hollows you didn't expect. The surface modelling (also done by Howard) was a long and tedious job, but as this part of the village grew, its changes in level — from Lower Mill and the pond, the veteran inn, past a disused quarry to Badbury Farm at the top of a rise — promised to make a scene that was particularly full of character.

From the planning of the Brook section we turned to the Gosditch scene, which was to join Brook in the yard of the mill. This latter building Paddy proposed making for us and in due course it was measured by Richard Roper who lived there. I myself wanted to build Packer's smithy from Childrey which I planned would stand beside the mill yard, and when Paddy and I went there we found, to our relief and surprise, that it was not only still standing but hardly altered at all from the photographs I had taken more than eleven years before.

In the middle of December, still planning Gosditch, I wanted to find a cottage to top a bank beside the smithy, and, as I had in mind a possible one from Childrey, Tony Smith offered to drive me there to assess it. But before we reached Wantage, desultory rain had turned to a continuous downpour. So we side-tracked to give it time to clear and found ourselves in Letcombe Regis. There, facing us

The primitive cottage that Roye and Tony Smith discovered at Letcombe Regis in 1969 — a remarkable survivor from a bygone age.   A. E. SMITH

across the end of the village street, stood a very primitive half-timbered cottage, dated 1698, which was exactly the sort of building I was seeking. Restoration had already started, but the frontage was as yet intact. There was no time to be lost, and Tony and I went there again soon after to measure up. The weather this time was even more unkind and we spent two hours with steel tape and sketch book in falling snow, during which time three biros froze in my hand. *[In a subsequent revision of the Vale scene plan, this cottage was relocated to the High Street section and two small thatched cottages placed in its stead alongside Packer's smithy.]*

So we came to the end of 1969 and with it, to the end of the 'sixties'. Nine years on from the hostel, six years from the crisis with Cope. But things were going well now. Village modelling was again to the fore whilst, on the railway side, Tony was still producing wagons, signals for the station had been started experimentally by John Clark in Bristol, and Paul King had prefabricated much of the new track for the station area. Our £500 loan from Cope had been cleared completely and Howard reported that in having reduced the bank loan from £2,500 to £1,000, our repayments were actually a little ahead of schedule. We still had big commitments but if the upsurge could be maintained, it offered the prospect of major advance in the coming year.

With this improved position in mind, the chief topic in the air at the start of 1970 was the prospect of rebuilding Marilyn. This, we now believed, might be nearer than we thought. We had conceived the idea of constructing a larger building around Marilyn which, once enclosed would be dismantled from within. An Upper Hall, placed above Dartmoor and the Relic Room would then provide the home for the Vale scene. After three months, however,

the steel firm that we had engaged to advise on construction gave a discouraging reply, and in May, another consultant raised unexpected difficulties, saying our proposals were not practical. The large span was one problem — not a constructional one as such, but the difficulty of erecting the building in a form that we could afford. An equally serious obstacle was the height involved in a two-storey building and its attendant cost, plus the likelihood that in a country village, such a structure would be refused planning permission.

One Saturday in June we were discussing these multiple troubles when Philip Rickard came up with a brainwave that was largely to solve the height problem besides considerably altering the character of the future building. We were already agreed that the Vale scene must be set at a level of about four feet above the viewing walkway which would surround it on three sides. Philip's argument was that if the floor of this walkway were built no higher than three or four feet above the ground floor, there would still be seven or so feet of headroom beneath the Vale scenery, in which to accommodate Dartmoor, the relics and the Madder Valley. By this arrangement two floors could be collapsed into not much more than the height of one. Philip became a hero on the spot and both Howard and I began working out detailed schemes for the 'undercroft'. There remained the question of spanning it, but we could only hope that this might somehow be resolved in due course. By early July I had evolved a two-tier ground plan which I believed gave us everything. It formed essentially the basis of the building as we know it today.

The type of construction required to surround this interior was the next subject for discussion, and we began to think of an agricultural barn-type or other prefabricated shell. A round of enquiries over a couple of months brought us to the conclusion that if we could afford it, a Crendon concrete portal-frame structure (with block walls and asbestos cladding) would be ideal for our needs. We decided that a building of 75ft by 40ft would be the most practical size, with an eaves height which we eventually fixed at 16ft. This was a compromise on Philip's original plan but it allowed us to create a decent-sized main entrance whilst still leaving the height of the building several feet lower than we had originally dared to hope.

It was now October and prices would almost certainly go up in the new year, but Crendon promised that if we could place a provisional order before then, they would hold the price for a further three months, The quotation for their part of the work was £3,000 and we estimated that not far short of a further £2,000 would have to be found to complete the main structure with walls and a ground floor. The provision of the Upper Hall might have to wait. Could we ever do it?

We had already been in touch with Mr. Morris of the National Provincial Bank, who had said that though the squeeze was still so tight that he was refusing loans every day, our repayments were well ahead of schedule and if the guarantors would extend their cover, he was willing to put back our loan to the original £2,500 over a five-year term.

Donald Mackay then told us he had persuaded the Hendon Building Society to offer us a 15-year loan for two-thirds of the value of the building and they might consider giving us more if the house were mortgaged as well. This was wonderful news and Howard judged that though repayments would put us right on the edge, it should just be possible to take it on if we were willing to make the sacrifices it would entail. So we signed the Crendon contract, subject, of course, to finance and to planning permission. It was the crystallizing of a year's thought and effort and a vital step towards fulfilment.

Although our chief energies had been centred on the building, very good progress was made in 1970 in other ways, particularly with the village. Tony Smith helped me measure Holburn Farm at Letcombe Bassett and Culham Station (which was to become the station for Pendon Parva), David Manders helped with the 15th-century Champ's Chapel and Priest's House from East Hendred, and, on my own, I completed measurement of Ivytimber at Idstone.

Peter Buddle finished modelling Corner and Fern Cottages from Fernham for the Brook group and started work on Holburn Farm. John Shingleton began the Hurdlemaker's Cottage from Fernham, though, owing to shortage of time and trouble with his sight, he asked me to take it over. My own sight was very gradually getting

Roye, photographed in about 1968, shortly before the model of 'The Waggon & Horses' was set within its surroundings in the village. PENDON MUSEUM COLLECTION

worse, but a pair of magnifying glasses which came to me by chance, did away quite unexpectedly with the double edges and proved the salvation of my modelling, for the time being, at least.

A second salvation followed at the beginning of October when I accepted voluntary redundancy at MG. It came at a providential time for Pendon and included a small pension which, together with the state one that was due in another year, made it possible for me now to give Pendon the whole of my time. Its first result was the completion of the immediate surroundings of the 'Waggon and Horses' inn — the veteran model begun at Wanborough in 1931, assembled in Western Australia in 1936, rethatched by Paddy in the early 1960s and now, 37 years after the start, in its setting which included a thriving vegetable garden modelled by Howard. It looked none the worse for its age, which gave great hope for the permanence of Pendon Parva as a whole.

Almost at the end of the year, Howard finished modelling the scenery of the Brook group. Its pond looked extraordinarily wet and the whole scene captured the unhurried, almost timeless atmosphere of the 1920s and the early 1930s. It was the culmination of our best year to date, a year that had also seen a new engine from Guy (a Dean Goods) and the completion of the lighted train with

Guy (left), Howard Fuller (right) and Paddy Burridge (below) working on the task of dismantling part of the Relics Room within 'Marilyn'.   A. E. SMITH

THE ERECTION OF
THE NEW MUSEUM BUILDING.

The erection of the new museum building. The site cleared and ready for the construction to begin. By now the signal had been relocated but its new position could not have been ideal for the construction that was to follow.   A. E. SMITH

The view from the top of the signal, with Roye watching progress from his room in 'The Three Poplars' (the upper window on the right side of the building).

The main piers being assembled over 'Marilyn', the Dartmoor extension and the small toilet block.   A. E. SMITH

The main structure in place.   A. E. SMITH

Stewart's model of the only 12-wheel Brake Third constructed by the GWR.

On the last day of 1970, Paddy knocked down the ruined walls of Pompeii and a couple of weeks later, I undertook the barrowing away of the blocks. Crendon then lodged our planning application, and to support it I submitted some very carefully thought-out points in our favour, together with a photograph showing the disreputable Marilyn, which we were now seeking to replace. When I took these to Mr. Lane, the Building Inspector, he said that if there were no hitch at all, the earliest we could expect a decision would be the beginning of March, but if there were difficulties, we would be approached before then. Consequently, when the Crendon representative came out unexpectedly on 25th February, my heart sank. He handed me a document. More than a glance was needed to get the gist of it and my eyes jittered over the lines of print with apprehension. Then I saw the words 'hereby PERMIT the above development.' Almost afraid to believe it, I read the conditions. The building must be used as a museum and not for industrial purposes and the exterior colouring must be to the Council's satisfaction. That was all. We had approval.

At a meeting of our own Council the following Sunday, Donald announced that, subject to there being four guarantors for the instalments, the Hendon Building Society were now offering a loan of no less than £4,500 on a 20-year term. This included £250 for the redemption of the additional car parking land from Mr. Heard. We went deeply into the contingencies which could affect our power to repay, during which discussion Howard announced that, thanks to good attendance figures, the original bank loan of £2,500 had been reduced, in record time, to a mere £100. The promise of the Hendon loan meant that we should not now need to take up Mr. Morris's offer to renew the original loan, and, with attendances showing no sign of slackening, we should be able to meet the Hendon loan, even though a rigid economy might become the price. Regarding guarantors, rather than place a burden on any four individuals, our Council as a whole accepted responsibility for the payments. The way was clear as never before.

It was the start of a new era. To prepare the site for the new building, the Relic Room section of Marilyn had to be dismantled and a new temporary end wall erected to protect Dartmoor. Similarly, the J.H.A., which had served us well since it had been erected but which now also lay in the path of new construction, was also taken down and stacked near the signal. Outside, an old apple tree, one of the last remnants of the garden of the old Three Poplars, and the remains of Cope's dividing fence were also cleared away. We were ready for the builders.

The start came early the next day 13th April, a day before schedule — when the Crendon lorry drove in.

Pegging out began soon after and when it was done, the digging commenced of huge holes for the columns. The weather was perfect and the ground bone dry. Had the winter floods come later, there could have been two feet of water to combat in every hole.

The three men doing the job were excellent workers, very pleasant fellows as well, and the progress they made was surprising. By the end of the second day all but one of the twelve main holes had been dug and half of them filled with concrete, the socket for each pier being set in place as they went. The ones at the back needed to be filled from the lane owned by Mercy Ward, our former antagonist in the saga of the signal. But the past had left no scars and she very obligingly gave us full permission for access which saved a vast amount of barrowing and enormously simplifying the erection of the rear pillars.

The following day the bigger of two cranes came in and the assembly of its tremendous jib began soon after arrival. A large low-loader then appeared with the first of four loads of the main pre-cast concrete frames. Everything was going well and the remaining holes had been concreted when Mr. Lane, the building inspector, suddenly appeared. He had only just received the inspection cards, Crendon having sent them in error to the Abingdon office rather than Didcot, and he had to see what was under our foundations. He was sorry, but the concrete must come out again. The men were dismayed and protested loudly the concrete had set and it would be a week's work to dig it out. But Mr. Lane was adamant. Had it been an agricultural building he might have overlooked it, but this was a building for the public and he could take no risks. There was much telephoning and next morning a Crendon director and the manager came out in person. Under their patient persuasion Mr. Lane at last began to unbend a little, agreeing in the end that by digging beside some of the holes and refilling with concrete, he could satisfy himself with what lay beneath. This done, we had permission to proceed and, as it turned out, this proved to be the only crisis in the building's construction.

Work on the building ceased over the weekend, and with the unexpected number of 83 visitors, we sampled the first of many exceedingly difficult showings. Fortunately, everyone was very understanding of our troubles and they seemed thoroughly impressed by what we had taken on. Throughout the whole of the rebuilding we were obliged to continue showing (if we were to pay our way), but looking back to this particular weekend, one shudders at the thought of such crowding when the sole exit from Dartmoor was one narrow escape door.

The Monday saw fantastic progress. Just before nine the same three men arrived, together with the drivers for the two cranes that were needed to assemble the main frame. At that time, there was not a thing that was new above the foundation holes. Marilyn stood resigned, but still unrivalled. Then the larger crane moved in, slung a shapely pier slowly into the air, then down again, finding its socket almost, one felt, by instinct. It was a fantastic sight as frame after frame went up, without effort and neither hurrying nor wasting time. We were told later that this was a hand-picked team that had been booked for a simpler job but were transferred to ours because of the extra problems of building over an existing structure. They certainly knew how to tackle it.

So the new columns rose in front of Marilyn and from the lane behind her and then the cross members were hoisted up and slotted in place, high above her leaky roof. I was appalled by the nonchalance with which the men walked and worked on those sloping beams. They were a mere six inches wide, and stretched, unsupported, forty feet across the void in which Marilyn stood.

By the time the men left at five, the frame of the whole building was standing, lacking some verticals and sheeting rails, but looking its full self and immensely impressive. Marilyn had shrunk beneath the high beams until it seemed quite insignificant. It was revealing now to remember how thrilled we had been when Marilyn first went up — how vast it seemed — and now how puny. In the future we might forget this comparison, but at the moment, seeing through the columns of the new to the low length of the old, the contrast was most striking.

Superb weather held until the basic portal frame structure was complete, though as yet without wall in-fills or roof, and then a week later there followed 38 hours of continuous rain. It produced, in addition to the usual leaks in Marilyn, yet another major one, this time beside the trains of Dartmoor, missing the Barnum engine by no more than inches. But it was the last emergency of this kind, for, early in May, contractors from another firm, Cape Universal, put up a double-skin asbestos roof, like a huge umbrella, over the lot, together with green fluted asbestos cladding on the upper half of the walls. The old reproach that we were keeping magnificent models in a leaky shed was overcome at last.

Amidst all the construction work, progress continued with the modelling. Howard was engaged on the surroundings of Holburn Farm and the Gosditch group and Paddy had turned to the unfinished 'Snobbing Cottage' *[The 'Snobby' was the village cobbler.]* This had been largely built some years earlier, then left, by Alan. It needed a good deal of exterior attention, but in the interior of the shop, Paddy produced his masterpiece, catching perfectly the dusty, fusty, grubby atmosphere, with boots and shoes everywhere. He also cleverly arranged the internal lighting so that the light appeared to shine from a minute hanging oil lamp. The building was thatched with plumber's hemp, an experimental change which Paddy

'The Three Poplars' in 1971.

ROYE ENGLAND

Holburn Farm, as modelled by Peter Buddle (buildings) and Howard Fuller (the surrounds).　　　A. E. SMITH

introduced to try to overcome the high cost of human hair and its need for mothproofing. Besides being decidedly cheaper, the hemp also had a more natural look and it became our standard thatching material thereafter.

For the railway, Fred Rogers presented us with an exquisite little engine which had been built for him by Guy — *Fair Rosamund* — the only engine of the '517' class that carried a name. The prototype spent almost all its life running to Woodstock from Oxford, so it would be out of place on Dartmoor. But when we could lay the Oxford line in the Vale scene, it would be very nearly at home. Another interesting vehicle, a 'Balloon' Full Brake of the old LB&SCR was commissioned for us by Philip Rickard from Teddy Francis, in memory of a friend and it added yet more colour and variety to our milk and parcels train.

The engines and rolling stock of the Madder Valley had not run for a long time, but, in anticipation of a day when they might again do so, we gladly accepted an offer of servicing and any necessary repair. This came from Harry Germaine, a Friend of Pendon and a semi-professional modeller, and he was helped by David Kitchiner, who also had the welfare of the Madder Valley very much at heart. July came before we were able to make a start on the block in-fill walls to the new building. We had given this job to a local builder, R. Hancock of Drayton, who had a name for good work and we soon saw that the choice had been a correct one. By October, all the walls were complete and the concrete floors laid throughout, except, of course, where Marilyn still stood. We then began the ticklish task of the demolition of Marilyn inside the new building. Howard and others worked on top, stripping off the asbestos roof whilst I barrowed away as much as I could of all and everything that came down. The din

inside the newly enclosed building was unbelievable, but, when it subsided, the whole roof was off, leaving only the hardboard inner ceiling.

The next day, a larger working party got busy on this, removing it completely from above the village showcases and the Madder Valley (which had its own ceiling) and then knocking down Marilyn's side wall. This went on, deafeningly, through three showings, but was completed without damage to the models. Then, on the last Saturday in October, with seven helpers, we shored up the Madder Valley with many cross-braces, jacked it onto industrial rollers and, with Marilyn's wall gone, moved it sideways and clear of the old building, following it with both village showcases. At the same time, Howard and Paddy stapled a black polythene 'ceiling' on the underside of Marilyn's rafters and above Dartmoor, the intention being to catch dust, birds' nests and anything else that might come down when the hardboard ceiling was finally removed.

Work on the new building now progressed more slowly. Gradually we removed walls that had formerly divided the different areas of the old Museum, whilst new ones were erected to match the planned configuration of the new. Surviving sections of Marilyn were supported on scaffolding poles. The dust and the noise were often overwhelming, but we pressed on. We also hired a bulldozer and driver to level the site for the Museum car park. Christmas Day (1971) was the fiftieth anniversary of the formation of the Australian Central Railway and of the project that was to become Pendon. It had been an uphill road almost all the way. But now the land was ours and paid for and the new building was essentially complete. 1971 was breakthrough year.

The steelwork for the upper gallery being delivered, watched in the background by Howard, Paddy and Tony Smith. ROYE ENGLAND

'Marilyn', entombed within the new building and awaiting final demolition. ROYE ENGLAND

CHAPTER FOURTEEN

1972–1974
THE NEW MUSEUM

ON the first day of 1972, a recent recruit named Mike Townsend took over the Treasurership from Howard who, in turn, became our Secretary, releasing Guy to concentrate on his more productive work as Chief Mechanical Engineer. Mike, a London bank manager in his forties, was portly in figure, with greyish hair brushed back and horn-rimmed glasses. His voice was soft, his personality delightful and his knowledge of finance consummate. No one could have made a more expert treasurer, or a more sensible one, which was the ideal combination. Howard had done a wonderfully good job in the past, but it was one of many skills that he was using for us, and, as our affairs grew and the burden increased, he handed it over with relief.

Steelwork for the upper floor of the new building had now become our main concern. Many consultations took place and we eventually accepted a quotation of £843. There was no question of our paying for erection, which we must somehow do ourselves. Even so, it was a lot of money and we thought of trying to get another loan. But one of Mike's first tasks when he took over as Treasurer had been sorting out two or three years of our Friends' covenants, on which we had never found time to claim. It was a daunting task demanding weeks of concentrated work, but Mike waded into it and seven days before we accepted the quotation for the steel, we received a cheque from the Inland Revenue for £893! The steel was paid for in advance, and with a little left over.

Before we could accept delivery, however, the remains of Marilyn had to be dealt with and this final demolition we decided to leave to Hancock's men. So on Sunday, 16th July, we gave Marilyn's last five showings and as soon as the visitors had gone, we took out the trains, vehicle by vehicle, storing them on the under-floor of the village showcases in what would become the new Relic Room.

Two days later Hancock arrived with a couple of his workers and the kill began. Hardboard walls, nest-ridden ceilings, the roof trusses themselves — all gave way before them. I had covered the Dartmoor tracks with newspaper and as clutter accumulated on top of the black polythene sheet that was still pinned over the model, it broke away and descended gently onto the hills, giving them closer and rather improved protection. The concrete walls of the Dartmoor extension were being retained but had to be cut down by two courses and a whole section removed to give access to a newly-built stairwell. The debris was unbelievable, with loose rubble six inches deep on some of the floors, but before leaving on the third day, the men swept up the lot and left it unexpectedly clean.

Marilyn was no more. Once again her trusses and sections lay stacked in what now remained of the garden, in almost the same place as they had lain 18 years before when the task of erecting them was still a problem that lay ahead — under apple trees then, now on the edge of a spick-and-span car park, beside a new building. Marilyn had caused many crises but she had kept us going through all those years to make the progress that we had achieved possible.

Before the steelwork for the upper gallery could be brought in, the Madder Valley had to be dismantled. In the whole of the new building, there was only one door by which the massive steelwork could be introduced — and Madder Valley stood directly in its path! Tony Smith photographed its entire layout as a guide for future reassembly, then dismantled it piece by piece and section by section, again sawing it in half at the spot where John Ahern himself had severed it, the last time it was stored. By evening the whole scene was once more packed away.

Saturday, 19th August 1972, saw the arrival of the steel. A hired crane and quite a gathering were at Pendon very early to meet it — Tony Smith, Howard, Mike, Paddy and Frank George, the latter a retired Friend of Pendon with first-hand knowledge of steel erection, who had come from Wembley with his son-in-law, Brian. The low-loader came in soon after 8.30am with a weighty consignment of red-primed girders and stanchions, together with sacks of large bolts, nuts and washers. It was too long to get into the car park but the crane coped with the task from its position in the yard, laying everything neatly beside the Museum building. Some of the longer girders had to be turned in the process. There would be no turning once they were inside.

The lorry departed. Then the crane picked up the girders one by one and positioned them neatly onto skates inside the near-end door, from where they were rolled to a transverse position in the future Relic Room. It went so smoothly that all were stacked indoors in less than four hours after their arrival.

Much poring over working drawings followed, and then the giant-Meccano exercise of erection started, going on thereafter, day after day, as time and opportunity allowed. Stanchions were propped up, cross-beams lifted into place and bolts dropped, or otherwise encouraged, into waiting holes. The great girders, 30 feet long and each weighing as much as a third of a ton, were hauled up with a chain hoist at the top of a lightly-guyed pole until, swaying and clanking, they could be perched high on a couple of 'roller skates' awaiting them. The skates ran on

Howard positioning one of the girders. The working conditions were precarious, to say the least, and the Dartmoor layout (which may be glimpsed below the girder) was, for a time, largely unprotected from the work overhead.   A. E. SMITH

temporary angle-iron tracks and having got a beam onto its skates, Howard and Paddy 'rode' it, propelling it the length of the Museum into its precise position for bolting.

Two factors made the rapid progress possible. The first was the skilled organisation of the work, and for this we owed almost everything to Frank. The second factor was the sheer application of the four indefatigable workers, Frank, Howard, Paddy and Brian. On one peak weekend, three of them worked a total of 23 hours each. No wonder their achievement astonished everyone. From the beginning to the end the whole thing went without a hitch. We had estimated the job taking ten weeks but three weeks from the start, it was done.

A week after the steel marathon was concluded, innumerable lengths of timber and a great pile of flooring-grade chipboard began to be used regularly upstairs as, amid much sawing and hammering, the joists and flooring for the new gallery were installed. Downstairs, in preparation for the reinstatement of the Madder Valley, Tony now began to erect wooden framing to enclose it. We had decided, with Mrs. Ahern's approval, to make the layout L-shaped instead of the former U-shape, to give closer and much better viewing. In this form, we found that it fitted the available space almost perfectly.

Work on the building had to dominate our time, thought and energy that year, but things were moving nonetheless in other directions too. Peter Buddle had completed no fewer than four buildings before the end of the summer — Champ's Chapel and its adjoining Priests House from East Hendred, Letcombe Cottage from Letcombe Bassett and the Police Cottage from Uffington, although the last two still awaited thatching and weathering. Paddy produced Billy Goodman's tiny cottage from Knighton. My own modelling was mostly confined to the Baker's Arms from Badbury, but it went slowly as I was spending a lot of time measuring in the Vale. Altogether I recorded 18 buildings that year. During one of these visits I made sketches of St. Frideswide's at Knighton, the drawings using up the last page of my notebook. Forty-seven years earlier I had started the same notebook by measuring and sketching a bogie rail wagon of the Western Australian Government Railways for use on my projected Australian Central Railway. No wonder the book was somewhat tattered!

On the railway, Guy did much toward the completion of his model of the only GWR 'Pacific' engine, *The Great Bear*, but a little earlier (during the miners' strike), a more substantial task had been the refurbishment of the

Dartmoor timber viaduct. For nearly seventeen years, this had withstood the passing both of time and trains, but some of the piers had settled, the line had become less than flat and we were beginning to have running problems. So Guy and John Clark made replacement timber fans, Tony Smith a new deck and Paul King the baulk-road track. It took a 16-hour session throughout the whole of a Sunday to install, in which another new helper, Tony Reynalds, came with Guy from Bristol to help.

The existing viaduct was sawn into its original four sections and removed, leaving only the piers standing. Then suddenly, precisely at 3 o'clock opening time, came one of the power cuts that had been prompted by the strike — and total darkness. Paddy connected emergency lighting to his car battery, and work continued dimly and with difficulty. But the power cut was a blessing in disguise for during that Sunday afternoon, about 80 visitors came for showings which, in any case, we could not have given because of the work on the viaduct. But the cut removed the whole of the blame from Pendon!

By the time light returned, the new timberwork was in place and the handrail was being fitted. The inaugural run over the new bridge was made by No. 5624 which had opened the original viaduct in 1955, and Guy and his helpers left for Bristol after 12 hours' work, almost without a break. Paul stayed to trouble-shoot for another hour

and Stewart and I continued the work until 1.0 a.m., by which time everything was in good running order again.

At about this time, we also made an important revision to the plans for the Vale railways. When, years before all this, I designed the Vale layout with its branching main lines representing those to Bristol and Oxford, I included an independent single line crossing the GWR in the north-west corner of the scene and climbing along the face of the southern hills towards the village. As a remnant of my early ambitions to model as much as possible of all the railways which came together at the grouping of 1923, I proposed making this line an LMS one. That, I hoped, would allow the introduction of both LNWR and Midland trains.

But there was, of course, no LMS line in the Vale, or anywhere near it. Wishful thinking had apparently dulled my sense of the fitness of things, but when John Wiltshire (backed by John Shingleton) came to me and stressed the facts to which I had been closing my eyes, I opened them with a start. They said, quite plainly, that if Pendon was to be the historical record that I claimed for it, we could not include the LMS in the Vale scene. I had to agree with them.

If not LMS, what was the line to be? I realised, quite suddenly, that there was actually no choice. The former Midland & South Western Junction Railway crossed the

The new museum building, photographed several years after completion.   A. E. SMITH

A typical train on the MSWJR route. GWR 4–4–0 'Duke' class No. 3278 on a down Cheltenham passenger train approaching Chiseldon on 28th August 1935. L & GRP

Vale at Swindon, running through the Hodson Woods to Chiseldon, not half a mile (in the real world) from my Chapel group from Badbury. Nothing else had any claim like this, or in fact, any claim at all. Although the MSWJR was grouped with the GWR, it retained a lot of its individuality through our period and would be a most interesting and unusual subject to model and to keep within the memory at Pendon. I still wonder why it took me so long to come to this view.

Work on the building was naturally less spectacular in 1973 but it went on steadily and well. When Tony had finished the staging for the Madder Valley and had glazed it, he moved on to build similar staging for the Dartmoor scene. David Kitchiner then began reassembling the Madder Valley, taking care to alter nothing of John Ahern's original work. The one place where change was unavoidable was the former corner near the Moonraker's Inn, which we had straightened to give the layout its new L-shape. However, this corner had in the past been dismantled by John Ahern himself, and what David undid was merely our own reconstruction of the original setting. Through the summer David came frequently to work on the model and was making excellent progress when he was suddenly promoted by his firm and sent abroad for an indefinite period. It set back the restoration of the Madder Valley very considerably, but he did continue the work later, albeit at a reduced pace. To help our visitors enjoy the layout, we prepared an automatic taped commentary, spoken by Bob Symes-Schutzmann of the BBC.

From the railway point of view, the highlight of 1973 was the completion by Guy of a magnificent model of 'King' class engine No. 6000 *King George V*, commis-

sioned from him by David Kearsey. The engine was finished in the 1934 livery with the new GWR monogram on the tender. David had been working on a model of the 'Cornish Riviera Limited' with the Centenary stock of 1934, which we hoped the new engine would pull, although, in the end, the coaches were never finished and instead the new 'King' worked a more mixed (though entirely typical) GWR express.

In order to have a suitable stretch of mainline for the 'King' (and other express engines) to show its paces, we decided to extend Dartmoor with a loop through the tea room, where we would reproduce a section of the famous sea wall between Teignmouth and Parson and Clerk Tunnel. At the Teignmouth end, this would pass through a narrow repair workshop and would curve into the main line side of Pen Tor Road station, where there would be a very effective broadside view, at right angles to the rest of the Dartmoor scene. This sounded easy in theory, but as soon as we tried to achieve it, a whole crop of complications arose and not a little argument and disagreement, and it actually took many months to work out the logistics for the extended layout and many years before the sea wall finally became operational.

So we reached the end of 1973, another extraordinarily successful year. On all fronts the Museum now seemed to be making excellent progress, but early in 1974 we suffered a tragic loss. At the end of February, being due for a short holiday, Mike Townsend went to a travel agency and asked them to book him five days abroad. "Where do you want to go?", asked the clerk. "Oh, I haven't thought about that", replied Mike, rather naively. "We have a trip to Istanbul", offered the clerk. "Right", replied Mike, "I'll

The branch platforms at Pen Tor Road. The model of Yelverton station building by George and Doris Iliffe Stokes can be glimpsed beyond the footbridge, together with two fine scratchbuilt model buses in the yard.   A. E. SMITH

go there." Had they suggested any other place in the world, Mike would probably have accepted it just as readily. But he went to Istanbul and came back on the DC10 that crashed outside Paris, at the time the world's worst air disaster. There were no survivors.

It was a stunning blow. Mike was a pillar of all that was best in Pendon. He was approachable and pleasant, enthusiastic yet level-headed, with a profound business sense, an incomparable treasurer and an exceptionally good friend to all of us. In due course we persuaded John Wiltshire, who had accounting experience, to become our Treasurer and, although reluctant, he agreed to see us through. The depth of Mike's attachment to Pendon was shown by his leaving us a duty-free legacy of £1,000.

Thanks to Tony Smith's continuing efforts with our showcases and staging, the Dartmoor scene was now safely behind glass and fitted with new fluorescent lighting by Paddy and Geoff Hembrow. Guy now decided that the time was right to concentrate on the construction of the station, Pen Tor Road. The initial results of this drive were the staggered branch line platforms, including an attractive station shelter and a typical GWR 'pagoda' style lock-up on one of them, a water tower and cranes, and a beautiful footbridge. In the station yard stood two Western National buses, scratchbuilt for us by Jim Holt of Gosport.

There were to be two station buildings in addition to the shelter — one to stand in the triangle between the branch and the main lines, for which the prototype would be Yelverton on the former Launceston branch, while the other would occupy the main line platform, being taken from Ivybridge, an interesting example of the architecture of the South Devon Railway.

For the latter we were not yet ready, but we had begun planning the Yelverton building as much as three years earlier. Guy had thought of building it, but his real love was engines. We also felt that Pendon should rightly have an example of the work of the famous modellers George and Doris Iliffe Stokes, despite the fact that as professionals, they would have to be paid for their work. However, Donald Mackay was trying to persuade Guy to build for him a model of No. 6029 *King Stephen*, so we agreed a three-sided agreement. Donald would pay the Stokeses to build Yelverton and later Ivybridge whilst Guy would build *King Stephen* for Donald at a greatly reduced cost. The theory was that the time taken in building the 'King' would more or less balance what Guy would have spent on the two station buildings.

In practice, however, this did not pan out and Guy could have built much more than Yelverton and Ivybridge in the time that the 'King' took. Also when, a year later, he had completed the engine, very little had been done to the first station building and it was another eight months before it finally appeared. We knew the Stokeses had a lot on their hands, but we had waited too long and Donald had to do some very insistent prodding to make them get down to it even then. We heard that they were frequently working into the small hours to complete the model.

The result was not their best work, though in actual construction it was very good. The interior had not been fitted, the valance was incomplete as the tool had broken, and the colouring was unbelievably bad. What should

Guy's model of King George V *flanked by the model of* King Stephen *and No. 6005* King George II. *No. 6005 was not completed until the 1990s, but much of the basic work was done at the same time as the other engines. The standard of modelling on these scratchbuilt models is breathtaking.*

Tony Reynalds' model of No. 3560.

A. E. SMITH

have been the soft, tawny shades of the GWR station livery came out as something approaching LMS maroon and the slates on the roof were royal blue! Guy completed the model and repainted it, when it became a delightful building. But it had been anything but a good bargain, especially as we now deemed it best to cancel the follow-up order for Ivybridge which had been part of the deal.

However, the finished Yelverton building was the making of the branch line station. The shelter had also come from Yelverton, only a couple of miles up the line from the Walkham Viaduct, so both were thoroughly in keeping. Pen Tor Road — junction for Burracombe, Trezellion Moors and Porthkerrick (names I had invented, making quite sure they were not actual ones) — in its colouring of 'light and dark stone' caught the true Great Western atmosphere. It vividly brought back the charm of many such out-of-the-way stations in the days of steam.

We were also heartened by the news that Tony Reynalds *[soon to become one of the most outstanding builders of locomotives in 4mm and, particularly 7mm scale]* had started building engines for us, taking some of the pressure off Guy. To show his progress, he brought to Pendon the sandwich-framed tender from No. 3560 — a 4-4-0 engine of the fascinating '3521' class. It was an exquisite creation. The completed engine followed in due course — one of the most characteristic of all the engines that ran on Dartmoor and one of the most appropriate for the district.

The village sections were still being shown in the tea-room area, but Tony's constructional work was going ahead there and more space was needed for it if he were not to be held up. Also, access for the public was rather cramped, forming a difficult bottleneck on busy days. So plans were laid, safety factors considered and, on the morning of Good Friday, we made the long-awaited advance of moving the village upstairs. The three large cases, with the models temporarily removed, were hauled up endwise through a gap in the ceiling — there being no other way of getting them into the upper floor — and they were installed, end-to end, across a single bay of the

upper hall. We had divided off this area from the rest with a hardboard screen, intentionally keeping the viewing passage narrow to restrict to about thirty, the number of visitors seeing the village at any one time. No more could comfortably do so, but this temporary arrangement was a great success, showing for the first time the three village sections that were then complete, in their correct sequence.

The move turned out to be providential for that Easter holiday broke every record we had previously set, totally more than 900 over three days with 357 on Easter Monday. The previous record for a single day had been 301 on Spring Bank Holiday Monday the year before. Then the Museum had been so full that many visitors went out through the emergency door without ever attempting to see the village models, trapped in the wedge of humanity within the tea-room area. But this time, with additional visitors, there was no trouble. Dartmoor and the Relic Room were solid, a queue stretched away from the main door, but we regulated a steady flow up the stairs, past the village and down to the tea room which, now freed of the village showcases, was for the first time able to provide our visitors with drinks and biscuits.

Three years had now passed since the portal frames of the new building went up and they had been years of intense effort by us all. Inevitably the progress that we impatiently awaited had seemed slow and at times even frustrating, yet looking back we could now see how solid it had been and how truly rewarding.

It was at Easter that year that we felt the new Museum had become a fact, for it now contained a comfortable Relic Room, the Dartmoor scene operating within its own showcase, the village being shown in the upper hall (albeit in a temporary configuration) and the tea-room, although as yet unfinished, was functioning in its own appointed surroundings. Outside the building, visitors came and went by a neat and cared-for car park. Pride in the new Museum could well run high at that Easter of 1974.

Roye, photographed in 1978.

A. E. SMITH

CHAPTER FIFTEEN

1974–1979
SO MUCH AHEAD

The up-beat mood of Easter 1974 was, however, soon replaced by a crisis that threatened to engulf Pendon and, for a time, placed in jeopardy the continuation of the project. At the centre of the crisis was a young man whom we shall call Tim Hancock, although that is not his real name. Tim (whom Roye had met in Bristol) had recently lost his mother in tragic circumstances, and to help him overcome the loss, Roye invited him to stay at the Poplars. The visit turned into an extended one, during which Tim began to help out in the Museum, almost becoming an unpaid and unofficial caretaker. Unfortunately, he was prone to moods of deep depression, and when suffering, could be rude and aggressive. Some personal items, including some of Roye's mother's jewellery went 'missing', for which Tim was held to account. Roye, with his usual Christian charity, was prepared to make allowances, but others in the Museum found this difficult young man less to their liking.

After some eight months, some members of the Museum Council became anxious, fearing that having stayed so long, Tim might be establishing a de facto right of tenancy. Roye was disinclined to make an issue of the matter, but the Council decided that Tim should be asked to leave and very much against Roye's wishes, he was given a month's notice. As Roye expected, he reacted badly, refused to go and then made a number of threats against the safety of individuals and Museum property, which didn't help the situation.

Roye then sought legal advice and established that if Tim signed a statement to the effect that he was a guest at the Poplars and helping Pendon voluntarily and in an unpaid capacity, there was no question of a tenancy and he could be legally evicted at any time. Tim agreed to sign, but, much to Roye's dismay, there remained a majority of Council members who felt that Tim's presence was not conducive to the proper running of the Museum and, notwithstanding the agreement, he should still be required to leave.

The situation was eased somewhat when Tim was offered a room in a house in the village and it was then agreed that he could still help around the Museum in the week, when other workers were generally not present. However, because of the irreconcilable differences of personality with several key Pendon workers, Tim was asked to stay away at weekends. Unfortunately, he chose to ignore the request and when the inevitable confrontation took place, the majority of the Council threatened to leave Pendon unless Tim was completely excluded.

In a desperate attempt to resolve the matter, Roye agreed that since his presence was probably the main factor that was encouraging Tim to remain around Pendon, he should take an extended break away from the Museum. Accordingly, and without forewarning Tim, Roye spent nearly three weeks in the Vale, measuring and recording. In retrospect, Roye admitted that it was a

heartless thing to do, but it did bring the resolution that Pendon, by then, so desperately needed. Tim, realising that there was now little purpose in attempting to remain at Pendon, arranged to go back to Bristol and much to Roye's relief, when Tim came to the Poplars later, to collect a few remaining possessions, the two friends were readily reconciled.

The whole saga had been drawn out over nearly six months and at its worst, had threatened the survival of the Museum. The thing that distressed Roye the most, however, was that for the first time, the threat (as he saw it) came from within the Museum and the strands of disenchantment and disappointment that begin to seep into Roye's account of the later phases of Pendon's development can, in some respects, be seen to stem from the unhappy experience surrounding Tim Hancock. Outwardly, things quickly returned to normal, but for Roye, it was never quite the same after Tim. It is also revealing to note that Tim was one of only four individuals who were named as beneficiaries in Roye's will. We take up Roye's own account with the visit to the Vale that he made at the height of the Hancock crisis.

IT was three in the afternoon, on Thursday 22nd August, before I finally got away. I cycled to Marcham, starting my safari by recording the ruined dovecot there and then going on to Goosey where I photographed elms. The disease (Dutch Elm) was getting bad in the Vale now and soon there might be few left. What a disaster it was becoming. After recording the Friends' Meeting House at Uffington and part of Pound Farm at Goosey on the Friday and Saturday respectively, Sunday morning found me at Watchfield church, near Shrivenham. I felt desperately in need of spiritual help — I was concerned for Tim and for Pendon — so I prayed and, to my joy, found that help was truly forthcoming. I returned to my measuring with a new zest, completing work previously started on Lilac Cottage at Bishopstone and a small cottage at Shrivenham that I named 'Littlecot'.

The most vital work of the whole trip, however, I did at Shrivenham, measuring the picturesque thatched row in the High Street which included a butcher's shop. The entry in 'Outline' was prophetic: 'The rain cleared early and I have done eight hours' measuring of the butcher's shop. The Hursts are selling it and change is bound to come, so I have done it fortunately in time.' Fortunately indeed, for only a year or so later, the whole of that part of the row was destroyed by fire. Later I returned to Goosey to complete the record of Pound Farm. The young couple who owned it, Patrick and Patsy Taylor, were extraordinarily helpful, giving me hospitality for three nights until the survey was complete. I then cycled

The Shrivenham row, as photographed in 1933. The butcher's shop is indicated by the small awning which shaded a set of simple boards on which the meat was displayed, uncovered and open to the road.
PENDON MUSEUM COLLECTION

to Swindon to spend the last part of my trip with my old friends, the Lomases. It was the first (and only) time that the cycle ride from Long Wittenham to Swindon had taken sixteen days!

Amongst several new recruits at this time was David Hyde. He had been writing a book on GWR goods stock and he came to return about 80 photographs which Pendon had lent. As it happened, we were discussing the MSWJR line, and David, who had known the line since boyhood, offered his immediate help with information, photographs and train details.

The point of discussion had been the selection of a suitable MSWJR station for the Vale scene. Chedworth and Collingbourne had been suggested but David Kitchiner gave such an enthusiastic account of Savernake (High Level), most of which still stood, that we decided it must be seen at first hand. So one perfect day in February, 1975, Paul Karau drove me there. It was all, and more than, we had hoped. The main station building, now converted into a dwelling, was changed, though still largely recognisable, while on the opposite platform the smaller structures were almost unaltered, except that their formerly varied and mellow brick work had been whitewashed. Down the line, now just a weedy path-like stretch, stood a fine brick water tower, in its own way quite beautiful, and a weatherboarded signal box in very good condition considering its 15 years of disuse. We took between us over a hundred photographs, and while Paul measured the signal box, I tackled the water tower.

A fortnight later we returned to complete the record, after which we went to find the tunnel between Savernake and Marlborough. It was set most impressively, in a very deep, steep-sided cutting through the chalk and flint. The

blue brick portal was beautifully weathered, in places crumbling to red, with an inscription above the arch — 'Opened by Georgiana, Marchioness of Aylesbury'. We walked through the tunnel, perhaps half a mile, to the Marlborough end, which was also impressive though not quite so attractive, then back again, before returning to Pendon, very content with all that we had found.

A year before this, I had found myself talking to a young and attractive American girl from California named Helen Buckland. She told me she had cut out a newspaper account of Pendon ten years earlier and had vowed to come ever since. Now she was here, loved everything and only wished she could help. "What are you doing for animal life?", she asked. I admitted that we should have to use commercial products, even though they were not up to the standard we needed. " I'm a commercial artist", she replied, "and I do animal sculptures in my spare time. I've never made anything so small, but if I can find the right medium, I'd love to try".

Helen was very busy and it was well into 1974 before we heard anything further. Then a little packet arrived, with a letter enclosed headed 'Pendon Rural Industries Inc. (California Branch)'. Inside was contained an exquisite young cart horse, modelled to Pendon's scale in fired clay. Ten weeks later came a whole set of animals and human figures. They included another horse and a workman, two cows, a pig and two dogs. There was also a small boy and his stout mother supporting, in a most natural attitude on one hip, a younger child. These formed an ideal group to complement the young cart horse which was now placed in a small field in the Brook group. Under the elm behind the hurdlemaker's cottage, Helen's cows replaced the commercial ones, with greatly improved nat-

Two vintage views of rick building in the 1930s. Even with the help of machines, farm work then was still highly labour intensive, there being at least nine men working on or alongside the threshing machine. It is also worth noting the small size of the tractor driving the thresher with a belt, as compared to a modern machine.
MUSEUM OF ENGLISH RURAL LIFE

A rick-building scene as recreated in miniature in the yard of Badbury Farm, Pendon Parva. The elevator is the work of Austin Attewell, whilst the figures came from Helen Buckland in California.

A. E. SMITH

uralness. Generally speaking, Helen's contribution was of people and larger animals. Some of the smaller ones, cats, hens, geese, waterfowl and at least one heron, were the work of Nick Britton, who carved them most effectively from plastic.

At about the same time, we were joined by Austin Attewell, a quiet, capable man who had long since been a Friend of Pendon and a regular visitor since 1958. He now volunteered to come onto the rota of drivers for Dartmoor, and at the beginning of December, I gave him his first practice. He soon became not only a very reliable driver but one of our most competent and interesting commentators. Austin was also interested in the farming of the Vale and knew a great deal about how the land had been worked in the 1930s, and in this area (amongst many) he was able to provide invaluable help in the years ahead.

One Sunday, in the spring of 1975, Philip Rickard was taking the upstairs showing and this left me free to talk with a family from High Wycombe. The mother, Penny Thompson, looked unusually young to have a grown-up son who towered over her, but she struck me as both very interested and very capable. She was a trained draughtswoman and had already done architectural modelling in 4mm scale. She said she would be pleased to model a building for us, and when she later brought a sample of her work, it left us in no doubt what she could achieve. We had nothing measured at the time, but Penny assured us that she could work with photos alone and that reminded me of a cottage demolished more than twenty years ago for which we had no measurements. A search realised just three colour transparencies and one black-and-white print of the house, Mount Pleasant, Bishopstone, but Penny went away quite happily to produce the model.

Meanwhile, I turned my attention to detailing of the yard at Badbury Farm. Helen had recently sent some more sculptured figures, and, one afternoon, Howard turned up unexpectedly with a large elm, a corn stack which he had modelled as though being built, and other bits and pieces to make a working scene. We spent an evening putting them in place, colouring the farmyard and re-spraying the

A photograph of building a real rick shows how precisely the scene in the model of Badbury Farm reflects real practice. The two farmhands in the foreground were forking the hay from the back of a truck onto the elevator, whilst the men on the stack were distributing the bundles to build the rick.   MUSEUM OF ENGLISH RURAL LIFE

Apart from the substitution of a steam engine with a small tractor, threshing scenes like this one had changed little for more than a century. The location is not recorded.   MUSEUM OF ENGLISH RURAL LIFE

elm to get the colour right. In time, a splendid elevator modelled by Austin Attewell would help to complete a charming scene.

It is a very long way back that the Ramells last appeared in the story. For the past nineteen years they had been living at Colerne, between Chippenham and Bath, where Lewis was in charge of two parishes. We had never lost touch, but both they and I had been chronically short of time and our contacts were confined to occasional meetings and the odd telephone call. Towards the end of 1974, however, Lewis underwent a serious, though successful, operation and this drew us closer together again. In turn, it reawakened Mario's interest in Pendon. After all, this was the infant guild that long ago she had served so devotedly, now grown in early maturity. So I was pleased that in the summer of 1975, while Lewis went to London for four days, Mario was able to spend them at Pendon, catching up with progress and meeting some of our helpers. I was also pleased to learn that Tim Hancock, whom the Ramells had known for some time, was staying at the Rectory in Colerne, whilst he looked for work.

For the past eighteen months I had been getting increasingly frustrated by the over-long hours of showing and the fact that by being the only person on the spot, everything seemed to fall to me. Everything had begun to lose its sparkle. I was jaded and becoming easily depressed, and for the first time, I felt too close to Pendon. In a long telephone chat to Guy, he echoed my feelings that I might be happier if I could find somewhere to live and work that was away from the Museum. The problem was to find somewhere, for there seemed little that was available locally.

I thought hard and the answer came — from Lewis and Mario at Colerne. They offered me a large room if I cared to accept it. The disadvantage was the distance to Pendon but, after all, the former GWR main line connected both Bath and Chippenham with Didcot and there were trains every couple of hours. So three days after the Ramells' offer, I dropped my bombshell at a routine meeting of Council. The reaction was one of undisguised surprise — most assumed nothing would induce me to move away from Pendon — but there was general approval. I made it clear that as Lewis was likely to retire within the next few years and that circumstances might then change, I must retain my room in the Poplars to come back to as necessary. This was agreed. We also agreed to end midweek

A beautifully tranquil scene at Ginge on the edge of the Vale, east of Wantage.   MUSEUM OF ENGLISH RURAL LIFE

Another threshing scene that is almost timeless. Only the motor and the clothing of the farm contractor's men give clues to the date.
MUSEUM OF ENGLISH RURAL LIFE

Elms beside the backwater at Long Wittenham.

ROYE ENGLAND

Elms photographed near Pearith Farm, Long Wittenham, in March 1959. Within 25 years, most of the elms in the Vale had gone.
ROYE ENGLAND

showings which I had generally taken alone and that incoming telephone calls would only now be answered when the Museum was open or workers happened to be present.

It was proposed that I would make the move in three weeks time, but plans changed and I moved nine days later, on 14th July. Paul Karau very generously used his free day to transport me by car, with all my modelling and other paraphernalia, and we arrived to a great welcome from Lewis, Mario and Tim. They had made ready for me a big room at the top of the house, complete with a tremendous table made of deal that was just right for my modelling and design work, and, from the start, I found myself eagerly looking forward to settling down and using it. The deadweight of frustration seemed already to have lifted and I knew that once again, there was so much ahead. The only cloud on the horizon was that I now found my eyesight worsening, and as I returned to design work on the Finch Hill section of the village that I had begun, but put down some nine months previously, I now found I needed the aid of a magnifying glass to re-read my earlier notes.

My stay at Colerne, however, was not to be an extended one. In January 1976, Lewis decided that the time had come to retire, and proposed to find a small property to which we could all go, either near to Swindon or in south Oxfordshire. I gave particulars of our needs to an estate agent in Didcot, who then sent details of two bungalows,

one in Abingdon and a second, rather more attractive, at Steventon. The Ramells were definitely interested by the latter one and although it was under offer from another buyer, the agent said nothing had been settled, so Lewis and Mario arranged to go and see it. About a fortnight later, the deal went through. We were thrilled. The house was modern, though not unattractive, and, although the rooms were generally small, the setting, a short cycle ride from Pendon, was a source of particular rejoicing for me. It was also a few streets from Howard's house, which would be most useful. But most of all, I would again be close to the Vale.

However, Spring 1976 was an unhappy one in the Vale itself. With half the elms dead and many of those that were coming into leaf probably doing so for the last time, the landscape of England would never be the same again. The impression of bareness was accentuated at the moment by the ash, which were so late that many were still leafless, or almost so. The oaks, on the other hand, had been in full leaf for some time, so according to the old addage, 'oak before ash, it will only be a splash'. And so it proved, with 1976 turning out to be the year of a record drought.

On Wednesday, 2nd June, we all made the move to Steventon. It all went well and when we arrived at Steventon, we confirmed that the bungalow was all that we had hoped it would be, and we had every reason to think we should be happy there. The following Saturday,

I cycled the eight miles to Pendon and it was a great feeling to be close again. A few weeks later, on 17th July, I was at Pendon to greet its 100,000th visitor, a member of a party of rail enthusiasts who arrived in a van from Bristol. A reporter from the *Oxford Mail* took photos of the special presentation of a leather-bound copy of our handbook to the lucky visitor, as Guy (who has also come for the occasion) looked on.

Now that I was close to the Vale once more, I was able to resume my measuring work. In about 1940 I had paced out the rough dimensions of Knighton Farm. But now I needed to know the precise dimensions for my village planning work, so I returned to the site to measure it properly. It proved fortunate that I had my original estimates, for since 1940, much of this lovely group had been pulled down, including some of the cow sheds, stables and pig sties. For these, we would have to reconstruct the dimensions, as best we could, from my original estimates. In all, I spent eight days in perfect weather, measuring and photographing buildings in the Vale. 'Outline' records 'an almost luminous heat haze on the hills that we have not had since 1949 — or in Australia. Fields and gardens are

The Causeway at Steventon. Roye included several buildings from this remarkable street in his plans for the Vale, including the Old Vicarage, the Priory Cottages and Godfrey's.

Part of Priory Cottages, Steventon, photographed in 1938.   H. O. VAUGHAN

an almost uniform beige and some trees are dying through the drought'. A little later, I also measured the ground plan for the Priory Cottages at Steventon, an extremely beautiful building, now partly in the care of the National Trust, which I proposed to build once I had completed work on Packer's smithy from Childrey.

My sight, by now, was gradually getting worse. I had known for some time that I was developing cataracts, and now, at Mario's insistence, I went to consult an eye specialist in Bristol, a Mr. Dallas. He was a tall, quiet, sensible man, in whom I immediately felt confidence. His wish was to operate on the worst eye in a couple of month's time and the second one a little later. Since I was doing skilled work for which good eyesight was essential, he felt the sooner I had an operation, the better.

Early in 1977, we recruited several valuable new helpers. First, Guy brought Tony Reynalds and Andrew Field to the Museum from Bristol. Tony, of course, was already building engines for us and Guy assured me that Andrew was also a builder of the highest possible standard. His first project was to be a model of a GWR 'Duke' class engine that would be just right for the Dartmoor scene. Then, a little while after, Martin and Mary Heard, who lived in Didcot, came to discuss with Howard an offer they had recently made to do village measuring for us. The Heards proved to be extremely knowledgeable and were meticulous workers, and their help was a godsend. Their first task was to measure Breakspear's Cottage at Knighton, the size and contours of which I needed urgently for design work that I was doing at the time.

The planning, however, was then suspended, as on the 20th March, I entered the Bristol Eye Hospital for the first cataract operation. After the operation, Tim Hancock spent the evening with me and Lewis and Mario came the following afternoon. Two days later, I was home again. All had gone well and immediately I could see better than I had expected.

Over many years we had been having problems with car parking at the Museum and several of our neighbours had become weary of the congestion that was caused on busy days. Eventually, matters came to a head when a public meeting was called to discuss the problems. The police were in attendance to advise, whilst Tony Smith, Howard and myself went along to speak for Pendon. Some of the villagers wanted Pendon's already limited opening restricted still further, but Tony quite rightly pointed out that shorter opening hours would only make the problem worse when we were open. The police also confirmed the view that Pendon had no responsibility for visitors who were parking off the Museum property. In the end, it was agreed that a joint approach to the District Council to provide a proper car park for the village might be the best way forward.

At the close of the meeting, I was offered a lift back to the Museum by a Mr. and Mrs. Nockels, who lived close by. On the way, they told me their son Aubrey, who was a qualified accountant, would like to help the Museum. When I went into the Library, I found that Aubrey was already there, discussing with Howard what help he might provide. As John Wiltshire, our existing Treasurer, was somewhat unsettled in the post, we felt sure he would welcome additional help or even relief from the position. This, in time, proved to be the case, and after an initial spell as Assistant Treasurer, Aubrey eventually took over full responsibility. It was reassuring to have someone in place who, like Mike Townsend, knew all the intricacies of running the finances of an organisation such as Pendon.

The second cataract operation took place in February 1978 and as before, everything went well and Mr. Dallas announced himself to be very pleased with the results. I returned to Pendon as soon as I felt able, and in March, whilst watching our Dartmoor scene, I was greeted by a visitor whose face I knew quite well. Angus Pilton was a man of late middle-age, stocky of build and full of enthusiasm for Pendon. A Friend of many years standing, Angus had visited us regularly over a period of twenty years from his home in Lincolnshire, and having recently lost his wife, he now felt the time had come to offer assistance. "Anything from sweeping the floor to running the trains", as he put it. Pendon had gained a dedicated helper.

Not long after, we gained another village modeller. Howard brought Stephen Williams, who lived in Staffordshire, to see me at Steventon. Stephen brought a sample model of a small house that he had built especially. It was one of the best first attempts we had seen, with exquisite brickwork and the colouring beautiful. There were, of course, some criticisms, but with no doubts as to his ability, we asked him to build the Jacobean almshouses from Lyford. These were not yet recorded but the following weekend I photographed them whilst Martin and Mary Heard did the measuring.

A little before this we had held a successful AGM of the Trust, following which quite a number of new models were available for viewing. Penny Thompson had recently completed a beautiful reconstruction of Mount Pleasant cottage from Bishopstone, whilst for the railway there were several new fish wagons and, in pride of place, Andrew Field's superb model, not quite complete, of the 'Duke' class engine The Lizard. I had photographed the original at Bath in 1928.

For some time, we had felt the new museum building would need to be extended, to provide a proper meeting space, storage facilities and workrooms that could not be accommodated within the existing structure. There was also the opportunity to reconstruct the old stable block and an adjacent building left over from the days of the

A distant view of some of the cottages built by Penny Thompson, with 'Mount Pleasant Cottage' from Bishopstone on the right and a part of Pound Farm from Goosey on the left. In the background, the massive form of Pen Castle (based on the Iron Age fort at Liddington) helps to provide a sense of scale and depth in the model that is perhaps unique to Pendon's Vale of White Horse Scene.

A. E. SMITH

A 1937 photograph of one wing of the group of almshouses in the tiny hamlet of Lyford, in the middle of the Vale of White Horse. The part of the building half-seen at the end of the courtyard was a small chapel which formed a link to a second line of cottages which faced those seen in this view, to complete a secluded and intimate little community.

H. O. VAUGHAN

hostel, to provide an accommodation unit for helpers who might need to stay over and much-needed office space. Several helpers had been actively working behind the scenes to realise this new goal, and by the third week of May (1978), we had both planning permission and, thanks again to Donald Mackay, a loan from the Hendon Building Society to finance much of the work. The work would again be done largely by Pendon volunteers, but we engaged Crendon to erect the main structure. The actual commencement of work was still some months away, but it was good to know that the way was now clear.

In the meantime, I felt able to take a short holiday with Angus. We went first to Bristol where the eye specialist fitted new contact lenses. It was a great joy to be able to see clearly again, after so much trouble. Then, through beautiful scenery we made our way to Newquay, staying with Peter and Sylvia Denny at St. Newlyn East, where Peter was the vicar. They made us extremely welcome and later Peter showed us his famous 'Buckingham Branch — Great Central' model railway. It was one of the most beautiful layouts in the country and was operated to a timetable with working signals, full bell-codes and some most ingenious electronic devices. I was fascinated to see that an automatic apparatus took the place of one operator, using the pianola-roll principle to set routes and signals and ring out the bell codes, much as I had patented for my Automotive Control system in 1925!

Three days later we went to visit the Lomases, who now lived in Paignton, and on our last day, we spent an interesting morning on the preserved steam railway that ran down to Kingswear. We watched a seven-coach train in primrose and chocolate depart behind a Prairie tank and a 52xx 2-8-0 tank was also in steam, having just passed a boiler test only the day before. We reached Steventon in the evening. It had been a wonderful trip, with scenery and sights that I could really enjoy through being able to see clearly again.

During July, a film crew from the BBC spent two whole days at Pendon, filming scenes for a programme on modelling by Bob Symes Schutzman. They took infinite trouble in filming Dartmoor including scenes as they would be seen from the train window and with close-ups following trains across the viaduct and through Pen Tor Road station. At some time on the first afternoon, Bob Symes asked me to go upstairs to talk about the next day's filming of the village models. After standing in silence for a few moments in front of the Chapel group, he turned and said, "I think this is the finest model ever made. You can see the love in every part of it". The next day the crew worked for ten hours, obtaining some marvellous close-up views of the model and, as a final gimmick, they contrived a scene in which a miniature Bob Symes walked up to the 'Waggon and Horses' and sat down at one of the benches outside! This was achieved by projecting a slide of the model onto a huge screen, against which Bob then walked. The deception was most effective but the thing that pleased and astonished me most was how lifelike the enlarged inn appeared.

By the end of the year, I was again at work on the model of Packer's smithy, but, as the colouring that I was doing depended upon daylight, I decided to use the evenings to start on the model of Priory Cottages and its neighbour (Godfrey's) to which it was joined. The Priory was not completely measured and I was hopeful that information would in due course be forthcoming from the Institute of Historical Research in London, whom someone had suggested I contact. But all the photographs were taken and I had fully recorded the brick, Regency-style end of the building, which would be a good place to start. So I began the construction by marking out this end.

A month or so later, on 22nd February 1979, I finished the model of Packer's smithy, having taken exactly five years and four months to do it. There had, of course, been many interruptions — I had spent many months in designing a sequence of trains for the Vale scene and further long months in working out a plan for the village and its contours. I had also been through two cataract operations. There was, of course, work still to be done on the model's surroundings but that did not diminish the sense of rejoicing at the completion of the building.

Part of the delay to Packer's was also occasioned by taking over models that others had started but had been unable to complete. One of these — Spring Cottage — was needed quite soon. It was ready for furnishing but I had no detail of the original. At Chilton Cantelo, in 1948, I had made a small interior to go into the proposed model of the Old Rectory at Liddington, which was never completed. The interior was still in store at my room at the Poplars, so, in pouring rain, Lewis drove me across to Pendon to retrieve it. Fortunately, it fitted almost exactly into Spring Cottage — a big chimney breast with a fire illuminated from beneath, a spiral stair, a grandfather clock and a three-piece suite. The little interior, so long placed on one side, saved many hours of detailed work.

It was in May that work began on the extension to the Museum building. Lewis drove Mario and myself over to Pendon, and we found that, unknown to me, work had actually started the previous day. The main frames were already standing and men were at work attaching the asbestos sheeting to the roof. Work was also in hand under Tony Smith's supervision on the dismantling of the old outhouses. We proposed to re-use the old bricks and tiles in the new work, so these were being carefully removed and stacked to one side.

Having completed Mount Pleasant, Penny had been working on the much larger model of the Butcher's Shop that I had recorded in Shrivenham at the height of the Tim Hancock affair. She now brought the model to show me the progress that she had made. Although unfinished, it was already a beautifully detailed model with the butcher in his blue and white striped apron, the carcasses

'Godfrey's Cottage' from Steventon, photographed in 1942.
H. O. VAUGHAN

and joints of meat in the shop looking horribly real, and a cart and sets of harnesses in the stable. Like the Greeks, who sculpted the hidden backs of statues, Penny insisted on modelling the rear of the building as meticulously as the front and she was setting the whole in a beautifully detailed yard and garden. We talked about her next project and although a huge undertaking, she agreed to take on Pound Farm which, coincidentally, I had also recorded on the same visit to the Vale as the Shrivenham shop.

I had received good news about drawings of the Priory Cottages at Steventon and one Monday in July, I went by train to Paddington and then to the Institute of Historical Research in Malet Street. There I met with Christopher Currie who came down to see me bearing drawings of the Priory, some of them his own work, others being copies of drawings prepared by an architect who had renovated the building. They were even more valuable than I had expected. There were lots of cross-sections giving details such as roof heights, yet the greatest treasure of all was the architects elevations of the building in 1939, before alterations were made. I found that the south-west side had been changed considerably — some of which affected the work I had already begun! But I was so thankful that the drawings had come to light.

The last day of August 1979 (St. Aidan's Day), I wrote in 'Outline' a telling passage. 'Forty years ago today, with the world on the brink of cataclysm, I founded the Guild of St. Aidan. I was convinced that the project had big possibilities and would work if only it could be given time — a lot of time — and nothing could seem less certain then than a stable future. But my prayers were answered and though the Guild of St. Aidan became Pendon, time has proved the possibilities. Looking at it now, though so much remains to be done, I am filled with overflowing for the way it has been led and prospered despite many difficulties. We have all played our part, but its success is the gift of God.'

Whatever prospects the future might hold, at least the 1970s had been for Pendon a wonderful decade. At the start we still had only a part of the present Dartmoor scene in a leaking hut, a couple of sparsely detailed showcases in the JHA and a tiny sales counter selling postcards and badges. Now the Museum was on two floors in a new building 70 feet long and being extended to 100 feet; attendances had risen up to 15,000 a year (and on occasions more) and we now had three finished sections forming the east side of Pendon Parva village ready to move into their final position within a new Vale showcase. We had replaced the simple sales counter with a formally-constituted sales company that sold our products across the world. Our reputation was established and the so-called impracticality of my early dreams had been replaced by a realisation on the part of all who knew Pendon that, short of any disaster, the dream would one day be fulfilled.

Two photographs of Roye's model of Packer's Smithy from Childrey. Unseen in these views, the open sheds contain all the paraphernalia of a village smithy, meticulously copied in miniature.
A. E. SMITH

Part of the yard at Pen Tor Road. The engine shed (based on Launceston) was built by Guy, whilst Pendon's first engine, No. 5624, can be seen on Tony Reynalds' beautiful model of a GWR turntable, alongside another veteran engine, No. 4908 Broome Hall.   A. E. SMITH

CHAPTER SIXTEEN
1980–1987
LIGHT AND SHADE

EARLY in 1980, I was called to a special meeting at the Museum where, together with Howard, Martin and Mary Heard, we discussed the selection of the church for Pendon Parva. For some time I had been intending to use the one at Hinton Parva and, indeed, it had featured in outline on the Pendon logo for several years. However, someone had questioned whether Hinton Parva church was too small for a village of the size of our model. So Martin and Mary had spent a day photographing and taking notes on almost every church in the Vale. For one reason or another, very few were suitable, and, in the end, we were left with a shortlist of Drayton, Bishopstone and the original choice, Hinton Parva. A little later, we added East Hendred to the list which, on a visit to the village, Martin and I both agreed was a beautiful building, with a wealth of styles — although perhaps rather too large for our purposes. *[The eventual choice, made some time later, was Bishopstone. In view of Roye's deep faith and the extensive nature of his travels through the area over many years, it comes as something of a surprise to find him apparently unsure or even unaware of the merits of the different Vale churches. However, it is possible that having made an early decision to model Hinton Parva, alternatives may not have been consciously evaluated thereafter.]*

In contrast to the problems in choosing a church, I had had no difficulty over a suitable station for the GWR lines in the Vale model. Culham, with its beautiful station buildings and imposing goods shed (both by Brunel) had been my preference for many years, and, although strictly not in the Vale of White Horse (being on the Oxford line north of Didcot), it was too good to miss. At Easter, 1980, we found a modeller to make the station. Stephen Clinch came from his home in Hazlemere to show me a small station he had made, based on Watlington. It was first class, clean work and very natural. I immediately suggested to Stephen that he might tackle Culham station and, although a difficult subject, I felt it would be very rewarding. To my joy, Stephen gladly accepted the challenge.

Two weeks later, I spent a most interesting day with the Oxford Museums Group, at which I asked Martin and Mary to join me. We started at East Hendred where Champs Chapel (which we had already modelled for Pendon) had been most beautifully restored and was in use as a local museum. What captivated me there was an oil painting, many years old, which took the view from the corner of Horn Lane, looking down the hill past Meadow Cottages, with magnificent trees and a country atmosphere that poignantly brought home how very much we had lost.

The summer and autumn of 1980 saw steady progress on both the Dartmoor and Vale scenes. In August, Council decided on a concerted effort to complete the Dartmoor scene and bring as much as possible of it up to standard. Guy brought his model of Pen Tor Road East Signal Box, beautifully done with the signalman looking out, as well as a new tunnel mouth for the main line. This was installed by Howard, who also spent time improving the scenery in and around the station. Sometime later, Tony Reynalds completed a working turntable, a beautiful and ingenious piece of work that would go alongside the engine shed (to be based on Launceston) that Guy was also building.

There was a steady trickle of new cottage models for the Vale scene, too. Stephen Williams completed Squareside and Square End (from Knighton), whilst I finished Peacock and Elderberry Cottages. These had been started by Alan Chapman (who had begun modelling for us again after many years in which his affairs had gone very wrong and he had been temporarily excluded from Pendon), but he had been unable to complete them in the time that Howard had set. Two new modellers, Ron Rising and Rupert Godfrey, had started work on Benjy's shop from Uffington and Littlecot respectively, whilst Penny, whose husband Ron had died unexpectedly, found the strength to resume work on Pound Farm and Keeper's Cottage from Fernham.

Early in 1981, the village modelling received another boost when Chris Pilton joined the team. He had known Pendon since childhood and now he was coming to help Angus who, at the time, was helping with the dismantling of the old stable block. Chris had lived for a time on canals and when he heard that we intended to include a stretch of the disused Wilts and Berks canal in the Vale scene, he offered his help with research and construction work. We also persuaded him to try his hand at architectural modelling, and, after a trial piece on a stable from Denchworth (which he did well, with lovely colouring), he began work on Breakspear's Cottage from Knighton.

Personally, however, that summer saw me very much below par. It was partly due to recurring eye trouble, but also persistent giddiness, a lack of staying power and permanent tiredness. Even cycling, though I missed it dreadfully, was too much effort. In the end I spent ten days in hospital, although nothing particular was diagnosed.

There were, though, still pleasures to be enjoyed. To my surprise and delight, a phone call from Pendon told me that Jack Butler and his wife were at the Museum, very anxious to see me. It was Jack who had lived at Middlecot (in the Chapel group) when Peter Lomas and I were measuring it in 1952-3, since when we had completely lost touch. They came across to Steventon and we had a most enjoyable couple of hours before they had to return to their home in Bournemouth. I learned that Tony Butler, the small boy who used to call me the 'Measure Man' and whose scribbled character on the wall of White Cottage I

sooner had I finished than Donald Mackay asked me to go along to the Library, where I found everyone assembled. I was told that I was to receive a belated 75th birthday present which I would find under a small box on the table. Gingerly I lifted it and revealed a perfect model of an old friend, engine No. 1335, as she would have appeared in her MSWJR days in mahogany-red livery. It had been

Chris Pilton's model of Canney Row from Chiseldon. A. E. SMITH

had captured in my model, was now married with a family, living in South Wales. At about the same time (mid-August), Martin and Mary went to Hinton Parva to complete the measuring of the old school that I had begun to record in 1953, but left unfinished. After 28 years, the same people were still there and they remembered the 'man on a bike' who had taken photographs. Martin had the prints with him and he said the adults to whom he was talking were quite clearly the children in my photographs.

But the year also brought sadness. Back in June we had word that Philip Rickard, after a period of extended ill-health during which he had only occasionally managed to get to Pendon, had suffered a stroke and lapsed into a coma. Six days later, and without regaining consciousness, he died. He had been such a very good friend to Pendon. He had known me since the days of the hostel. He was one of our first helpers, had later become a Council member, our Librarian, and, for a time, the Chairman of Pendon Sales Company. We would miss him.

For a few years now, I had been showing copies of my Pendon Saga to Members and helpers whom I thought might be interested. Chris Pilton had just read it and rang me, saying he was so moved by my account of the destruction, as I worked, of Canney Row, that he would like to build the model. I was delighted. He had just finished Breakspear's and the quality of his work, his sense of colour and the special ability to make a miniature building look old, gave me confidence that he would do a fine job with Canney Row.

On the last Saturday in October, I was at Pendon early to give a driving lesson to a trainee Dartmoor driver. No

Roye at the presentation of Tony Reynalds' model of MSWJR 2–4–0 No. 11, a few weeks after his 75th birthday. A. E. SMITH

commissioned by Donald from Tony Reynalds and had taken two years to build. It was a superb model and a great start to our MSWJR engine programme. Although given to me personally, it would of course run at Pendon and become Pendon's in the end. What struck me as so wonderful was that its fine lining and script lettering was as perfect as its construction, yet both were done by Tony — a rare combination of skills.

Before year's end, another milestone was reached. Arriving at Pendon on the second Saturday in December, I was ushered upstairs by Howard. To my astonishment, the village showcases that previously had been arranged

Part of the sea wall scene that represents one of the best-known sections of the GWR between Parson's Tunnel and Teignmouth, with its distinctive road bridges. A. E. SMITH

across the temporary gallery at one end of the building, were gone. Now visitors were being directed around the Vale showcase where, along its far side, the first three village sections now stood in their final position. They had been moved in the week by Howard, Angus and Chris. I could hardly believe it, but there it was, looking incredibly attractive with its sections joined together for the first time and under the new lighted ceiling, more natural than ever before. Further along the viewing gallery, a new enclosed modelling room set within the Vale showcase contained the village section that would house Penny's model of Pound Farm, and, alongside it, Peter Buddle's Harrow group, which proved to be his last contribution to the project as he had decided to become a professional modeller.

Soon after, another landmark was reached when work began on the trackwork for the Vale railways. Ray Hammond had been overseeing the construction of our track and had already laid the running lines for the Teignmouth Sea Wall scene, including the very characteristic super-elevation of the tracks as they left the sea wall proper and entered the cutting that in reality led to Teignmouth station. However, because of many pressures, Ray now felt unable to do more, and in his place, John Copsey, who had been a Dartmoor driver and Pendon helper for several years, took over the co-ordination of this vast job.

The sea wall scene itself was coming together well at this time, although there were some disagreements over the best method of modelling the cliffs. In the end these were very effectively modelled by Penny, using the same method that was used in the Vale scene, with cardboard

profiles to establish contours and then a covering of mutton cloth and a plaster-PVA mix to form the surface proper. Frank George, who was also modelling the well-known road bridges at the Teignmouth end, provided a beautifully-built model of the Parson and Clerk Tunnel mouth and the underbridge that stood just west of the tunnel. These were installed by Howard, who also contrived an interesting diorama effect to suggest the steep gully that was cut into the cliffs at this point. A little later, Stuart Johnson brought a nice model of the small signal box which stood immediately outside the entrance to the tunnel.

Christmas allowed me the chance to get back to modelling and I returned to modelling the Priory. Unfortunately, I discovered that some 6,000 tiles that I had painted whilst in hospital earlier in the year, needed a good deal of modification in colour, the penalty of working on them when I was unable to refer to the model. I managed to get them right the next day, but, as daylight hours were so short, I then made a tentative start of modelling Godfrey's. In the model it would become a continuation of the Priory and was going to be a demanding subject — fascinating but full of difficulties.

For the first half of 1983, things progressed well, but then we suffered a major setback. For some months we had felt concerned that Penny was losing interest. Apart from her modelling, she had taken on responsibility for Pendon's library and had also been editing the monthly in-house newsletter, the Pendon Link. I feared that she had put in too much, too soon and had burnt herself out, but I realised, also, that she was a victim of the clashes of personality that had intermittently bedevilled our work for many years and had lost Pendon the services of other skilled and knowledgeable people before Penny. I wished she had gone on helping, despite the problems, which, as I saw it, was the only way to win through in the end. But I knew she felt very unhappy at the way things had gone and we could only hope that if she took a break, she might come back to modelling. *[Penny did return to model and also*

to undertake valuable work on the cataloguing of Pendon's photographs.]

More positively, the task of completing Dartmoor advanced significantly in the autumn. First, after a Council meeting in September, I was called down to Dartmoor where Stewart asked me to press a button on the control panel. Without any idea of what would hap-

Roye, photographed in his room at the Ramells' home in Steventon, working on his model of 'Priory Cottages'. In later life, rather than modelling at a table, Roye preferred to have his work on his lap, usually resting on a pile of old 78 rpm records.

Roye's last masterpiece — 'Priory Cottages' and 'Godfrey's' from Steventon. Although now almost 80 years old, Roye seemed to have lost none of his skills in colouring and texture. The rear of 'Priory' cannot be seen by the public at Pendon, but it still received the same meticulous attention as the front. 'Godfrey's' was actually the last model that Roye completed, 54 years after he started work on the 'Waggon & Horses' from Wanborough.

A. E. SMITH

The model of the alms-houses from Lyford, built by Stephen Williams, after weathering by Roye.

pen, I did so and, as I did, the whole scene turned from day to night. The station buildings were lighted, as were the platform lamps, the overbridge, the signal cabin and the engine shed, as well as the yard. It was most effective, especially when the lighted train came through.

Then, in October, no less than five new engines arrived to complete the Dartmoor engine programme and several of the trains were remarshalled to provide, at last, correct formations for a Devon branch line. All the new engines were exquisitely built. They consisted of a Mogul 2-6-0 tender engine from Tony Reynalds, a 44xx Prairie tank from Paul Morgan and the slightly larger 45xx by Andrew Field, together with a 51xx Large Prairie and a steam railmotor from Guy.

Six months later, in March 1984, we held an equally successful evening for the village modellers. Chris Pilton brought the partly finished model of the Old Vicarage from Steventon which he had measured the previous autumn with the help of Tony Smith, Stephen Clinch had the first stages of Culham Station and Stephen Williams showed the work he had done on Duck's Stores from East Hendred and the Hinton Parva school. I showed the Priory and Godfreys which had been at Pendon to allow Howard to mark out their positions in the scenic tray on which he was now at work.

Easter 1984 was brilliantly fine, so, as always when the weather was good, attendances were down! Among the visitors, however, was a youngish fellow named John Whiston, who lived near Aylesbury. I sensed immediately that here was someone who could help Pendon, without any suspicion of where it would lead us or of the times together that we would share. He seemed pleased when I suggested he might like to learn to drive the trains on Dartmoor, and when he came a few days later for his first practice, I realised what an unusually nice companion I had found. About three weeks later, he spent the evening

at Steventon with the Ramells and me, during which time Mario persuaded him to try his hand at modelling trees, something on which John had been quite critical.

But my joy in finding a new kindred spirit was tempered by the loss, not long after, of two more friends. The first was a shy man who had lived for many years as a tenant in a room in the Poplars, largely unnoticed by visitors and unknown even to many Pendon helpers. His name was Luke Callaghan, known as 'Cal', and for a long time he had acted as an unofficial caretaker, watching over the Museum in the many hours in which it was left untended. Sadly, he was now in hospital and early in July, he died from cancer, aged just 52. I immediately became concerned that I should move back to the Poplars so that Pendon would not be left unguarded but after some lengthy phone conversations with Guy, Aubrey and one or two others, I was persuaded that this was not a good idea. The house was now in a very poor condition and in honesty, I was not sorry to be spared the sacrifices that a move back to the Poplars would have entailed.

The second loss that summer was John Shingleton. Although he had been suffering for some time with both eye problems and poor circulation, John had been continuing to help at Pendon. One Wednesday in September, Chris phoned John to ask if he could repair some electrics that were giving trouble. John promised to come on Saturday, but the following morning, Thursday 20th September, his daughter rang the Museum to tell us that in the early morning, John had collapsed and died. For John, a devout Roman Catholic, after the many physical difficulties against which he had struggled, it may have been a happy release. But that did nothing to diminish the sense of loss. John had been a superb electrical designer and had given faithful service to Pendon in all kinds of capacities for more than twenty years. He would not be easy to replace. A few days later, David Hyde kindly drove

*Chris Pilton's model of
'The Old Vicarage'
from Steventon.*
A. E. SMITH

me to the little church in Dorchester-on-Thames for the funeral and I was pleased to see the church full to over-flowing.

It was now 1985, and on 7th March, 'Outline' recorded that I finished modelling the Priory — 2,639 hours of work, not counting the time that Mario must have taken to cut the 30,000 tiles for its roof. I had begun it at the end of 1979, nearly seven years earlier, but whilst building it I had also worked on Spring, Peacock and Elderberry Cottages, besides spending time weathering Stephen Williams's model of the almshouses and completing the ruined cottage from Garford, started by Alan Chapman.

With a growing need to record appropriate outbuildings for placing behind Godfrey's, Angus and Chris drove me one afternoon to the Vale in the hope of finding something suitable. I knew of a superb stable at Lyford, but it was at Baulking that we came on a long, low range of weatherboarded and slated sheds which were exactly what I wanted. The retired farmer and his wife were extraordinarily friendly, taking us all over the farmhouse, the furnishing of which seemed largely unchanged from Victorian times — an absolute treasure house of what life once had been like. Chris took quite a lot of interior views for future modelling.

At a meeting towards the end of June we decided to base our Midland & South Western station not on Savernake as had been intended, but instead on Ogbourne St. George. Savernake, we decided, was rather too imposing, although we decided to retain the signal box and water tower, as these were already recorded. In the model,

our MSWJR station stood close to a tunnel, so we selected the north portal of Chedworth tunnel as a prototype and asked Alan Butcher, a new village modeller from Gloucester, to make it for us. This he did with remarkably accurate brickwork and lovely colouring.

My own modelling progressed well that summer, and in November I completed the model of Godfrey's. The roof carried 20,000 tiles, cut, of course, by Mario and most of which I had painted individually. However, the last 2,500 on the back (which would never be seen except in photographs, I laid unpainted. These I then coloured en bloc, not even stopping to remix the blends and after less than two hours work, they came out looking rather better than those on the front that I had taken weeks to paint. How perverse things can be! So a good deal sooner than I had dared to hope, the model was finished and I could breathe again . . . *[This, as events transpired, turned out to be the last model that Roye would make for Pendon.]*

The work of rebuilding the old outhouses and then the stable block had been progressing well for some time, and as the work on the stable was now nearing completion, it was suggested by someone that we also rebuild the house, making it smaller to allow better access and also more suitable for a much-needed resident caretaker. This would leave me out completely as I should lose my present room in the house (which I still used occasionally) and have nothing to take its place, Always I had felt that if anything happened to Lewis and Mario there would at least be a haven for me at Pendon, but apparently, if this project was accepted, no longer so. There could be good reason for

The front of Roye's last finished model — Godfrey's Cottage from Steventon. Part of the original building is shown on page 202

The creeper on the front of Priory Cottages was modelled in the only way that Roye knew — leaf by leaf, with individual leaves cut from painted tissue paper. The model was completed in 1985.   A. E. SMITH

what was being proposed, but I felt that I should have been asked to take part in discussions since it would affect me directly. It had been my own home for twenty years, and but for Cope's perfidy, it still might have been so.

Sadly, the problem was brought to the fore sooner than any would have wished. For some time Mario had been gradually failing and, early in 1986, she became worse. The doctor sent her to hospital in Abingdon and on our first visit, she seemed a little brighter than we expected. The next day Angus and Chris drove me to see her again, but this time she was not conscious. When I held her hand and spoke to her she slowly replied "Yes", but obviously knew nothing about it. Audrey *[the Ramells' adopted daughter]* had come for one night and when she and Lewis went to see Mario, she was completely inert. It was Audrey's opinion that she was quietly slipping away. Though she never gave up, life was getting too difficult for her, and to leave like this would be what she would have wanted. For three days she remained unconscious, then at 7.30 in the morning of 12th January, the vicar came with the news that Mario had died in the night, without regaining consciousness.

Several times lately when she found it hard to cope, she had said "I wish I could go", and now it had been granted to her without any suffering at all. Despite our deep and inevitable grief at her loss, which was quite irreparable, we were thankful that it had been as it was. But life without her would never be the same. For more years than I could remember she had been my most consistently staunch friend and one to whom I could always turn if things were difficult. In the church at Steventon, a few days later, there was held for Mario a most beautiful funeral service, just as she would have chosen, and the church not far from full.

Shortly after I had a long talk with Howard in which he expressed concern over my future with Lewis. He feared that Lewis would be unable to look after himself now Mario was dead, in which case I would be out. Howard urged me to enquire as to the possibility of going into one of the sheltered homes in Abingdon, from which he could continue to take me to Pendon. But the idea was distasteful to me — living alone, yet with many old people — as it were, and I didn't want to be in a town. But after only three hours, John Whiston rang, inviting me, when the crunch came, to share with him his home at Cuddington, near Aylesbury. It was a gift from God and I felt overwhelmed.

On the following Sunday, John drove me to Cuddington to see what he was offering, and on the way we were able to discuss contingencies, made with the best of intentions on both sides, that I should also keep open alternative plans. The house was semi-detached, set back from the road with a lawn and some garden and with an upstairs bedroom that could be mine. Although no larger than my room at Steventon, there was enough storage space in another room alongside, and the free and easy impression that the whole place gave, encouraged me in the belief that I would be happy there. When I returned to Pendon, I received the welcome news that planning permission to demolish the Poplars and build a smaller house in its place had been refused. So even if its interior had to be redesigned, the attractive outer shell would be retained.

In March, Lewis suffered a slight stroke and the doctor's advice was that he was no longer to be left untended. Audrey had arranged that when the need came, he would be able to enter a home for clergymen, and this was now agreed. I began planning the move to Cuddington, but no sooner had I done so than I became aware that several members of Pendon were pulling every string they knew to forestall my going. Apparently the theory was that John and I would soon fall out, and, with nowhere else to go, I would try to return to the Poplars — an inconvenience, no doubt, to all and sundry.

I rang Guy and repeated what I had been told. He saw no intrigue but rather a genuine desire to do what was best for Pendon and for me, that had simply been misunderstood. I was not convinced for I saw it as a culmination of a gradual process in which my feelings and views had been increasingly ignored and discounted. After a 55 year struggle to make Pendon what it was, the first 21 years single-handed, I felt I was now being covertly ostracised.

Meanwhile, there was further discussion of plans for the house. After having permission to demolish refused, the District Council had then sent a buildings inspector who had advised that the structure was actually unsafe. So after all, it could not be renovated but should be taken down and rebuilt. The outside appearance would be largely retained in the new house and we would re-use as much of the existing materials as were suitable, but, even so, the cost would be around £30,000. With sufficient borrowing, Aubrey advised that we could afford to undertake the work, so we agreed to proceed. It was a mark of Pendon's maturity and financial stability that we could even contemplate such an expenditure which, perhaps even ten years before, would have been out of the question.

As a first step towards demolition, John removed most of my possessions from my room in the Poplars and transferred them to Cuddington. Several car loads were necessary but John was incredibly helpful and understanding and his unfailing support at the time was a great comfort. By the end of May, I had a new home.

Cuddington, when I came to know it, was a very pretty village, old and mostly unspoilt, and I soon felt the urge to explore the area. For several years I had been riding a tricycle after the doctor advised me to give up bicycling when I was suffering from giddiness. But I never felt happy with the trike, and one fine day in July, I took out my Dawes bicycle into the back garden, where we replaced the Brooks saddle that had been transferred to the trike, and pumped up the tyres. John walked the bike to a quiet lane between lines of chestnuts and I got on. At first, I felt giddy but gradually things improved and after a quarter of an hour I felt sufficiently confident for John to leave me while I carried on up and down the lane. The entry in 'Outline' records my pleasure — 'Joy! I have ridden the Dawes again after five years.' If I could now regain my confidence in traffic, all kinds of possibilities would open up. Two days later, John took me as far as Chiselhampton, from where I cycled the 5¼ miles to Pendon, arriving to the astonishment of those present.

But hardly more than a fortnight had passed when everything changed. It was early morning on Sunday, 3rd August, and I was cycling to a Communion service held in a neighbouring church in Haddenham. My route crossed the main A418 Thame to Aylesbury road, less than a mile from home. At the crossroads I waited for two cars, the first of which signalled to turn to Haddenham whilst the second slowed behind it. But as I started to cross, I was hit by a third car that I had not seen. It was travelling at speed and swung out to overtake on the crossroads. I remembered nothing but the witnesses recounted that both the bike and I were thrown over the car. The cycle was a write-off and I was unconscious for ten days. *[According to the police report on the accident, the vehicle that hit Roye was travelling at 43mph and within the speed limit for the road. Despite the view of some witnesses that the motorist had overtaken in a dangerous manner, the police saw no reason to prosecute and they took the matter no further.]*

The medical opinion was that I would not recover, but I woke up in Stoke Mandeville hospital, the right leg and a collar bone broken and feeling good for nothing. When eventually I was able to get up, I managed to walk with a frame and the many visitors I received, including Tim Hancock who came from Bath, greatly helped.

My 80th birthday came while I was still in hospital, but arrangements were made to take me by ambulance to Pendon, where celebrations were being held. The ambulance was delayed but we arrived eventually, and, to cheers, I was taken into the Museum. *[Roye's memory of the evening is wrong on this point. The celebrations were actually held at Long Wittenham Village Hall, to accommodate the numbers that wished to be present.]* Slides were shown of the earliest days, bringing back many happy memories, after which we saw further film of the models. It was a wonderful occasion although, of course, far too short.

I stayed in hospital until the end of October, when I was able at last to return to Cuddington. The following Sunday, John drove me to Pendon, and whilst he showed the village, I sat in the corner by the Chapel group and chipped in as best I could. Helen Buckland had sent from

Roye, posed with his beloved Dawes bicycle in early 1986.
PENDON MUSEUM COLLECTION

California a tiny model of me as I looked in the past, in shorts and my favourite beret, which she hoped we could place outside the Chapel group. Apart from two small slips, it was excellent, but she had given me long stockings instead of the ankle socks that I always wore, and the shorts had no turn-ups. Chris Pilton agreed to put these right and the figure was placed, as Helen intended, in the lane at the corner of the Chapel group.

At this point, Roye's own account of his life and work effectively stopped. The remaining page of the manuscript for his 'Saga' contains some disjointed references to various activities, amongst which one is worth adding here:

In the middle of February (1987), John drove me to East Hanney, where we measured and photographed the huge stump of the Cross Tree, an elm which had reputedly been several hundred years old and in its prime had been bigger than anything I could remember. We intended to model the stump of this great tree for School Green, more or less in front of my model of Godfrey's.

It seems most appropriate that almost the last action that Roye himself recorded was of him measuring one of his beloved elms in a village of the Vale of White Horse.

The countryside that inspired the vision and the dream — the Vale of White Horse from the White Horse Hill, Uffington.

H. O. VAUGHAN

1987–1995
THE FINAL YEARS

ALTHOUGH Roye's own account of his life did not go beyond the early months of 1987, the story did not, of course, end there. He recovered remarkably well from his accident and, for a while, he was able to continue to visit Pendon regularly with John, sitting in his favourite corner and conversing with visitors very much as he had always done. The facts, figures and anecdotes that once had tripped so freely off the tongue perhaps did so now with rather less certainty than of old, but he still retained much at his fingertips and he remained deeply interested by all that went on in the Museum. He continued to sit on various Museum committees, and although he tended to say little within these meetings, he took much of it in and often discussed matters at length at home in Cuddington. In July, Radio Oxford chose to broadcast an hour-long programme of music and interviews from Pendon, in which Roye gave a very clear and lucid account of the Museum's origins and development and (to the surprise of several present) selected Stravinsky's 'Firebird' as one of his favourite pieces of music.

He remained at Cuddington until October of that year, when John, who had been made redundant from his work and could no longer afford the upkeep of the house, decided to move back to his home area in Herefordshire. In view of the level of care that Roye now required, it seemed best if he could be placed in a retirement home. Roye, of course, was very unhappy at this prospect, and for a brief period, the best that seemed available appeared to be a depressing local authority home in Aylesbury. Fortunately, however, a new home for the elderly had recently opened at Haddenham, no more than a mile or so from Cuddington, and Roye was fortunate in being offered a room there. So with good grace, and resolved to make the best of it, Roye moved the short distance to Haddenham.

As had so often been the case before, his many papers, books and other possessions threatened to swamp the space that was available, but once settled, he was quite happy there, and being still close to Pendon and with several Museum helpers who lived locally, he was able to go often to the Museum. There was, of course, no modelling, and, strangely, he ceased to listen to music, until then one of his mainstays in life, but the writing, with which he had always been so busy, continued. Before his accident he had been engaged in editing and rearranging a selection of his verse that had now been published in the anthology *The Vale That Inspired Pendon*, and he continued to spend time revising and correcting his 'Saga'. He also took regular walks around the village, often at dusk, moving slowly with the aid of his walking frame.

Roye stayed at Haddenham for two years. However, as his faculties became less certain, the staff at the home became more concerned. His walks became a source of anxiety over his safety during these outings, and his refusal to allow his room to be tidied also caused difficulty for the staff. The home was primarily intended for the 'active retired' and was rather rule-bound. Roye had no time for rules and was no longer active in the sense that the home expected, and it became apparent that somewhere else — somewhere that could give him the care and attention that he needed — would have to be found.

It was one of the many friends that Roye had made in Cuddington who suggested the Dalecare Centre at Stockcross, just outside Newbury. Dalecare was a big old house with some new extensions, set within its own grounds, and it seemed to John to be very suitable. The

Roye, caught in characteristic pose, in his favourite corner at Pendon, alongside the Chapel group in the Vale Scene – 1988.

A. E. SMITH

atmosphere in the home was far more easy-going than at Haddenham, whilst the staff were very genuine and had the right skills and excellent facilities to look after Roye. He would be able to have his own room and would still be relatively close to Pendon and to the Vale. There were also, at the time, several Pendon helpers who lived in the area and who could help to bring Roye to the Museum. So the move was made.

The years spent at Dalecare were a period of gradual decline. At first, Roye remained quite active. He walked within the grounds and continued what had become a seemingly endless process of sorting through, editing and correcting his various writings. He read from his large collection of religious books, often marking passages or placing bookmarks so that he could return again to things that interested him. Owing to deteriorating eye conditions, he had taken to wearing a green eyeshade to protect his eyes from bright light, and the curtains of the room were now kept firmly shut at all times, with a curt note to staff pinned in place, to the effect that they should not be touched! So visitors often found themselves sitting (assuming there was a chair free of papers) in comparative gloom.

Later, however, things were not so good. Several Pendon helpers who had been in the area moved away and Roye became rather cut-off from Pendon. Although he still had good days when he would scribble away at (correctly dated) notes of what he had done, the bad days — when his mind refused to focus and he couldn't even remember the names of people that he knew well — became more frequent. He grew more visibly frustrated with his situation. He felt that he still had a lot to give to Pendon and was probably saddened that he was no longer involved in the way that he wished. Sometimes, the frustration came across almost with a touch of bitterness, and on occasions, he no longer showed any interest in the news of Pendon that people brought. But he always returned to the home after the increasingly rare visits to the Museum, reinvigorated by the experience. Throughout it all, he remained genuinely grateful to those who cared for him, and the Matron at Dalecare said that, to the end, he was always polite and always a gentleman.

Roye's last three visits to Pendon were all made in 1994, the fortieth anniversary year of the first public showings of the models in the old Long Wittenham Youth Hostel. In February, John came specially from his home near Hereford to collect Roye from Newbury and then to take him on to Pendon. Despite his infirmity, Roye nevertheless managed the stairs and the walk round to his favourite corner by the Chapel group, where he brightened visibly amidst familiar surroundings.

Then, on Monday 11th July, the exact anniversary of the opening, a special gathering of the surviving Founder Members and a few old friends was held at the Museum.

On this occasion Roye was largely confined to a wheelchair, but he was in good spirits and enjoyed a couple of glasses of Australian 'Great Western' label champagne, as well as several helpings of cake. He was also able to watch trains working on the Teignmouth Sea Wall scene and later to walk through the Vale gallery, although sadly, his memory of his own models was now very patchy. He did, however, remember the cat whose discarded whiskers he had used to make the stems of the hollyhocks outside the Waggon and Horses inn — the model that had been the start of it all, more than sixty years before.

His last visit was on 5th October when two Pendon helpers, Ron Collins and Ken Surman brought him to the Museum. Once again, Roye was initially disorientated but gradually familiar objects seemed to register — the nameplate of *Westminster Abbey,* the first Great Western engine that he travelled behind on his arrival in England in 1925, the Madder Valley layout that had meant so much to the fledgling museum when it arrived in 1961, and then the Vale scene that he, personally, had done so much to inspire and create. On his way down to the tea room, he paused in front of a static display of new engines and coaches and asked (in that slightly hesitant way that would be familiar to all who had ever shown a model to Roye that was not quite right), whether the red paint on the buffer beams of some of the engines was quite the right shade? As he left the Museum the last thing he said was: "Now, is there anything I can do to help?"

Roye died peacefully at the Dalecare Centre on Sunday, 3rd September 1995, a few days short of what would have been his 89th birthday. *The Times* printed a notice of his death but *The Guardian* and *The Independent* both carried full obituaries by Guy and by Austin Attewell respectively. The funeral service took place at Oxford Crematorium on 7th September. The service was conducted by Archdeacon Basil French, and Michael French led the mourners — the two young boys whom Roye had first met in 1925 outside Bath Abbey and whose home at Wanborough he had then shared, with such far-reaching consequences. About 35 members of Pendon were also present at a service that was simple and dignified, very much as Roye would have wished. Later the same day, Roye's ashes were interred at St. Mary's Church, Bishopstone, a few feet to the south of the tower. Basil French conducted a brief ceremony and Michael carried the casket and placed it in the ground. The setting could not have been more appropriate for, as Martin Heard observed (writing in the 'Pendon Link'), Roye's final resting place was 'just a short distance from his first home in England, in the midst of the countryside he loved and in a situation that will actually be represented in his dream village, Pendon Parva'.

Some seven months later, on 27th April 1996, a memorial service was held at the parish church of Long

Wittenham. Archdeacon French again conducted the service and the address was delivered by Guy. In it he spoke of Roye's astonishing character and his many talents — his infectious enthusiasm, his charisma, his artistry, his caring for others and his unshakeable faith. Roye's influence, he concluded, would always be present. Ken Surman read the poem 'The Passing From The Vale' that Roye had composed on the train during his departure from England in 1931 which, despite (or perhaps because of) its hurried and spontaneous creation, captured most powerfully his love of the countryside and his deep sense of loss at the parting. Music from John Rutter's beautiful 'Requiem' was played and the congregation sang several of Roye's favourite hymns, ending with 'Dear Lord and Father of Mankind', sung to Hubert Parry's great tune, 'Repton'. Outside, it was a glorious spring morning of the kind that Roye would surely have cherished and celebrated — the hedgerows dusted with blossom and bursting with the first flush of summer green, the larks soaring in a clear, blue sky, and bright, cumulus clouds towering over the hills that border the Vale of White Horse — the countryside that had inspired the visions and dreams of a great man.

Near Uffington Castle.

H. O. VAUGHAN

PENDON MUSEUM

Pendon Museum is open throughout the year, except at Christmas and the preceding two weeks.

Saturdays and Sundays: 2.00 p.m. — 5.00 p.m.
Bank Holiday weekends Easter to August: 11.00 a.m. — 5.00 p.m.
Wednesdays in July and August: 2.00 p.m. — 5.00 p.m.

Groups can be accommodated at other times by special arrangement. Please write for details.

For further information and details of special events:
Telephone 01865 407365
or visit Pendon Museum's website at *www.pendonmuseum.com*

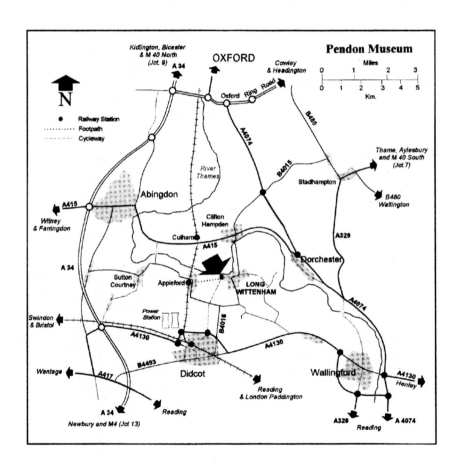